INSTANT POT TOP 500 RECIPES

Written by: Jamie Stewart

Copyright © 2016

All Rights Reserved

Warning-Disclaimer

****

Download a FREE PDF file with photos of all the recipes.

Link located at the end of the book.

*****

Table Of Contents

DESSERTS   217

INTRODUCTION

If you think that cooking good and healthy food is difficult, think twice. How about an electric pressure cooker? Are you curious? Instant Pot electric pressure cooker utilizes the pressure, steam, and high temperatures to speed up the cooking time. You can cook a wide variety of delicious meals with your multi-cooker and save your precious time and hard-earned money!

If you are lucky enough to own an electric pressure cooker and have an experience with pressure cooking, you will enjoy this book. Further, if you are planning to purchase an Instant Pot, you will have a great opportunity to get knowledge about pressure cooking and its benefits. If you love healthy homemade food but you don't have hours to spend in the kitchen, the Instant Pot electric pressure cooker might be for you!

In this cookbook, you will have an amazing opportunity to explore the surprising variety of nutritious and delicious recipes that you can make with an electric pressure cooker. Are you eager to start cooking with your Instant Pot? Go ahead, step into the magical world of pressure cooking!

Getting Back to Grandma's Way of Eating

Some of the most beautiful childhood memories are of our grandmother's kitchen that was filled with sweet smells of steamed vegetables, smoky meat, and delectable desserts. Chili beans, hearty stew, homemade chicken soup, mashed potatoes, sticky pork ribs, Christmas pudding, Thanksgiving turkey, and other great-tasting meals... If you are desirous of old-fashioned meals and you would like to cook like your grandma, the Instant Pot electric pressure cooker is your first choice. This recipe collection will bring a spirit of the good old times into your kitchen!

A definition of pressure cooking according to Wikipedia is: "Pressure cooking is the process of cooking food, using water or other cooking liquid, in a sealed vessel, known as a pressure cooker. As pressure cooking cooks food faster than conventional cooking methods, it saves energy."

As a matter of fact, the first type of pressure cooker was invented in the late 1600s. It was the form of a large cast iron vessel with a lock top. Throughout the years, this revolutionary way of cooking has been developed to suit the taste of the modern consumers and their lifestyle. Today, Instant Pot electric pressure cooker is an amazing tool with a number of cooking functions for fast and easy cooking. Use this multi-function cooker to prepare delicious meals that otherwise would take hours in the kitchen.

This recipe collection is chock-full of hand-picked recipes that are written in an easy to follow fashion. The vast majority of the recipes can be prepared in less than 30 minutes. Further, you will find a lot of one-pot meals, making meal planning and cooking a breeze. Once you try the pressure cooker recipes, you and your Instant Pot are sure to become "best friends". The book will guide you every step of the way in order to make the perfect meals and add some WOW factor to your everyday cooking. Yes, you can be comfortable in the kitchen and your meals can be absolutely delicious. Afterward, it all boils down to easiness and variety.

10 Things You Should Know About Your Instant Pot

The Instant Pot is a multifunctional programmable cooker that can do the job of an electric pressure cooker, steamer, warming pot, yogurt maker, porridge maker, sauté pan, and slow cooker. There are lots of reasons to love the Instant Pot, but there are a few things you should know before you start cooking. Here are ten tips for getting the most out of your Instant Pot and take advantage of this automated cooking process without the fuss.

Preparation is half the battle.

This may be a cliché, but it's also true in most cases. First and foremost, if you are new to the Instant Pot, it is very important to read instructional guides provided by the manufacturer in order to understand how to best use your Instant Pot. However, if you are a skilled chef, you still need to consult the manual on a regular basis.

How does the Instant Pot electric pressure cooker work?

Cooking liquids come to a boil under a sealed lid; consequently, the heat is evenly distributed inside a cooking pot and Voilà! Instant Pot cooks your meals as much as 70 percent quicker than other traditional cooking methods.

A modern hands-off functionality.

The Instant Pot is designed to use an intelligent programming so that it automatically regulates the pressure and time to control the entire cooking process. In other words – select your favorite recipe, set your cooker and go wherever you want! Instant pot is a digital electric pressure cooker so you don't need to stand by the stove to regulate pressure or stir your meal. Easy!

Healthy and flavorful meals.

A pressure cooking requires very little fat and water so that your meals retain most of their valuable nutrients. The short cooking time also helps you to cook great meals without nutrient loss. An extra tip to eat healthier – use as little liquid as possible and chop your vegetables into large pieces or cook them whole. Moreover, you can also preserve food in your Instant Pot. Home-canning allows you to keep your food for extended periods (for several years) on an easy and healthy way.

This is one of the best ways to cook economical cuts of meat, root vegetables, beans and other delicious and healthy food with minimal effort.

Instant Pot is eco-friendly.

In comparison with other cooking methods, this magnificent kitchen gadget uses two to three times less energy. Go green!

Which Instant Pot button to use?

The Instant Pot is one appliance that can do the work of even seven devices. However, practice makes perfect. "No one is born a great cook, one learns by doing." – Julia Child.

Remember, this is a journey of trials and errors. Don't be afraid to experiment a little bit with your cooker. Explore new ingredients, substitutions, combinations, and so on. However, if you are new to the pressure cooking, simply follow the recipe directions. For instance, "Sauté" function is the perfect flavor-enhancing technique. You should sauté your veggies and meat before pressure cooking. Then, you can use the "Manual" button to increase or decrease the cooking time. "Keep Warm/Cancel" – turn off your machine or cancel a function. "Soup"– high pressure and 30-minute cook time, and so on.

A Natural release or Quick release.

When it comes to the Natural pressure release, press the "Cancel" button and let your cooker stand until the float valve sinks. You can also release the steam manually for the Quick pressure release. Keep in mind that it takes 15 to 20 minutes to release the pressure after the cooking has been completed. An extra tip – keep your hands away from the steam as it's released!

The Instant Pot is ideal for busy households.

Pressure cooking is an easy and handy technique to save time, energy and money while making four-star recipes every day. With the Instant Pot, making comforting one-pot meals has never been easier. This is the new way of healthy eating, the new fast food for people who take good care of themselves and their health. Just try giving your family a new way of enjoying food!

Instant Pot accessories – must haves!

A steamer basket (for steaming vegetables and fish);

A metal trivet for the steamer basket;

An Instant Pot silicone lid (you can place leftover meal in the refrigerator in the cooking pot because this lid creates an air-tight and water-tight seal on your cooker);

An immersion blender for pureeing your soups right in the inner pot;

Instant Pot silicone mini mitts;

Individual heatproof molds (such as custard cups, ceramic ramekins, soufflé dishes, etc.)

A seven-in-one multi-cooker for a minimal kitchen.

If you have a limited kitchen space, the Instant Pot is a great versatile gadget for you. You can build the sauce, you can sauté, brown or braise without another skillet or pan. Further, the Instant Pot will keep your kitchen and the entire home warmer in the winter and cooler in the summer.

We have got 500 Instant Pot recipes ahead: a delicious porridge to oatmeal and bread puddings, hearty soups to flavorful chilies, homey snacks, fresh salads and appetizers to family desserts, and so on. Remember, grandma's secret ingredient to any kind of cooking is – LOVE. Bon Appétit!

BREAKFAST

Medjool Date Morning Bread Pudding

(Ready in about 45 minutes | Servings 4)

Ingredients

Nonstick cooking spray

6 slices bread, torn into bite-sized pieces

For the Custard:

3 cups milk

3 eggs

1/4 teaspoon pure orange extract

1/2 teaspoon pure vanilla essence

A pinch of kosher salt

1/2 cup brown sugar

1 tablespoon honey

1/4 teaspoon grated nutmeg

1/2 teaspoon cinnamon powder

1/2 cup dried Medjool dates, pitted and chopped

Directions

First, brush a 5-cup bowl with a nonstick cooking spray. Then, drop the bread pieces into the bowl.

In another bowl, prepare the custard by mixing all of the remaining ingredients, except chopped dates. Pour the custard mixture over bread pieces.

Scatter chopped dates over the top. Allow the mixture to rest at least 15 minutes to let the bread absorb the custard mixture.

Cover the bowl with a piece of buttered foil. Add a steaming rack to the inner pot; pour in 2 cups of water.

Lock the lid. Press the "Manual" button and let it cook for 25 minutes under HIGH pressure. Afterward, use a natural release method. Serve at room temperature.

Cinnamon Oatmeal with Apples

(Ready in about 30 minutes | Servings 4)

Ingredients

3 tablespoons butter, softened

1 cup steel-cut oats

2 ½ cups water

1 apple, cored, peeled, and chopped

1 tablespoon maple syrup

1/2 freshly grated nutmeg

1 teaspoon ground cinnamon

A pinch of kosher salt

Directions

First, select "Sauté" mode. Now, melt the butter. Stir in the oats and cook for 2 minutes, stirring frequently.

Add the water, apple, maple syrup, nutmeg, cinnamon, and kosher salt. Secure the lid and select "Manual" mode; cook for 7 minutes at HIGH pressure.

Once cooking is done, use a natural release in order to release any pressure. Your oatmeal will continue to thicken as it cools.

Serve the oatmeal topped with fresh fruits.

Quick and Easy Summer Oatmeal

(Ready in about 15 minutes | Servings 2)

Ingredients

2 apricots, pitted and halved

2 peaches, pitted and diced

2 figs, chopped

1 cup steel-cut oats

1 cup coconut milk

1/4 teaspoon pure orange extract

1 teaspoon vanilla essence

1 tablespoon rum

2 cups water

2 tablespoons agave syrup

1/2 teaspoon cinnamon powder

Directions

Simply drop all ingredients in the inner pot.

Now, press "Manual/Adjust"; set the timer for 3 minutes.

Then, perform a natural release for 10 minutes. Serve warm and enjoy!

Coconut French Toast Casserole

(Ready in about 35 minutes | Servings 4)

Ingredients

1 ½ cups water

1 tablespoon margarine or butter, melted

3 eggs, beaten

1 cup milk

2 tablespoons agave nectar

1/2 teaspoon pure coconut extract

1 teaspoon vanilla extract

3 cups stale cinnamon-raisin bread, cut into small chunks

Coconut flakes, for garnish

Directions

Prepare your Instant Pot by adding the water to the inner pot; place the steam rack on top.

Then, grease a soufflé dish with melted margarine or butter. In a large-sized mixing dish, thoroughly whisk the eggs, milk, agave nectar, coconut, and vanilla extract.

Fold in the chunks of bread; let it sit for 5 minutes; make sure to stir once or twice.

Pour your mixture into the soufflé dish; using a wide spatula, push down to submerge the bread. Lower the soufflé dish onto the steam rack, and secure the lid.

Select "Manual" mode and pressure cook for 15 minutes using a HIGH pressure. Afterward, use a quick release method. Open the cooker carefully.

Scatter coconut flakes over the top and serve.

Quick and Easy Summer Oatmeal

(Ready in about 15 minutes | Servings 2)

Ingredients

2 apricots, pitted and halved

2 peaches, pitted and diced

2 figs, chopped

1 cup steel-cut oats

1 cup coconut milk

1/4 teaspoon pure orange extract

1 teaspoon vanilla essence

1 tablespoon rum

2 cups water

2 tablespoons agave syrup

1/2 teaspoon cinnamon powder

Directions

Simply drop all ingredients in the inner pot.

Now, press "Manual/Adjust"; set the timer for 3 minutes.

Then, perform a natural release for 10 minutes. Serve warm and enjoy!

Savory Porridge with Tomatoes

(Ready in about 40 minutes | Servings 4)

Ingredients

2 cups water

2 cups vegetable broth

1/2 cup jasmine rice, rinsed and drained

A pinch of sugar

1 tablespoon butter, melted

4 eggs

1/2 teaspoon sea salt

1/2 teaspoon cayenne pepper

1/4 teaspoon ground black pepper

1 tablespoon soy sauce

1/2 cup tomatoes, diced

Directions

Add the water, broth, jasmine, and sugar to the Instant Pot; mix to combine. Secure the cooker's lid.

Press "Porridge" button and cook for 30 minutes at HIGH pressure. Perform a natural release for 15 minutes.

In the meantime, in a cast-iron skillet, melt the butter over medium flame. Now, fry the eggs in the warned butter, for 3 to 5 minutes, or until the yolks are still runny.

Season with salt, cayenne pepper, and ground black pepper. Drizzle soy sauce over all and serve with tomatoes on the side.

Soft-Boiled Eggs with Toasted Bread

(Ready in about 15 minutes | Servings 4)

Ingredients

1 cup water

4 eggs

2 tablespoons butter

8 bread slices

Salt and ground black pepper, to taste

Directions

Prepare your cooker by adding the water to the pot; lay the steam rack on top.

Lay the eggs on the steam rack; secure the cooker's lid. Select "Manual" mode and cook at LOW pressure for 6 minutes. Perform a quick release.

Meanwhile, butter and toast the bread slices. Cut them into strips. Carefully remove the eggs from the pot; put them into egg cups.

Season with salt and ground black pepper of choice, and serve with the buttered toast.

Sausage and Cheddar Frittata

(Ready in about 40 minutes | Servings 4)

Ingredients

1 ½ cups water

1 tablespoon butter, at room temperature

4 eggs, beaten

2 tablespoons sour cream

1/2 cup cooked sausage, crumbled

1/4 cup Cheddar cheese, grated

Salt and ground black pepper, to your liking

1/2 teaspoon paprika

1 tablespoon fresh parsley, coarsely chopped

Directions

Add the water to your Instant Pot; place the steam rack on top. Lightly butter a soufflé dish.

In a medium-sized mixing bowl, beat the eggs with sour cream. Fold in the sausage and grated cheese. Season with salt, black pepper, and paprika.

Pour the mixture into the buttered soufflé dish. Cover with foil and lower onto the steam rack. Secure the cooker's lid. Press the "Manual" button and cook for 17 minutes at LOW pressure.

Once cooking is complete, perform a quick release. Afterward, remove the soufflé dish from the pot, and scatter chopped parsley over the top. Enjoy!

Pear and Apricot Oatmeal

(Ready in about 15 minutes | Servings 4)

Ingredients

2 Bosc pears, cored and diced

2 apricots, pitted and diced

1 cup steel-cut oats

1 cup milk

1 teaspoon vanilla essence

2 cups water

2 tablespoons honey

1/4 teaspoon grated nutmeg

1/4 teaspoon ground anise star

1/2 teaspoon cinnamon powder

Directions

Simply put all ingredients into the inner pot.

Now, choose "Manual/Adjust" function; set the cooker's timer for 4 minutes.

Afterward, perform a natural release. Serve warm and enjoy!

Bacon and Swiss Cheese Frittata

(Ready in about 30 minutes | Servings 4)

Ingredients

Water, for the pot

1 tablespoon vegetable oil

4 eggs, slightly beaten

2 tablespoons cream cheese

3-4 slices of bacon, fried and crumbled

1/4 cup Swiss cheese, grated

1/2 teaspoon salt

1/4 teaspoon ground black pepper, or to your liking

1 teaspoon granulated garlic

Directions

Pour the water into Instant Pot; place the steam rack on the top. Treat a baking dish with vegetable oil.

In a mixing bowl, beat the eggs together with cream cheese. Fold in the crumbled bacon and grated Swiss cheese. Sprinkle with salt, black pepper, and granulated garlic. Beat until everything is well mixed.

Pour the mixture into the greased baking dish. Cover with foil and lower onto the steam rack. Close the cooker and choose "Manual" mode; cook for 17 minutes at LOW pressure.

Lastly, perform a quick release. Serve warm.

Easiest Hard-Boiled Eggs Ever

(Ready in about 10 minutes | Servings 4)

Ingredients

1 cup water

8 eggs

Salt and freshly cracked black pepper, to taste

Paprika, to taste

Directions

Add the water to the inner pot; now, position a steamer basket atop the rack.

Carefully put the eggs into the steamer basket; you can use canning lids to hold the eggs.

Seal the cooker's lid. Press "Steam" button and adjust time to 5 minutes. Lastly, quick release the steam valve.

Season the eggs with salt, black pepper, and paprika to taste. Serve with toasted bread or English muffins. Enjoy!

Aromatic Sweet Risotto with Sultanas

(Ready in about 30 minutes | Servings 6)

Ingredients

1 ½ cups basmati rice

1/2 cup sugar

1 tablespoon agave nectar

A pinch of kosher salt

A pinch of cinnamon powder

5 cups milk

2 eggs

1 cup half-and-half

1 cup sultanas

1/4 teaspoon ground anise star

1/4 teaspoon freshly grated nutmeg

Directions

In the inner pot, mix together the rice, sugar, agave nectar, kosher salt, cinnamon, and milk. Choose the "Sauté" mode and bring it to a boil. Stir until sugar fully dissolves.

Cover your Instant Pot. Choose the "Rice" mode and cook 15 minutes; perform the Quick pressure release.

In the meantime, beat the eggs and half-and-half in a mixing dish.

Remove the lid and fold in the egg mixture. Now add sultanas, anise, and grated nutmeg. Press the "Sauté" button again. Cook, uncovered, until the mixture begins to boil. Lastly, turn off your Instant Pot.

Serve right away. Bon appétit!

Easiest Hard-Boiled Eggs Ever

(Ready in about 10 minutes | Servings 4)

Ingredients

1 cup water

8 eggs

Salt and freshly cracked black pepper, to taste

Paprika, to taste

Directions

Add the water to the inner pot; now, position a steamer basket atop the rack.

Carefully put the eggs into the steamer basket; you can use canning lids to hold the eggs.

Seal the cooker's lid. Press "Steam" button and adjust time to 5 minutes. Lastly, quick release the steam valve.

Season the eggs with salt, black pepper, and paprika to taste. Serve with toasted bread or English muffins. Enjoy!

Classic Creamed Oats

(Ready in about 10 minutes | Servings 4)

Ingredients

1 cup water, for the pot

1 cup oats

1 2/3 cups water

A pinch of kosher salt

1/2 teaspoon ground cardamom

1/4 teaspoon ground cinnamon

Cream, to serve

Directions

Pour 1 cup of water into the pot; now, lay the trivet on the bottom of the pot.

Put oats and 1 2/3 cups of water into a heat-proof bowl; sprinkle with salt, cardamom, and cinnamon, and stir until everything is well incorporated.

Next, lower the bowl onto the trivet. Press "Manual" button; cook 7 minutes. Afterward, quick release steam.

Divide the oatmeal among individual bowls and top with cream. Enjoy!

Potato White Wheat Berries

(Ready in about 15 minutes | Servings 4)

Ingredients

6 ½ cups water

2 cups white wheat berries, soaked overnight in water

2 tablespoons canola oil

2 medium-sized shallots, peeled and thinly sliced

2 cloves garlic, smashed

1/2 teaspoon dried thyme

1/2 teaspoon dried dill weed

4 medium potatoes, cubed

Salt and ground black pepper, to taste

Directions

Mix 6 ½ cups water and white wheat berries in your cooker.

In a pan, warm canola oil over medium-high flame. Now, sauté the shallots and garlic until tender and fragrant. Add the thyme and dill, and cook for 1 more minute, stirring constantly.

Stir in the potatoes; press the "Multigrain" button. When it is done, add sautéed shallot/garlic mixture. Sprinkle with salt and black pepper. Serve warm and enjoy.

Easy and Yummy Cashew Oats

(Ready in about 10 minutes | Servings 4)

Ingredients

1 cup water

1 cup steel-cut oats

2 cups water

1/8 teaspoon kosher salt

1 tablespoon agave nectar

1/2 cup cashews, chopped

Directions

Pour 1 cup of water into your cooker. Put a trivet into the pot.

Throw the oats, together with two cups of water and kosher salt, into a heat-proof bowl; place this bowl on the trivet. Lock in the lid. Use the "Manual" setting, and cook 6 minutes.

When your oats are done, add agave nectar; stir well to combine. Serve topped with chopped cashews. Enjoy!

Morning Wheat Berry with Sour Cream

(Ready in about 15 minutes | Servings 4)

Ingredients

2 cups white wheat berries, soaked overnight in lots of water

2 tablespoons olive oil

2 medium-sized shallots, peeled and sliced

1/2 teaspoon sea salt

1/4 teaspoon ground black pepper

1/2 teaspoon dried basil

1 celery stalk, chopped

2 medium carrots, thinly sliced

Sour cream, for garnish

Directions

In the cooker, combine white wheat berries with 6 ½ cups water.

Then, in a saucepan, heat the oil over medium heat. Then, sauté shallots until translucent. Add salt, ground black pepper, and basil.

Next, choose the "Multigrain" button; add the celery and carrots, and cook until they have softened. Stir in sautéed shallots. Serve garnished with sour cream. Enjoy!

Walnut and Raisin Congee with Seeds

(Ready in about 45 minutes | Servings 6)

Ingredients

1/2 cup rice

1/2 cup walnut, minced

1 tablespoon nut butter

2 tablespoons sesame seeds

1 teaspoon pumpkin seeds

1/4 cup raisins

7 cups of water

Directions

Add all of the above ingredients to your Instant Pot.

Now press the "Rice" button. When it is ready, carefully open the cooker. Serve warm, sprinkled with some extra seed, if desired. Enjoy!

Delicious Spring Steamed Eggs

(Ready in about 15 minutes | Servings 2)

Ingredients

2 eggs

2/3 cup milk

1 tablespoon olive oil

1/2 cup green onions, chopped

1/4 cup carrots, shredded

1/2 teaspoon dried dill weed

Salt and crushed red pepper flakes, to taste

Directions

Whisk together the eggs and milk in a small-sized mixing dish. Transfer the mixture to a heat-proof bowl.

Stir in the rest of the above ingredients; stir until everything is well combined.

Pour 1 cup of water into the inner pot of your Instant Pot. Add the trivet to the Instant Pot. Lay the heat-proof bowl on the trivet.

Close the cooker and close the vent valve. Press the "Manual" button and use HIGH pressure; cook for 5 minutes.

Afterward, manually release the pressure. Serve warm with English muffins and enjoy!

Swiss Cheese and Ham Omelet

(Ready in about 25 minutes | Servings 4)

Ingredients

4 medium-sized eggs

1/3 cup whole milk

1 medium-sized sweet onion, finely chopped

1 clove garlic, peeled and minced

1 cup cooked ham, chopped

1 red bell pepper, seeded and thinly sliced

1 green bell pepper, seeded and thinly sliced

1/2 cup Swiss cheese, grated

1/2 teaspoon dried basil

1/2 teaspoon dried oregano

1/2 teaspoon dried thyme

Salt and black pepper, to taste

Directions

Begin by whisking the eggs and milk in a large-size mixing dish. Stir in the rest of the above ingredients; stir until everything is well mixed.

Pour the egg mixture into a heat-resistant dish; cover with a lightly buttered foil.

Add 1 cup of water to the base of Instant Pot. Lay the trivet inside. Lower the heat-resistant dish onto the trivet.

Close the lid and choose "Manual" setting; cook for 20 minutes using HIGH pressure. Serve immediately with your favorite mustard. Enjoy!

Date and Almond Sweet Risotto

(Ready in about 45 minutes | Servings 6)

Ingredients

1/2 cup rice

1 tablespoon nut butter

2 tablespoons sunflower seeds

1 teaspoon pumpkin seeds

1/2 cup almonds, minced

1/4 cup dates, pitted and chopped

7 cups of water

Directions

Throw all ingredients into your Instant Pot.

Now, choose "Rice" setting. When the rice is ready, open the lid. Serve right away.

Coconut and Peanut Rice Pudding

(Ready in about 45 minutes | Servings 4)

Ingredients

1/4 cup wild rice

1/4 cup white rice

1 tablespoon orange juice

1 tablespoon coconut sugar

1/2 cup peanuts, minced

1/2 cup coconut flakes

Zest of 1 orange

7 cups of water

Cream, to serve

Directions

Place all ingredients in your Instant Pot.

Now, select "Rice" mode. Afterward, open the lid and divide the mixture among individual bowls. Serve right away.

Hot Spicy Cheesy Eggs

(Ready in about 30 minutes | Servings 6)

Ingredients

6 eggs, beaten

6 tablespoons milk

1/2 cup scallions, chopped

1 chipotle in adobo sauce, finely minced

1 bell pepper, seeded and thinly sliced

1/2 cup Colby cheese, grated

Salt and freshly ground black pepper, to your liking

1 teaspoon cayenne pepper

Directions

In a mixing dish, whisk together the eggs and milk. Stir in the rest of the above items; stir until everything is well incorporated.

Pour the egg mixture into a heat-resistant dish; cover.

Pour 1 cup of water into the cooker. Place a rack on the bottom of the cooker. Lower the dish onto the rack.

Choose "Manual" mode and cook 20 minutes using HIGH pressure. Serve immediately.

Mocha Latte Breakfast Quinoa

(Ready in about 10 minutes | Servings 4)

Ingredients

1 cup quinoa, rinsed well

1 heaping cup brewed coffee

1 cup water

1/2 teaspoon grated nutmeg

1/4 teaspoon ground cloves

1/2 teaspoon ground cinnamon

1/4 cup vegan chocolate chips

Directions

In your Instant Pot, place all ingredients.

Close and lock the lid. Press the "Manual" button and cook for 2 minutes. Then, perform the Natural pressure release.

Taste and adjust for seasonings. Serve warm and enjoy!

Cheddar and Leek Morning Risotto

(Ready in about 15 minutes | Servings 8)

Ingredients

2 tablespoons olive oil

1 cup leeks, chopped

2 cloves garlic, finely minced

2 cups dry Arborio rice

2 tablespoons dry white wine

4 cups roasted-vegetable stock

Salt and ground black pepper, to taste

Shredded Cheddar cheese, to serve

Directions

Grease the inner pot with olive oil. Combine the leeks and garlic in your electric pressure cooker. Stir to coat and turn the cooker on to the "Sauté" setting; then, sauté it, stirring frequently, until the veggies are softened.

Stir in the rice; cook and continue stirring frequently for 1 minute.

Add the wine and continue cooking till the liquid has evaporated. Pour in the stock; place the lid on the cooker.

Season with salt and ground black pepper. Close and lock the lid; set the timer for 7 minutes.

Release pressure and carefully remove the lid. Stir before serving, garnish with Cheddar cheese and enjoy!

Two-Mushroom Breakfast Pilaf

(Ready in about 40 minutes | Servings 8)

Ingredients

1 package dried porcini mushrooms

4 cups warm water

1 tablespoon butter, softened

1 cup yellow onion, chopped

2 cups button mushrooms, sliced

2 cups dry Arborio rice

2 tablespoons dry white wine

1/2 teaspoon dried dill weed

Sea salt and freshly cracked black pepper, to taste

Directions

Soak the porcini mushrooms in 2 cups of warm water about 30 minutes.

In the meantime, add the butter, yellow onion, porcini mushrooms, and button mushrooms to the pressure cooker. Turn the cooker to the "Sauté" mode; cook, stirring continuously, until the onions are translucent and the mushrooms are fragrant.

Add the rice, wine, dill, salt, and dill weed; cook until the liquid has evaporated.

Pour in the remaining 2 cups of warm water. Close and lock the cooker's lid; set the timer for 7 minutes. Afterward, release the pressure naturally in order to remove the lid. Eat warm and enjoy!

Quinoa with Mulberries and Yogurt

(Ready in about 10 minutes | Servings 6)

Ingredients

1 ½ cups quinoa

1 cup fresh orange juice

1 tablespoon coconut oil

Pinch of salt

6 cardamom pods

1/2 teaspoon cinnamon

1 vanilla bean

3 tablespoons dried mulberries

Yogurt, to serve

Directions

In your Instant Pot, place all ingredients, except mulberries and yogurt.

Close and lock the cooker's lid. Select "Manual" setting; cook for 2 minutes. Lastly, perform the Natural pressure release.

Taste and adjust for seasonings. Serve warm, topped with mulberries and yogurt.

Pineapple and Carrot Sweet Rice

(Ready in about 30 minutes | Servings 8)

Ingredients

Water, for the pot

2 cups basmati rice

1/2 canned pineapple, chopped

2 large-sized carrots, grated

2 tablespoons coconut sugar

2 teaspoons coconut butter

A pinch of salt

1/2 teaspoon ground cardamom

1/4 teaspoon ground cloves

Directions

First, fill the water to the level 2 mark on the inner pot of Instant Pot.

Next, simply dump all ingredients into your cooker. Turn the "Rice" mode and cook until the rice is softened. Eat warm.

Apricot and Cranberry Oatmeal

(Ready in about 20 minutes | Servings 4)

Ingredients

3 cups water

1 cup toasted metal-reduce oats

2 teaspoons coconut butter

1 cup orange juice

1 tablespoon dried apricots, snipped

2 tablespoons dried cranberries

1 tablespoon agave syrup

1/4 teaspoon ground cloves

1/4 teaspoon ground cinnamon

1/2 teaspoon ground cardamom

A pinch kosher salt

Directions

Place the rack in your cooker; pour 1/2 cup of water over the rack.

In a metallic bowl, combine the remaining 2 ½ cups water, oats, and coconut butter. Now, add the orange juice, apricots, cranberries, and agave syrup,

Next, stir in the cloves, cinnamon, cardamom, and salt. Lock the cooker's lid into place. Then, keep strain for 8 minutes. Eat warm.

Apple Maple Oatmeal with Walnuts

(Ready in about 20 minutes | Servings 6)

Ingredients

2 cups water

1/2 cup steel-cut oats

3/4 cup dried apples, chopped

1/4 cup walnuts, chopped

1/4 cup maple syrup

1/4 teaspoon grated nutmeg

1/4 teaspoon ground cloves

1/4 teaspoon ground cinnamon

1/8 teaspoon salt

Directions

Combine everything in your Instant Pot.

Lock the lid onto the pot and set your cooker to cook at HIGH pressure. Set the timer to cook 18 minutes.

Reduce the pressure. Turn off the machine. Allow the pressure to return to normal.

Afterward, open the pot and serve warm. Bon appétit!

Vegan Banana Coconut Oatmeal

(Ready in about 20 minutes | Servings 4)

Ingredients

3/4 cup water

1 cup soy milk

1 cup fast-cooking oats

2 bananas, sliced

2 tablespoons coconut sugar

1 teaspoon cinnamon powder

2 tablespoons shredded coconut

1/2 teaspoon ground cloves

1/2 teaspoon pure vanilla extract

Directions

Combine all ingredients in your cooker.

Lock the lid onto the pot; set your cooker to cook for 18 minutes at HIGH pressure.

Turn off the machine and allow the pressure to return to normal.

Take away the lid and stir the oatmeal before serving. Serve with a splash of soy milk, if desired.

Sunday Morning Rice Pudding

(Ready in about 20 minutes | Servings 4)

Ingredients

1 ½ cups Arborio rice

3/4 cup sugar

A pinch of kosher salt

5 cups milk

2 eggs

1 cup half-and-half

1/4 teaspoon grated nutmeg

1 cup dried apricots, snipped

Directions

In the inner pot, combine Arborio rice, sugar, kosher salt, and milk; stir until everything is well combined.

Select the "Sauté" button, and bring to a boil. Stir constantly till the sugar dissolves. Now, cover and lock the lid. Press the "Rice" key.

Meanwhile, whisk the eggs, half-and-half, and nutmeg in a small-sized mixing bowl.

Next, use the Quick pressure release and carefully remove the lid. Stir the whisked egg mixture into the pot. Add the apricots here.

Choose the "Sauté" mode and cook uncovered. Keep in mind that the pudding will thicken as it cools.

Potato and Sausage Breakfast Casserole

(Ready in about 20 minutes | Servings 6)

Ingredients

2 tablespoons canola oil

1 yellow onion, diced

2 cloves garlic, minced

1 bell pepper, chopped

8 ounces sausage, crumbled

3 cups potatoes, peeled and shredded

6 eggs, beaten

2 cups Cheddar cheese, shredded

Salt and freshly cracked black pepper

1/2 teaspoon dried basil

1/2 teaspoon smoked paprika

Directions

Add the canola oil to the cooker, and sauté the onion, garlic, and bell pepper till tender and fragrant. Stir in the sausage and cook for 3 minutes extra.

Add the remainder of the items to your cooker.

Then, pressure cook on "Manual" setting for 10 minutes using HIGH pressure. Now, quick release pressure. Taste, adjust the seasonings, and serve warm.

Easy Country Grits

(Ready in about 30 minutes | Servings 4)

Ingredients

2 cups water

2 cups non-dairy milk

1 tablespoon butter

1/2 teaspoon salt

1 cup corn grits

A pinch of freshly grated nutmeg

Directions

Put the water, non-dairy milk, butter, and salt into the Instant Pot. Choose the "Sauté" button, and bring it to a boil.

Gradually stir the grits into the boiling liquid. Sprinkle the nutmeg over the top and stir to combine.

Cover and press the "Manual" button; cook it for 7 minutes. Afterward, release pressure naturally about 15 minutes.

Stir before serving and eat warm.

Cauliflower and Tofu Scramble

(Ready in about 20 minutes | Servings 2)

Ingredients

16 ounces firm tofu, drained

1 teaspoon vinegar

1/2 teaspoon black pepper

1 teaspoon salt

1 tablespoon olive oil

1 clove garlic, minced

1/2 cup scallions, chopped

1 cup cauliflower florets, blanched

1/2 cup tomato, diced

1 quarter cup water

2 tablespoons fresh cilantro, chopped

Directions

In a mixing bowl, mash the tofu with a fork; stir in the vinegar, black pepper, and salt.

Choose "Sauté" function. Then, bring the oil to medium warmth in your cooker. Now, sauté garlic, scallions, cauliflower florets, and tomato until the cauliflower is tender.

Add the water, cover and cook till everything is warmed through. Take away the lid and serve topped with cilantro.

Sausage and Pepper Casserole

(Ready in about 20 minutes | Servings 2)

Ingredients

1 pound ground pork sausage

1 yellow onion, peeled and diced

1 yellow bell pepper, seeded and diced

1 bell pepper, seeded and diced

1 red bell pepper, seeded and diced

2 tablespoons olive oil

1/2 cup flour

2 cups half-and-half

1/2 teaspoon dried marjoram

Salt and freshly ground black pepper, to your liking

Directions

Using the "Sauté" setting, brown the sausage along with the onions and bell peppers.

Lock the lid into place and cook for 10 minutes. Add the oil and flour; stir-fry it for 1 to 2 minutes, stirring repeatedly.

Now, stir in the half-and-half, marjoram, salt, and ground black pepper. Bring to a boil; then, simmer for 3 minutes more. Eat warm.

Spiced Millet with Sautéed Candy Onion

(Ready in about 20 minutes | Servings 6)

Ingredients

1 tablespoon olive oil

1 bay leaf

1 large-sized candy onion sliced into strips

2 cups husked organic millet

3 cups water

1/4 teaspoon freshly cracked black pepper

1/2 teaspoon red pepper flakes, crushed

1 teaspoon salt

Directions

Start by preheating your pressure cooker on "Sauté" function. Now, heat the oil and sauté the bay leaf and candy onion for 5 to 6 minutes or until they become soft.

Add the millet, water, black pepper, red pepper, and salt. Close and lock the cooker's lid. Cook for 1 minute longer using HIGH pressure.

Release the pressure and fluff millet with a fork.

Aromatic Spiced Grits

(Ready in about 30 minutes | Servings 4)

Ingredients

2 cups water

2 cups soy milk

1 tablespoon ghee

1/2 teaspoon kosher salt

1/4 teaspoon seasoned pepper

1 cup stone-ground grits

A pinch of ground allspice

1/2 teaspoon paprika

1/2 teaspoon dried thyme

1/2 teaspoon dried basil

Directions

Add the water, soy milk, ghee, kosher salt, and seasoned pepper to the Instant Pot. Select the "Sauté" function, and bring it to a boil.

Gradually stir the grits into the boiling liquid. Add all seasonings.

Cover and select the "Manual" function; cook covered for 8 minutes.

Afterward, release pressure naturally. Serve warm.

Polenta with Roasted Figs

(Ready in about 30 minutes | Servings 4)

Ingredients

2 cups water

2 cups almond milk

1 tablespoon butter

1/2 teaspoon salt

1 cup polenta

1 tablespoon maple syrup

1/2 teaspoon crystallized ginger

1 teaspoon ground cardamom

A pinch of cinnamon

A pinch of freshly grated nutmeg

2 fresh figs, roasted and diced

Directions

Throw the water, almond milk, butter, and salt into the Instant Pot. Choose the "Sauté" mode, and bring it to a boil.

Gradually and slowly stir the polenta into the boiling liquid. Add the maple syrup and crystallized ginger.

Sprinkle the cardamom, cinnamon, and nutmeg over the top and stir to combine.

Seal the cooker's lid and select the "Manual" mode; cook it for 7 minutes. Afterward, release pressure naturally about 15 minutes.

Stir before serving and serve topped with roasted figs.

Wheat Berry Porridge with Sweet Potatoes

(Ready in about 20 minutes | Servings 8)

Ingredients

2 cups white wheat berries, soaked overnight in lots of water

2 tablespoons olive oil

2 candy onions, peeled and sliced

1/2 teaspoon basil

1/2 teaspoon oregano

1 teaspoon fresh sage, minced

A pinch of allspice

A pinch of sea salt

4 large-sized sweet potatoes, cubed

Directions

Add white wheat berries along with 6 ½ cups of water to your Instant Pot.

Then, heat the skillet over medium-high heat; add olive oil and swirl it around to coat the bottom. Now, sauté the onions in hot oil until they become tender, or 3 to 4 minutes.

Add the remaining items and stir until everything is well incorporated. Choose "Multigrain" function. When your mixture is cooked, add sautéed candy onions. Serve and enjoy!

Smoked Sausage and Cheese Frittata

(Ready in about 25 minutes | Servings 4)

Ingredients

1 ½ cups water

1 teaspoon lard, melted

4 eggs, beaten

2 tablespoons Ricotta cheese, crumbled

1/3 pound pork sausage, cooked and crumbled

1/4 cup smoked Cheddar goat cheese, grated

Salt and ground black pepper, to your liking

1/2 teaspoon red pepper flakes, crushed

1/2 teaspoon smoked cayenne powder

1 tablespoon fresh cilantro, coarsely chopped

Directions

Add the water to the electric pressure cooker; place the steam rack on the bottom. Lightly grease a soufflé dish with melted lard.

In a mixing dish, whisk the eggs and Ricotta. Fold in the sausage and goat cheese. Season with salt, black pepper, red pepper, and smoked cayenne powder.

Scrape the mixture into the greased soufflé dish. Cover the dish with foil and lower it onto the steam rack. Secure the cooker's lid and select "Manual" setting; now, cook for 17 minutes at LOW pressure.

Once cooking is complete, use release the pressure. Serve in individual serving dishes topped with fresh chopped cilantro. Enjoy!

Yummy Peanut and Date Congee

(Ready in about 25 minutes | Servings 4)

Ingredients

1/2 cup rice

1/2 cup peanuts, finely chopped

1 tablespoon peanut butter

2 tablespoons hemp seeds

1 teaspoon pumpkin seeds

1/4 cup dates, pitted and chopped

1/4 teaspoon ground cloves

1/2 teaspoon freshly grated nutmeg

1/4 teaspoon ground cinnamon

7 cups of water

Directions

Simply throw all of the above ingredients into your cooker.

Choose "Rice" setting. When it is ready, release the pressure, and carefully open the cooker.

Serve warm in individual bowls, topped with some extra peanuts, if desired.

Creamed Raspberry Rice Porridge

(Ready in about 25 minutes | Servings 4)

Ingredients

1/2 cup jasmine rice

1 tablespoon butter

1/2 teaspoon pure orange extract

1 teaspoon pure vanilla essence

1/4 teaspoon cinnamon powder

1/4 cup dried raspberries, chopped

1 tablespoon agave syrup

7 cups of water

Directions

Add all ingredients to your Instant Pot.

Now, select the "Rice" button. Carefully open the cooker.

Divide your congee among 4 individual serving dishes. Serve at room temperature and enjoy!

Buttery Ginger Morning Rice

(Ready in about 20 minutes | Servings 6)

Ingredients

2 ½ cups roasted-vegetable broth

1 (14-ounce) can tomatoes, diced

1 ½ cups long-grain white rice

1/2 stick butter, cold

1/2 teaspoon ground ginger

1/4 teaspoon salt

1/4 teaspoon ground allspice

Directions

First, combine the broth, tomatoes, white rice, and butter in an electric pressure cooker. Mix to combine well

Now, add the remaining ingredients and mix again until everything is well combined.

Click the "Rice" button and cook for 15 minutes at HIGH pressure.

Afterward use the Quick-release method; unlock and open the cooker. Stir before serving and serve warm with sour cream if desired.

Barley Porridge with Blueberries and Red Grapes

(Ready in about 30 minutes | Servings 6)

Ingredients

1 ½ cups pearl barley, rinsed and drained

1 tablespoon butter, melted

3/4 teaspoon salt

4 cups water

2 tablespoons orange juice

1 ½ cups fresh blueberries, picked over

1 ½ cups red grapes, halved

Heavy cream, to serve

Directions

In your Instant Pot, combine the barley, butter, salt, water, and orange juice. Stir to combine well.

Set your cooker to "Manual" and HIGH pressure for 20 minutes. Close and lock the cooker's lid.

Afterward, allow the pressure to release naturally for 10 minutes. Now, divide your porridge among six individual bowls. Top with blueberries, red grapes, and heavy cream. Enjoy!

Easy Aromatic Apple Sauce

(Ready in about 10 minutes | Servings 10)

Ingredients

4 Gala apples, peeled, cored, and sliced into wedges

1 teaspoon fresh lemon juice

1 tablespoon water

2 tablespoons brown sugar

1/4 teaspoon ground cloves

1/2 teaspoon freshly grated nutmeg

1/4 teaspoon vanilla paste

3/4 teaspoon cinnamon

Directions

Put the apple wedges into your Instant Pot along with the remaining items. Combine it all together.

Close and lock the cooker's lid. Use "Manual" setting; pressure cook for 4 minutes at HIGH pressure. Once the cooking is done, let your cooker release pressure; carefully open the cooker.

Then, blend the mixture using your food processor; blend until your desired consistency is reached.

Keep in your refrigerator and serve with English muffins. Enjoy!

Rich Rice Pudding with Sultanas

(Ready in about 30 minutes | Servings 4)

Ingredients

3/4 cup Arborio rice

1/3 cup sugar

1/4 teaspoon salt

2 ½ cups soy milk

1 egg

1 tablespoon butter

1 teaspoon orange zest

1/2 teaspoon ground cloves

1/2 teaspoon ground cinnamon

1/3 cup Sultanas

Directions

Add the rice, sugar, salt and soy milk to the Instant Pot. Stir until everything is well mixed.

Set the pot to "Sauté" function; bring it to a boil and stir constantly. Once it comes to a boil, press the "Rice" button.

Meanwhile, whisk together the egg, butter, orange zest, cloves, and cinnamon. Press the "Cancel" button. Let it stand covered for 10 to 15 minutes.

Add the egg/butter mixture and Sultanas. Stir until everything is mixed together. Serve warm or at room temperature.

Eggplant with Eggs and Tomatoes

(Ready in about 50 minutes | Servings 4)

Ingredients

1 eggplant, peeled and cut pieces

1 tablespoon salt

2 tablespoons olive oil

1 medium-sized red onion, chopped

3 large garlic cloves, minced

1 (28-ounce) can crushed tomatoes, drained

1 tablespoon harissa

Salt and freshly ground black pepper, to your liking

6 eggs

6 thick slices crusty bread

Directions

In a large-sized bowl, toss the eggplant with the salt. Let it sit for 30 minutes. Rinse the eggplant.

Preheat your cooker by selecting "Sauté" mode.

Once hot, add olive oil. Stir in the eggplant and cook for 4 minutes. Add the onions and garlic and cook for 3 minute longer.

Add the tomatoes, harissa, salt, and ground black pepper. Seal the lid and select "Manual"; cook for 10 minutes at HIGH pressure.

Afterward, use a quick release. Choose "Sauté" setting. Crack the eggs into a cup and lower them into the Instant Pot.

Now, cook, loosely covered, about 6 minutes. Lastly, serve with bread and enjoy!

Grits with Goat Cheese

(Ready in about 35 minutes | Servings 4)

Ingredients

1 cup coarse-ground cornmeal

3 ½ cups water

1 teaspoon salt

1/2 teaspoon cayenne pepper

1/4 teaspoon ground black pepper

4 tablespoons butter, cut into pieces

1 cup goat cheese, shredded

Directions

Add all ingredients, except for goat cheese, to the Instant Pot. Stir to combine; secure the cooker's lid.

Select "Manual" function and cook for 15 minutes at LOW pressure.

Once cooking is done, naturally release pressure for 10 minutes; make sure to release any remaining steam.

Stir in the goat cheese and whisk until it is well incorporated. Serve warm.

Morning Risotto with Butternut Squash

(Ready in about 25 minutes | Servings 4)

Ingredients

1 tablespoon canola oil

1/2 yellow onion, chopped

3 green garlics, minced

1 bell pepper, diced

2 cups butternut squash, peeled and diced

1 ½ cups Arborio rice

1/2 cup dry white wine

3 ½ cups vegetable broth

8 ounces white mushrooms

Kosher salt and ground black pepper, to taste

1/2 teaspoon dried basil

1/4 teaspoon dried oregano

1 large handful fresh parsley, roughly chopped

Directions

Using the "Sauté" setting, heat the Instant Pot with canola oil.

Then, sauté the onion, green garlic, bell pepper and butternut squash for 5 minutes. Then, stir in the rice.

Add the remaining ingredients, except for the parsley, and stir well to combine. Close the cooker's lid. Click the "Manual" button and cook for 5 minutes

Next, carefully release the pressure and open the cooker. Serve warm, topped with fresh parsley.

Peach Oatmeal with Almonds

(Ready in about 25 minutes | Servings 4)

Ingredients

2 cups rolled oats

4 cups water

1 peach, chopped

1/4 teaspoon ground cloves

2 tablespoons flax meal

1/2 cup almonds, chopped

A splash of milk

Directions

Add rolled oats, water, and peach to the Instant Pot.

Now, add the cloves and flax meal; stir to combine. Adjust the times for 3 minutes. Allow the pressure to release naturally.

Divide the mixture among four bowls. To serve, top with slivered almonds and a splash of milk.

Savory Mushroom and Gouda Oatmeal

(Ready in about 25 minutes | Servings 4)

Ingredients

2 tablespoons olive oil

1/2 onion, chopped

2 cloves garlic, minced

1 cup steel cut oats

1 (14-ounce) can roasted-vegetable stock

1/2 cup water

1/4 teaspoon salt

1/4 teaspoon seasoned pepper

8 ounces white mushrooms, sliced

1/2 cup smoked gouda, grated

Directions

Preheat the cooker by selecting "Sauté" mode. When the oil is hot, add the onions and garlic; cook for 4 minutes. Add steel cut oats and sauté 1 to 2 minutes.

Throw in the roasted-vegetable stock, water, salt and seasoned pepper. Lock the cooker's lid in place. Select HIGH pressure and 10-minute cook time.

Next, brush a skillet with a nonstick cooking spray. Next, sauté white mushrooms until tender and fragrant.

Turn off the pressure cooker and use the Natural pressure release. Then, remove the lid. Stir in the mushrooms. Serve topped with smoked gouda.

Cranberry Farro Salad

(Ready in about 40 minutes | Servings 4)

Ingredients

3 cups water

1 cup whole grain farro, rinsed

1 teaspoon freshly squeezed lemon juice

2 tablespoons coconut oil

1/4 teaspoon sea salt

1/2 cup dried cranberries, chopped

8 mint leaves, minced

2 cups blueberries

Directions

Pour the water into the cooker. Stir in the farro. Lock the lid in place; cook using HIGH pressure for 40 minutes. Then, quick release the pressure. Drain the farro and transfer it to a bowl.

Stir in the remaining ingredients. Serve well-chilled.

Cherry Oatmeal with Brown Sugar Topping

(Ready in about 30 minutes | Servings 4)

Ingredients

1 tablespoon butter

1 cup steel cut oats

3 ½ cups water

A pinch of kosher salt

3/4 cup dried cherries

1/2 teaspoon pure vanilla extract

For the Topping:

1/4 cup packed light brown sugar

1/4 teaspoon ground cloves

1/4 teaspoon ground anise star

1 teaspoon cinnamon

Directions

Add the butter to the cooker; select "Sauté' mode. Melt the butter and stir in the oats; toast them, stirring constantly, until they start to smell nutty.

Stir in the water and kosher salt. Select HIGH pressure and 10-minute cook time.

Then, release the pressure and carefully remove the lid. Stir in toasted oats, dried cherries, and vanilla extract. Cover and allow it to stand approximately 10 minutes.

Prepare the topping by mixing all topping ingredients. Serve the topping over the oatmeal and enjoy.

Tofu Scramble with Sautéed Veggies

(Ready in about 30 minutes | Servings 4)

Ingredients

16 ounces firm tofu, drained and mashed

1 teaspoon vermouth

1 teaspoon salt

1/2 teaspoon red pepper flakes, crushed

1/2 teaspoon black pepper

1 tablespoon sesame oil

1/2 cup shallots, chopped

2 cloves garlic, minced

2 medium-sized carrots, blanched

1/2 cup tomato, diced

1 quarter cup water

2 tablespoons fresh cilantro, chopped

Directions

In a mixing dish, combine the tofu, vermouth, salt, crushed red pepper flakes and black pepper.

Click "Sauté" key. Now, bring the sesame oil to medium warmth in your Instant Pot. Sauté the shallots, garlic, carrots, and tomato until the vegetables are tender.

Add the water to the Instant Pot, cover and cook until it is warmed through. Remove the cooker's lid and serve topped with cilantro. Enjoy!

Mediterranean Polenta with Sun-Dried Tomatoes

(Ready in about 35 minutes | Servings 4)

Ingredients

2 tablespoons extra-virgin olive oil

1/2 cup green onions, finely chopped

2 cloves garlic, minced

2 cups vegetable stock

2 cups water

1/3 cup finely diced sun-dried tomatoes

1 teaspoon salt

1/2 teaspoon dried basil

1/2 teaspoon dried rosemary, crushed

1 tablespoon fresh coriander, chopped

1 tablespoon fresh parsley, chopped

1 cup coarse polenta

Directions

Preheat an electric pressure cooker and warm the oil until it is hot. Now, sauté green onions and garlic until the onions are translucent and the garlic is fragrant and slightly browned.

Add the remaining ingredients, and stir to combine well.

Select the "Manual" button and cook for 15 minutes at LOW pressure.

Afterward, naturally release the pressure for 10 minutes; release any remaining steam. Serve warm, topped with Kalamata olives. Bon appétit!

Spiced Chicken Sausage Casserole

(Ready in about 30 minutes | Servings 6)

Ingredients

1 pound chicken sausage, ground

1 onion, peeled and diced

1 celery stalk, chopped

1 medium-sized carrot, chopped

1 jalapeño pepper, seeded and minced

2 tablespoons vegetable oil

1/2 cup flour

2 cups half-and-half

1/2 teaspoon dried thyme

1/4 teaspoon dried marjoram

Salt and ground black pepper, to your liking

Cayenne pepper, to your liking

Directions

Using the "Sauté" setting, cook the sausage along with the onions, celery, carrot, and minced jalapeño.

Seal the lid and cook for 10 to 12 minutes. Stir in vegetable oil and flour; stir-fry the mixture for 2 minutes.

Now, stir in the rest of the above ingredients. Bring it to a boil; then, reduce the heat and simmer, uncovered, for 3 minutes more. Eat warm.

Tangy Quinoa with Tomato and Bell Peppers

(Ready in about 10 minutes | Servings 4)

Ingredients

1 ½ cups water

1 cup quinoa, rinsed and drained

2 tablespoons olive oil

3/4 teaspoon salt

1 tomato, finely chopped and seeded

1 bell pepper, thinly sliced

2 garlic cloves, minced

1/3 cup fresh parsley, finely chopped

Juice of 1 lemon

Directions

Add the water, quinoa, 1 tablespoon of oil, and the salt to the Instant Pot. Seal the lid.

Select "Manual" setting and cook at HIGH pressure for 1 minute.

After that, use a natural release. Transfer the quinoa to a bowl and let it cool slightly.

Add the remaining ingredients. Taste and adjust the seasonings. Serve and enjoy!

Grits with Bacon and Cheddar Cheese

(Ready in about 35 minutes | Servings 4)

Ingredients

3 ½ cups water

1 cup grits

1 ½ teaspoons kosher salt

3/4 teaspoon smoked paprika

2 tablespoons vegetable oil

4 ounces bacon, coarsely chopped

1 cup Cheddar cheese, shredded

Directions

Add the water, grits, kosher salt, smoked paprika, and vegetable oil to your Instant Pot. Now, secure the lid.

Select "Manual" setting and cook at LOW pressure for 15 minutes.

Meanwhile, preheat a nonstick skillet over medium-high heat. Then, fry the bacon till it is crisp, about 10 minutes.

Serve your grits warm, topped with bacon and Cheddar cheese. Enjoy!

Tomato and Ham Omelet

(Ready in about 25 minutes | Servings 6)

Ingredients

6 medium-sized eggs

1/2 cup whole milk

1 white onion, finely chopped

2 cloves garlic, peeled and minced

1 cup ham, cooked and chopped

1 Roma tomato, chopped

1/2 teaspoon smoked cayenne pepper

Salt and ground black pepper, to your liking

1/2 teaspoon dried thyme

Directions

Start by whisking the eggs along with milk. Whisk to combine well.

Add the remaining items; stir until everything is well mixed. Pour the egg mixture into a heat-resistant dish; cover.

Add 1 cup of water to the base of your cooker. Lay the trivet on the bottom of the cooker. Lay the heat-resistant dish on the trivet.

Close the cooker's lid. Select "Manual" button and cook for 20 minutes under HIGH pressure. Serve warm.

Old-Fashioned Chicken Liver Pâté

(Ready in about 15 minutes | Servings 8)

Ingredients

1 teaspoon butter, at room temperature

1 leek, finely chopped

2 cloves garlic

3/4 pound chicken livers

1/4 cup rum

2 anchovies in oil

1 teaspoon dried marjoram

1 teaspoon dried thyme

1 teaspoon spicy brown mustard

3/4 teaspoon salt

Ground black pepper, to taste

Directions

Melt the butter in your cooker; sauté the leeks and garlic until tender. Next, add the chicken livers; continue to cook until the livers are seared.

Add the rum. Close the lid and cook for 5 minutes under HIGH pressure.

Afterward, stir in the rest of the above ingredients. Serve with crusty bread of choice.

Polenta with Caramelized Onion

(Ready in about 25 minutes | Servings 4)

Ingredients

3 ½ cups water

1 cup polenta

1 ½ teaspoons salt

3/4 teaspoon lemon thyme

1 tablespoon vegetable oil

2 tablespoons butter, room temperature

1 yellow onion, halved and sliced into rings

2 ounces goat cheese, crumbled

Honey, to drizzle

Directions

Throw the water, polenta, salt, lemon thyme, and vegetable oil into your Instant Pot. Now, secure the lid.

Select "Manual" setting and cook at LOW pressure for 15 minutes.

Meanwhile, preheat a nonstick skillet over medium-high heat. Then, warm the butter and add the slices of the onion. Now cook, over medium-low heat, stirring periodically until they are caramelized.

Serve polenta warm, topped with caramelized onion and goat cheese, and drizzled with honey. Enjoy!

Greek-Style Mediterranean Quinoa Salad

(Ready in about 10 minutes | Servings 4)

Ingredients

1 ½ cups water

1 cup quinoa, rinsed and drained

1/2 teaspoon sea salt

2 tablespoons extra-virgin olive oil

1 teaspoon dried oregano

1/2 teaspoon dried basil

1/4 teaspoon ground black pepper

1 red bell pepper, thinly sliced

1 cucumber, thinly sliced

1 large-sized purple onion, thinly sliced

1 tablespoon red-wine vinegar

Crumbled Feta cheese, to serve

Pitted olives, to serve

Directions

Add the water, quinoa, and salt to the Instant Pot. Seal the lid. Choose the "Manual" button and cook it for 1 minute using a HIGH pressure.

Next, perform a natural release. Transfer the quinoa to a bowl and let it cool completely.

Gently and slowly stir in the rest of the above items. Taste and adjust the seasonings. Bon appétit!

Pork and Chicken Liver Pâté

(Ready in about 20 minutes | Servings 8)

Ingredients

1 teaspoon olive oil

1/2 onion, finely chopped

2 cloves garlic, minced

1/2 pound ground pork

3/4 pound chicken livers, trimmed of connective tissue

1/4 cup sherry

1/4 teaspoon powdered ginger

1 teaspoon dried marjoram

1 teaspoon dried thyme

1 teaspoon spicy brown mustard

3/4 teaspoon salt

Ground black pepper, to taste

Directions

Warm the oil in an electric pressure cooker; sauté the onion and minced garlic until fragrant and tender. Now, add the ground pork and chicken livers; continue cooking until the meat is browned.

Add the sherry. Seal the cooker; cook for 5 minutes using a HIGH pressure.

Lastly, stir in the remaining ingredients. Serve with sweet pickles. Enjoy!

Autumn Pumpkin Steel Cut Oats

(Ready in about 25 minutes | Servings 4)

Ingredients

1 tablespoon coconut oil

1 cup steel cut oats

3 cups water

1 cup pumpkin puree

1/4 cup agave syrup

1/4 teaspoon ground cloves

1/2 teaspoon grated nutmeg

1 teaspoon ground cinnamon

1/4 teaspoon vanilla paste

1/8 teaspoon salt

Directions

Add the butter to the preheated pressure cooking pot. Select "Sauté" function. Then, melt the butter and add the oats; toast them, stirring frequently, about 3 minutes.

Add the remaining items. Select HIGH pressure and 10-minute cook time.

Stir in oats, uncover, and let them stand approximately 10 minutes. Serve warm with a splash of milk. Enjoy!

Coconut Oats with Raisins

(Ready in about 20 minutes | Servings 4)

Ingredients

2 tablespoons coconut butter

1 cup steel cut oats

3 ½ cups coconut milk

A pinch of kosher salt

1/2 cup golden raisins

1/4 cup shredded coconut, toasted

Directions

Add coconut butter to your Instant Pot; choose "Sauté" button. When coconut butter has melted, stir in the oats; toast them, stirring often, until they begin to smell nutty, 3 to 4 minutes.

Pour in coconut milk; now add the salt and golden raisins. Select HIGH pressure and 10-minute cook time.

After that, turn off the cooker. Use the Natural pressure release and carefully remove the lid.

Divide the oats among individual serving dishes and top each serving with coconut. Enjoy!

Mixed Berry and Chia Seeds Morning Treat

(Ready in about 20 minutes | Servings 4)

Ingredients

2 tablespoons butter

1 cup steel cut oats

3 ½ cups rice milk

A pinch of kosher salt

1 cup fresh or frozen mixed berries

1/4 cup Chia seeds

Directions

Begin by preheating your Instant Pot on "Sauté" function. Now, melt butter; toast the oats in the melted butter; make sure to stir frequently until the oats begin to smell nutty.

Next, add the rice milk and salt. Use HIGH pressure and 10-minute cook time.

After that, turn off the cooker; perform the Natural pressure release and open your cooker. Stir in mixed berries and Chia seeds.

Put the lid back on the cooker and let the mixture rest 7 to 10 minutes until it reaches desired thickness. Serve warm and enjoy!

Spring Steamed Eggs

(Ready in about 15 minutes | Servings 4)

Ingredients

4 eggs

1 cup cold water

1 cup spring onions, finely chopped

1 clove garlic, minced

1 medium-sized tomato, chopped

1/2 teaspoon kosher salt

1/4 teaspoon freshly ground black pepper

Directions

Mix the egg with water in a small-sized bowl.

Then, strain the egg/water mixture over a fine mesh strainer into a heat-proof bowl.

Stir in the remaining ingredients; mix to combine. Pour 1 cup of water into the inner pot of your Instant Pot.

Place a steamer basket in the pot. Place the heat-proof bowl on the steamer basket. Seal the cooker's lid.

Select "Manual" setting and 5-minute cook time; cook under HIGH pressure. Serve with English muffins or some rustic bread.

Steamed Eggs with Spinach and Shallot

(Ready in about 15 minutes | Servings 4)

Ingredients

4 eggs

1/2 cup milk

1 cup shallots, finely chopped

1 clove garlic, minced

1/2 cup spinach, chopped

1/2 teaspoon dried dill weed

1/4 teaspoon cayenne pepper

1/2 teaspoon kosher salt

1/4 teaspoon freshly ground black pepper

Directions

Start by mixing eggs and milk in a small-sized bowl.

Now, strain the egg/milk mixture over a fine mesh strainer into a heat-proof bowl

Stir in the rest of the above items; mix to combine well. Pour 1 cup of water into the inner pot of your cooker.

Place a steamer basket in the pot. Lower the heat-proof bowl onto the steamer basket. Cover with the lid.

Select "Manual" mode. Cook 5 minutes using a HIGH pressure. Serve with sour cream or homemade rustic bread. Enjoy!

Pressure Cooker Eggs de Provence

(Ready in about 25 minutes | Servings 4)

Ingredients

6 eggs

2 tablespoons water

1/2 cup heavy cream

1 white onion, chopped

1 cup cooked ham

1 cup Swiss chard, chopped

1 cup Colby cheese, grated

1/4 teaspoon dried savory

1/4 teaspoon dried marjoram

1/4 teaspoon dried thyme

1/4 teaspoon dried oregano

1/4 teaspoon sea salt

1/2 teaspoon ground black pepper

Directions

In a mixing bowl, whisk the eggs along with water and heavy cream.

Add the remaining ingredients and stir till everything is well combined. Spoon the mixture into a heat-proof dish and cover with aluminum foil.

Add 1 cup of water to the bottom of your cooker. Place the trivet inside. Lower the dish onto the trivet. Close the lid according to manufacturer's directions.

Press "Manual" key; cook under HIGH pressure for 20 minutes. Afterward, perform the Natural pressure release. Serve warm.

Morning Summer Salad

(Ready in about 10 minutes + chilling time | Servings 6)

Ingredients

2 cups jasmine rice, soaked and well rinsed

3/4 teaspoon salt

3 cups water

1 large-sized candy onion, chopped

1 yellow bell pepper, seeded and thinly sliced

1 red bell pepper, seeded and thinly sliced

Coarse black pepper, to your liking

1/2 teaspoon dried oregano

1/2 teaspoon dried basil

1 tablespoon fresh sage, chopped

2 tablespoons extra-virgin olive oil

2 tablespoons fresh parsley, finely chopped

1 tablespoon white vinegar

1 tablespoon fresh lemon juice

1/4 cup olives, pitted and sliced

Directions

First, cook the rice along with salt and water using the "Manual" function and 4-minute cook time.

Then, perform the Natural pressure release. Allow the rice to cool slightly.

Add the rest of the above ingredients. Stir until everything is well incorporated and serve chilled.

Rice Pudding with Strawberries and Apricots

(Ready in about 25 minutes | Servings 6)

Ingredients

1 ½ cups basmati rice

1/2 cup sugar

1 tablespoon agave syrup

5 cups whole milk

2 eggs

1 cup evaporated milk

1/2 cup dried strawberries

1/2 cup dried apricots, chopped

1/2 teaspoon ground cardamom

1/8 teaspoon salt

Anise seeds, to taste

Directions

In the inner pot, combine the rice, sugar, agave syrup, and whole milk.

Now, select the "Sauté" mode and bring it to a boil. Stir until the sugar dissolves completely.

Then, cover the cooker according to the manufacturer's instructions. Select the "Rice" mode.

In the meantime, simmer the eggs and evaporated milk. After that, use the quick-pressure release. Stir in the egg mixture, along with dried strawberries, apricots, cardamom, salt, and anise.

Press the "Sauté" button. Continue to cook, uncovered, until your pudding starts to boil. Serve immediately or at room temperature.

Wheat Berry Salad with Cherries and Hazelnuts

(Ready in about 20 minutes + chilling time | Servings 6)

Ingredients

Cold water

1 cup wheat berries

2 cups water

1/4 cup dry white wine

1 tablespoon lime juice

1 teaspoon yellow mustard

1 teaspoon sea salt

3/4 teaspoon red pepper flakes, crushed

3 tablespoons extra-virgin olive oil

1 cup scallions, chopped

1 cup dried cherries

1/2 cup hazelnuts, chopped

Directions

The night before, soak wheat berries in cold water. Rinse and drain.

Transfer the soaked wheat berries to your electric pressure cooker; now, pour in 2 cups of water. Then, let it cook for 20 minutes using "Multigrain" function.

Drain wheat berries and transfer them to a large-sized salad bowl. Add the remaining ingredients.

Then, place your salad in the fridge at least 3 hours. Eat well-chilled and enjoy!

Soft Boiled Eggs

(Ready in about 10 minutes | Servings 6)

Ingredients

6 eggs

Seasonings, to taste

Croque Monsieur, to serve

Directions

Pour 1 cup of water into the inner pot. Place the steamer basket inside.

Add the eggs to the steamer basket. Close the lid according to the manufacturer's directions.

Press the "Manual" button and cook under HIGH pressure for 4 minutes. Transfer the eggs to a bowl of cold water. Peel the eggs and season them to taste. Serve with Croque Monsieur.

Potato Hash with Poached Eggs

(Ready in about 10 minutes | Servings 6)

Ingredients

1 cup water

1 cup red potatoes, peeled and cubed

2 tablespoons bacon fat

1 chili pepper, minced

1/2 scallions, chopped

1 tablespoon bacon, fried and crumbled

1 clove garlic, minced

1 teaspoon fennel seeds

Sea salt and crushed red pepper flakes, to taste

2 large-sized eggs

1 tablespoon fresh cilantro, chopped

Directions

Pour 1 cup of water into the inner pot; place the trivet inside. Place the dish with potatoes on the trivet. Close the lid tightly, choose "Manual" button, and cook under HIGH pressure for 2 minutes. Press the "Cancel" button. Reserve the potatoes.

Set the cooker on "Sauté" and warm the bacon fat. Now, cook chili pepper and scallions for a couple of minutes, stirring continuously.

Now, stir in the reserved potatoes, along with bacon, garlic, fennel seeds, salt, and red pepper flakes; stir until it is thoroughly warmed. Then, using a spatula, make a little crater in the middle of this mixture. Crack the eggs gently into the crater.

Close the lid tightly, and cook it for 1 minute under HIGH pressure. After that, carefully remove the lid. Serve topped with fresh chopped cilantro. Enjoy!

Broccoli Scrambled Tofu

(Ready in about 20 minutes | Servings 4)

Ingredients

16 ounces firm tofu, drained

1 teaspoon fresh lime juice

1/2 teaspoon cayenne pepper

1/2 teaspoon black pepper

1 teaspoon sea salt

1 tablespoon sesame oil

2 cloves garlic, minced

1/2 cup onions, chopped

1 cup broccoli florets, blanched

1 quarter cup water

2 tablespoons fresh parsley, chopped

Directions

In a mixing dish, mash the tofu using a fork; stir in the lime juice, cayenne pepper, black pepper, and salt.

Choose the "Sauté" button. Then, bring sesame oil to medium warmth in your cooker. Sauté the garlic, onions, and broccoli until they have softened.

Add the water, cover, and cook till the mixture is heated through. Take away the lid and serve topped with fresh parsley. Enjoy!

Cranberry and Pecan Oats with Cheese Topping

(Ready in about 30 minutes | Servings 4)

Ingredients

For the Oatmeal:

1 tablespoon butter

1 cup steel-cut oats

3 ½ cups water

1/4 teaspoon salt

1/2 teaspoon ground anise star

3/4 cup cranberries

1/2 cup pecans

For the Topping:

2 ounces Ricotta cheese, softened

2 tablespoons powdered sugar

1 teaspoon milk

1 teaspoon vanilla paste

A pinch of salt

A pinch of ground cloves

Directions

Add the butter to the cooker, and select "Sauté" function. When the butter is melted, toast the oats approximately 3 minutes; make sure to stir constantly.

Add the water, salt, and anise seeds to the cooker. Select HIGH pressure and 10-minute cook time. After that, perform the Natural pressure release for 5 minutes.

Stir in cranberries and pecans. Cover and allow the mixture to stand about 10 minutes.

Make the topping by whisking together all the topping components. Serve at room temperature.

Oatmeal with Fruits and Peanut Butter

(Ready in about 25 minutes | Servings 4)

Ingredients

For the Oatmeal:

1 cup soy milk

3/4 cup water

1 cup fast-cooking oats

2 tablespoons sugar

1/2 teaspoon pure coconut extract

1/2 teaspoon pure vanilla extract

1 teaspoon cinnamon powder

1/2 teaspoon ground cloves

1/4 teaspoon grated nutmeg

For the Topping:

Peanut butter

1 apple, cored, peeled and diced

1 pear, cored, peeled and diced

Directions

In your Instant Pot, combine all ingredients for the oatmeal.

Lock the lid according to the manufacturer's directions; set the Instant Pot to cook for 18 minutes under HIGH pressure.

Turn off the machine; release the pressure. Stir the oatmeal and divide it among 4 serving bowls. Top each serving with a dollop of peanut butter. Add the slices of apple and pear and serve.

Apple Maple Breakfast Quinoa

(Ready in about 10 minutes | Servings 6)

Ingredients

1 ½ cups quinoa

1/2 cup apple juice

1/2 cup water

1 tablespoon coconut butter

6 cardamom pods

1 vanilla bean

1/2 cup pomegranate seeds

Maple syrup, to serve

Directions

In your Instant Pot, place all ingredients, except for pomegranate seeds and maple syrup.

Close and lock the cooker's lid. Choose "Manual" setting and cook for 2 minutes. After that, perform the Natural pressure release

Serve warm, topped with pomegranate seeds and drizzled with maple syrup to taste.

Cheesy Spinach and Tomato Quiche

(Ready in about 25 minutes | Servings 6)

Ingredients

1/2 cup milk

12 eggs

3/4 teaspoon salt

1/2 teaspoon cayenne pepper

1/4 teaspoon ground black pepper

3 cups fresh spinach leaves, roughly chopped

1 cup tomatoes, diced

3/4 cup yellow onions, sliced

1/4 cup Parmigiano-Reggiano cheese, shredded

Directions

Lay a trivet in the bottom of your cooker; pour in 1 ½ cups of water.

In a large-sized bowl, whisk the milk, eggs, salt, cayenne pepper, and black pepper.

In a baking dish, combine the spinach, tomatoes, and onions; stir to combine. Pour the egg mixture over the spinach mixture; stir to combine. Top with Parmigiano-Reggiano.

Lock the lid in place. Use a HIGH pressure and 20-minute cook time. After that, use the Quick pressure release. Serve warm.

Sausage and Ham Quiche

(Ready in about 35 minutes | Servings 4)

Ingredients

6 eggs, beaten

1/2 cup milk

1/2 teaspoon dried dill weed

1/2 teaspoon cayenne pepper

1/4 teaspoon ground black pepper

3/4 teaspoon salt

1 cup ground sausage, cooked

1/2 cup diced ham

1/2 cup onions, finely chopped

1 cup Colby cheese, shredded

Directions

Put a trivet into the bottom of the Instant Pot; now add 1 ½ cups of water.

In a bowl, whisk together the eggs, milk, dill, cayenne pepper, black pepper, and salt. Stir the sausage, ham, onions, and Colby cheese into a soufflé dish; stir well to combine.

Pour the egg mixture over the top. Loosely cover the dish with foil. Seal the lid and cook under HIGH pressure for 30 minutes. After that, use the Quick pressure release.

Next, open the lid and serve immediately.

Yummy Carrot Oatmeal with Prunes

(Ready in about 15 minutes | Servings 6)

Ingredients

1 tablespoon coconut butter

1 cup steel-cut oats

4 cups water

1 cup carrots, grated

3 tablespoons agave syrup

1/2 teaspoon grated nutmeg

1/4 teaspoon ground cloves

1 teaspoon ground cinnamon

1 teaspoon pumpkin pie spice

A pinch of salt

3/4 cup prunes, pitted and chopped

1/4 cup chia seeds

Directions

Add coconut butter to the Instant Pot; now, select "Sauté" function. Then, toast the oats in melted butter about 3 minutes.

Stir in the remaining ingredients. Next, select HIGH pressure and 10-minute cook time.

Perform the Natural pressure release, and then, carefully remove the lid. Eat warm.

Rich Apricot Bread Pudding

(Ready in about 45 minutes | Servings 4)

Ingredients

2 tablespoons coconut butter, melted

7 thick slices bread, cubed

1/3 cup brown sugar

1 tablespoon raw honey

3 cups milk

3 eggs, well beaten

1/4 teaspoon ground cloves

1/2 teaspoon ground cinnamon

1/4 teaspoon salt

1/2 cup dried apricots, roughly chopped

Directions

First, brush a 5-cup bowl with melted coconut butter. Then, drop the bread pieces into the bowl.

In another bowl, prepare the custard by mixing all of the remaining ingredients, except chopped apricots. Pour the custard mixture over bread pieces in the bowl.

Scatter chopped apricots over the top. Let it rest about 15 minutes.

Cover the bowl with the buttered foil. Place a steaming rack in the cooking pot; pour in 2 cups of water.

Seal the cooker and choose the "Manual" setting; cook at HIGH pressure for 25 minutes. Afterward, use the Natural release method. Serve at room temperature.

Easy Berry Oatmeal

(Ready in about 10 minutes | Servings 4)

Ingredients

3 cups water

1 cup toasted metal-reduce oats

2 teaspoons canola oil

1 cup apple juice

2 tablespoons dried cranberries

2 tablespoons dried cherries

1 tablespoon agave nectar

1/2 teaspoon vanilla paste

1/4 teaspoon ground cinnamon

1/2 teaspoon ground cardamom

Directions

Lower the rack onto the bottom of your cooker; pour 1/2 cup of water over the rack.

In a heatproof bowl, place the remaining 2 ½ cups water, oats, and canola oil. Now, add the apple juice, cranberries, cherries, and agave nectar,

Then, stir in the remaining ingredients. Lock the lid into place. Cook for 8 minutes and eat warm. Enjoy!

Amaranth and Berry Oatmeal

(Ready in about 25 minutes | Servings 6)

Ingredients

2 tablespoons coconut oil

1/2 cup amaranth seeds

2 cups steel cut oats

3 cups milk

3 cups water

3 apples, diced

1 cup fresh mixed berries

1/2 teaspoon ground cinnamon

1/4 cup maple syrup

1/4 teaspoon ground cardamom

1/2 teaspoon ground anise star

Directions

Grease the bottom and sides of the Instant Pot container with coconut oil. Soak amaranth overnight.

Add all ingredients to the cooker and select "Porridge" setting.

Now, close the valve and cook for 20 minutes. Carefully open the Instant Pot and serve warm.

Amaranth Porridge with Blackberries and Cream

(Ready in about 25 minutes | Servings 4)

Ingredients

1/2 cup amaranth

1 cup coconut milk

1 cup fresh blackberries

1 tablespoon agave syrup

1 small-sized vanilla bean

1 cinnamon stick

2-3 whole cloves

Coconut whipped cream, to serve

Directions

Soak amaranth overnight. Brush the bottom and sides of the Instant Pot container with a nonstick cooking spray.

Add all ingredients, except whipped cream, to the cooker; choose "Porridge" function.

Now, seal the lid and cook 20 minutes. Eat warm, topped with coconut whipped cream.

Decadent Challah Bread Pudding with Walnuts

(Ready in about 50 minutes | Servings 4)

Ingredients

3 tablespoons butter, melted

1/2 cup brown sugar

1 teaspoon honey

3 cups milk

3 eggs, beaten

1/2 teaspoon pure almond extract

1/2 teaspoon vanilla extract

1/4 teaspoon grated nutmeg

1/8 teaspoon ground anise star

1/2 teaspoon ground cinnamon

1/4 teaspoon kosher salt

8 slices Challah bread, cubed

1/2 cup raisins

1/2 cup walnuts, toasted and coarsely chopped

2 tablespoons heavy cream

Directions

In a bowl, whisk together the butter, sugar, honey, milk, eggs, almond and vanilla extract; then, stir in the spices.

Fold in cubed bread and raisins. Let it stand about 20 minutes until the bread absorbs the liquid; press down occasionally.

Pour bread pudding into a greased baking dish that fits into your cooker. Cover the dish with foil and create a foil sling.

Pour 1 ½ cups water into the cooker; lay the trivet in the bottom. Now, lower the baking dish into the pressure cooker.

Cover and choose HIGH pressure and 20-minute cook time. After that, turn off your cooker; perform the Quick pressure release and carefully remove the cooker's lid.

Eat warm, topped with walnuts and heavy cream. Enjoy!

Peanut and Date Rice Pudding

(Ready in about 20 minutes | Servings 2)

Ingredients

1/2 cup jasmine rice

1 tablespoon peanut butter

2 tablespoons hemp seeds

1 teaspoon pumpkin seeds

1/2 cup peanuts, minced

1/4 cup dates, pitted and chopped

1/2 teaspoon vanilla essence

7 cups of water

Directions

Simply drop all ingredients into an electric pressure cooker.

Now, select "Rice" mode. When the rice is ready, carefully open the lid.

Serve warm, topped with some extra peanut butter, if desired. Enjoy!

Pear Challah French Toast

(Ready in about 20 minutes | Servings 6)

Ingredients

1 ½ cups water

2 tablespoons light corn syrup

1 tablespoon butter, melted

3 eggs, well beaten

1 cup whole milk

1 tablespoon honey

1 teaspoon vanilla extract

1 (29-ounce) can pear halves, cut lengthwise into 4 slices

1 pound stale Challah bread, torn into bite-sized chunks

Directions

Prepare your cooker by adding the water to the inner pot; add the steam rack to the cooker. Then, grease a soufflé dish using a nonstick cooking spray.

In a mixing bowl, thoroughly whisk the corn syrup, butter, eggs, milk, honey, and vanilla extract.

Place the pear halves on the bottom of the greased soufflé dish. Then, place the bread chunks on the top of the pears.

Pour the egg mixture over the pears and bread; using a wide spatula, push down to submerge the bread. Lower the soufflé dish onto the steam rack. Seal the lid.

Push the "Manual" button, and pressure cook for 15 minutes using a HIGH pressure. After that, use the Quick release method. Open the cooker carefully and serve warm. Enjoy!

Rich Apple French Toast Casserole

(Ready in about 35 minutes | Servings 4)

Ingredients

1 ½ cups water

1 loaf French baguette, cut into 1-inch thick slices

3 apples, peeled, cored and diced

2 tablespoons melted margarine

3 eggs, beaten

1 cup milk

1 tablespoon agave nectar

1/2 teaspoon coconut extract

1 teaspoon vanilla extract

1 tablespoon fresh lemon juice

1 teaspoon ground cinnamon

1 teaspoon ground cloves

Directions

Prepare your Instant Pot by adding the water to the inner pot; place the steam rack on the bottom of the cooker. Lightly oil a baking dish that fits in your cooker.

Arrange the bread slices and apples in your baking dish.

In a mixing dish, thoroughly combine all remaining ingredients. Pour this mixture over the bread/apple layer; let it stand about 15 minutes. Lower the baking dish onto the steam rack.

Seal the lid and use the "Manual" function; let it cook for 15 minutes under HIGH pressure. Lastly, perform the Quick release method. Serve right away.

Morning Pudding with Seeds and Prunes

(Ready in about 20 minutes | Servings 2)

Ingredients

1/2 cup basmati rice

2 tablespoons hemp seeds

1 teaspoon sunflower seeds

1 teaspoon flax seeds

1/2 cup pecans, minced

1/4 cup prunes, pitted and chopped

1/4 teaspoon ground cloves

1/2 teaspoon grated nutmeg

1/2 teaspoon pure almond extract

1/2 teaspoon pure vanilla essence

7 cups of water

Directions

Simply drop all ingredients into your Instant Pot.

Now, push the "Rice" button. When the cooking is complete, carefully open the lid.

Serve warm and enjoy!

Cajun Rice with Spinach and Sausage

(Ready in about 20 minutes | Servings 8)

Ingredients

2 pounds sausage, cut into 1/2-inch slices

1 tablespoon Cajun seasoning

1 teaspoon salt

3 tablespoons oil

2 cups shallots, chopped

2 cups Arborio rice, cooked

2 ½ cups beef stock

1 cup water

1 red bell pepper, seeded and diced

1 summer squash, seeded and diced

1 cup spinach, torn into pieces

Directions

Sprinkle the sausage with the Cajun seasoning and salt. Click the "Sauté" button and heat the oil. Then, cook the sausage for 3 minutes, stirring constantly.

Stir in the shallots and cook for 3 minutes until it is softened.

Then, stir in the remaining ingredients and cook for 5 minutes under HIGH pressure. Allow it to stand approximately 5 minutes.

Pressure Cooker Banana Bread

(Ready in about 30 minutes | Servings 8)

Ingredients

1/3 cup butter, at room temperature

3/4 cup sugar

1 egg

1 teaspoon pure vanilla essence

2 ripe bananas, mashed

1 ½ cups flour

1 teaspoon baking powder

1/8 teaspoon salt

1/3 cup cashew milk

1/2 teaspoon ground cloves

1/2 teaspoon grated nutmeg

1/4 teaspoon ground cinnamon

1 tablespoon cream of tartar

Directions

In a mixing bowl, cream together the butter and sugar. Fold in the egg and vanilla essence; mix to combine well. Then, stir in mashed bananas.

In another bowl, combine the flour, baking powder, and salt. Gradually add this mixture to the wet ingredients.

Add the rest of the above ingredients. Transfer the mixture to the baking pan and cover it with foil.

Add 2 cups of water to the bottom of your Instant Pot. Set a rack to the bottom of the Instant Pot. Lower the baking pan filled with batter onto the rack.

Close the lid and choose "Manual"; cook for 30 minutes. Afterward, allow the cooker to naturally release pressure. Allow the bread to cool slightly before removing it from the pan.

Black Rice Pudding with Figs

(Ready in about 35 minutes | Servings 4)

Ingredients

3 cups of water

4 cups rice milk

1 cup black rice

1 tablespoon flax seeds

1/2 cup dried figs, pitted and chopped

1/4 teaspoon ground cinnamon

1/4 teaspoon ground cloves

1/2 teaspoon grated nutmeg

1/2 teaspoon pure vanilla essence

Directions

Simply throw all ingredients into your Instant Pot.

Now, push the "Rice" key. When the cooking is complete, carefully open the lid.

Serve warm, topped with cream, if desired. Enjoy!

LUNCH

Flavorful Black Bean Soup

(Ready in about 45 minutes | Servings 6)

Ingredients

1 poblano pepper

2 tablespoons olive oil

1 leek, finely diced

2 bell peppers, finely diced

1 carrot, chopped

3 garlic cloves, minced

2 teaspoons ground cumin

1 teaspoon dried basil

1 teaspoon dried thyme

1 pound dried black beans, rinsed

2 bay leaves

7 cups vegetable stock

1/4 salt

1/8 teaspoon freshly ground black pepper

Directions

Preheat the oven to broil. Brush the poblano pepper with 1 teaspoon of olive oil. Broil it on all sides. Remove the seeds from the pepper, peel, and chop it.

Preheat your cooker by selecting "Sauté" button. Then, heat the remaining 1 ½ tablespoons of olive oil. Now, cook the leeks, bell peppers, carrot and garlic for 3 to 5 minutes, until they have softened.

Stir in the reserved roasted poblano pepper, cumin, basil, and thyme. Cook for another 1 minute.

Add the beans, bay leaves, stock, salt, and black pepper. Secure the lid, and select the "Manual" mode; cook for 30 minutes under HIGH pressure. Afterward, use a natural release.

Taste and adjust the seasonings. Lastly, purée the soup with an immersion blender. Serve topped with avocado slices or fresh cilantro leaves, if desired. Enjoy!

Traditional French Onion Soup

(Ready in about 35 minutes | Servings 6)

Ingredients

4 tablespoons butter

2 pounds sweet onions, cut into thinly slices

1 teaspoon kosher salt

1/2 teaspoon freshly ground black pepper

1 teaspoon white sugar

1/2 cup dry white wine

6 cups beef broth, preferably homemade

1 teaspoon granulated garlic

1 fresh rosemary sprig

1 fresh thyme sprig

1 loaf French bread, cut into slices and toasted

1 cup Gruyère cheese, grated

Directions

Preheat your cooker by selecting "Sauté". Then, melt the butter; sauté the onions until translucent, about 15 minutes.

Reduce the heat to low. Now, add the salt, black pepper, and white sugar. Continue to cook, stirring constantly, until the onions turn golden brown.

Add the wine, and scrape off any brown bits from the bottom of your cooker. Now, pour in the broth and stir to combine; add granulated garlic, rosemary, and thyme.

Secure the lid, and select "Manual" setting; cook at HIGH pressure for 7 minutes.

Preheat the oven to broil.

Ladle the soup into ovenproof bowls; top with toasted bread and grated cheese; place under the broiler for 7 minutes, or until the cheese is bubbly.

Creamed Cheesy Tomato Soup

(Ready in about 40 minutes | Servings 4)

Ingredients

2 tablespoons olive oil

1 large-sized onion, chopped

1 carrot, peeled and chopped

1 parsnip, chopped

2 garlic cloves, smashed

3 pounds ripe tomatoes, chopped

1 teaspoon sugar

1 cup roasted-vegetable broth

Kosher salt and freshly ground black pepper, to your liking

1/3 cup heavy cream

Grated Parmigiano-Reggiano cheese, to serve

Directions

First, select the "Sauté" button to preheat your Instant Pot. Now, warm the oil, followed by the onion, carrot, and parsnip. Cook about 7 minutes, or until the veggies are tender and fragrant.

Now, stir in the garlic, continue sautéing for 2 minutes more. Add the tomatoes, sugar, broth, salt and ground black pepper.

Close the cooker and select the "Manual" mode; cook for 15 minutes under HIGH pressure. Once pressure cooking is complete, use a naturally release for 10 minutes.

After that, stir in the cream. Use an immersion blender to purée the soup. Serve topped with Parmigiano-Reggiano cheese. Enjoy!

Cheesy Cauliflower and Potato Soup

(Ready in about 15 minutes | Servings 4)

Ingredients

2 tablespoons olive oil

1 yellow onion, peeled and sliced

2 garlic cloves, smashed

1 cauliflower head, broken into florets

1 pound potatoes, peeled and cut into ½-inch cubes

4 cups vegetable broth

Kosher salt

Freshly ground black pepper

1 cup half-and-half

1 cup sharp Cheddar cheese, shredded

Directions

Preheat the Instant Pot by selecting "Sauté" mode.

Once hot, add the oil, followed by the onion and garlic. Stir and cook for about 3 minutes, until the onion begins to turn translucent.

Add the cauliflower, potatoes, and broth. Season with salt and pepper. Secure the lid.

Select "Manual" mode and cook for 5 minutes using a HIGH pressure. Press the "Cancel" button; release any remaining steam.

Add the half-and-half and 1/2 cup of shredded cheese.

Blend using an immersion blender. Serve topped with a sprinkle of the remaining shredded cheese. Enjoy!

Smoky Cannellini Bean Soup

(Ready in about 35 minutes | Servings 6)

Ingredients

2 tablespoons vegetable oil

1 red onion, finely diced

1 red bell pepper, finely diced

1 yellow bell pepper, finely diced

1 parsnip, chopped

2 celery stalks, chopped

4 garlic cloves, minced

2 bay leaves

1 teaspoon ground cumin

1 teaspoon dried marjoram

1 pound dried cannellini beans, rinsed

7 cups roasted-vegetable stock

1/2 teaspoon cayenne pepper

4-5 black peppercorns

1 teaspoon smoked paprika

A few drops of liquid smoke

1/4 salt

1/8 teaspoon freshly ground black pepper

Directions

Preheat your Instant Pot by selecting "Sauté" button. Then, heat the oil and sauté the onion, bell peppers, parsnip, celery and garlic for 5 minutes, until they have softened.

Stir in the remaining items. Secure the lid and press the "Manual" button; cook for 30 minutes under HIGH pressure. Lastly, use a natural release.

Discard bay leaves and serve in individual bowls, topped with fresh chopped cilantro leaves, if desired.

Hot and Spicy Navy Bean Soup

(Ready in about 45 minutes | Servings 8)

Ingredients

1 cup dry navy beans

1 large bunch kale, stemmed and chopped

1 tablespoon vegetable oil

1 cup onion, chopped

2 cloves garlic, minced

4 cups beef broth

Kosher salt and ground black pepper, to taste

Hot sauce, to taste

Directions

First, soak the navy beans overnight. Drain and rinse.

Cook the soaked beans in your Instant Pot along with 4 cups of water for 25 minutes. After that, perform the Natural release method.

Meanwhile, bring a separate pot of salted water to a boil. Now, steam the kale until it is bright green, approximately 2 to 3 minutes. Drain in a strainer and rinse with running water. Reserve.

In a stock pot, heat the oil over medium-high heat. Then, sauté the onion and garlic until tender and fragrant. Now, pour in a splash of broth and scrape up any browned bits.

Next, add reserved beans, followed by remaining broth, salt, and black pepper, to the stock pot. Bring soup to a boil. Then, reduce the heat to low, and simmer for 15 minutes. Add the kale and cook until everything is heated through.

Serve warm with a few drizzles of hot sauce. Enjoy!

Red Lentil Soup with Vegetables

(Ready in about 35 minutes | Servings 10)

Ingredients

1 cup red lentils

1 cup yellow split peas

1 cup leeks, coarsely chopped

2 carrots, coarsely chopped

1 parsnip, coarsely chopped

4 cloves garlic, chopped

8 cups chicken broth

Kosher salt and freshly cracked black pepper, to taste

1 tablespoon white wine vinegar

Directions

Put the lentils, split peas, leeks, carrots, parsnip, and garlic into your cooker; mix to combine.

Now, pour in the chicken broth and seal the Instant Pot. Press "Soup" key and cook under HIGH pressure for 30 minutes.

Remove from heat, and add the salt, black pepper, and wine vinegar. Stir before serving and eat warm!

Creamed Root Vegetable Soup

(Ready in about 40 minutes | Servings 8)

Ingredients

4 yellow potatoes, peeled and cubed

3 stalks celery, chopped

1 turnip, chopped

1 parsnip, chopped

1 carrot, chopped

1 large-sized yellow onion, chopped

4 cups water, or as needed

1 (12-ounce) can evaporated milk

4 tablespoons butter

1/2 teaspoon dried dill weed

1 teaspoon red pepper flakes, crushed

Salt and ground black pepper, to taste

Directions

Place the potatoes, celery, turnip, parsnip, carrot, and onion in the cooker; now, pour in the water.

Cover the cooker, seal, and press the "Soup" button. Cook for 25 minutes.

Then, release the pressure and open the cooker. Mix in the milk, butter, dill, red pepper, salt, and ground black pepper; now, bring the soup to a boil over medium heat.

Reduce heat to a simmer; cook the soup about 15 minutes. Adjust the seasonings, serve hot and enjoy.

Lightly Spicy Super Yummy Corn Chowder

(Ready in about 20 minutes | Servings 4)

Ingredients

1 tablespoon vegetable olive oil

1 yellow onion, chopped

2 cloves garlic, finely minced

1 yellow bell pepper, finely diced

1 green bell pepper, finely diced

1/2 teaspoon crushed red pepper flakes

1 ½ cups roasted-vegetable stock

6 ears corn, cut the corn off the cob

1 (13.5-ounce) can coconut milk

1 tablespoon balsamic vinegar

Kosher salt and freshly ground pepper, to taste

Sunflower seeds, for garnish

Directions

Preheat the Instant Pot by using "Sauté" feature. Heat the oil; sauté the onion, garlic, and bell peppers until they're tender or about 3 minutes.

Now, add the red pepper and stir an additional 2 minutes. Add the broth and corn, and seal the pot. Select "Manual" mode and cook under HIGH pressure for 3 minutes.

Press "Cancel' button and use a quick release. Stir in the coconut milk, vinegar, kosher salt, and ground black pepper.

Blend about two-thirds of the soup with an immersion blender. Serve in individual bowls, sprinkled with sunflower seeds. Bon appétit!

Creamy and Cheesy Broccoli Soup

(Ready in about 35 minutes | Servings 4)

Ingredients

4 tablespoons butter, divided

2 onions, chopped

2 garlic cloves, smashed

2 carrots, chopped

1 head of broccoli, cut into florets

3 cups chicken stock

Kosher salt and freshly ground black pepper, to your liking

1 teaspoon cayenne pepper

3 tablespoons all-purpose flour

1 cup whole milk

1/2 cup Swiss cheese, grated

Directions

Select "Sauté" mode to preheat your Instant Pot. Then, heat 1 tablespoon of the butter; sauté the onions and garlic for 5 minutes, or until they are tender.

Add the carrots, broccoli, stock, salt, black pepper, and cayenne pepper. Secure the lid. Select "Manual" mode and cook under HIGH pressure for 6 minutes. Afterward, use a natural release

Meanwhile, in a skillet, melt the remaining 3 tablespoons of butter over medium flame. Whisk in the flour and whole milk.

Purée the broccoli mixture using an immersion blender. Return the puréed mixture to the pot; stir in the milk mixture. Stir until everything is well incorporated.

Serve in four soup bowls, topped with Swiss cheese. Bon appétit!

Potato Chowder with Sausage and Swiss Chard

(Ready in about 15 minutes | Servings 8)

Ingredients

2 tablespoons olive oil

10 ounces cooked Spanish chorizo, sliced

1 onion, chopped

2 garlic cloves, minced

2 pounds Yukon Gold potatoes, peeled and cubed

6 cups vegetable broth

Kosher salt and freshly ground black pepper, to your liking

1 bunch Swiss chard, stemmed and roughly chopped

Directions

Add all ingredients, except for Swiss chard, to the Instant Pot. Then, press the "Soup" button and set the timer for 8 minutes.

Use a potato masher to mash about 1/2 of the mixture.

Next, press the "Sauté" button and add Swiss chard. Cook for 4 to 5 minutes longer or until the chard is wilted. Serve at once.

Lentil, Shrimp, and Kale Stew

(Ready in about 35 minutes | Servings 4)

Ingredients

2 tablespoons olive oil

1 large-sized Vidalia onion, chopped

2 celery stalks, chopped

1 carrot, trimmed and chopped

1 parsnip, trimmed and chopped

2 garlic cloves, minced

1/2 teaspoon ground cumin

1 cup water

2 cups chicken stock

1 cup dried green lentils, rinsed and drained

Salt and freshly ground black pepper, to taste

16 large-sized shrimp, peeled and deveined

5 ounces fresh kale leaves, torn into pieces

Juice of 1 small-sized lime

Directions

Add all ingredients, except shrimp, kale, and lime juice, to the electric pressure cooker.

Then, select "Soup" setting; set the timer for 20 minutes.

Select "Sauté" setting. Add the shrimp and kale and bring to a boil; turn the heat off. Allow it to stand for 5 to 6 minutes. Stir in the lime juice and serve in individual soup bowls immediately.

Chipotle Black Beans

(Ready in about 25 minutes | Servings 8)

Ingredients

2 tablespoons olive oil

1 onion, finely diced

1 green bell pepper, finely chopped

1 red bell pepper, finely chopped

3 garlic cloves, minced

1 teaspoon ground cumin

1 canned chipotles in adobo, roughly chopped

1 pound dried black beans, rinsed, and soaked overnight

4 cups vegetable stock

4 cups water

1 teaspoon salt

1/2 teaspoon ground black pepper

Directions

Preheat your cooker by selecting "Sauté" mode. Add the oil to the pot and swirl it around.

Then, sauté the onion, bell peppers, and garlic. Stir in the ground cumin and continue cooking for 1 to 2 minutes. Add the chipotles and stir until heated through.

Add the beans, vegetable stock, water, salt, and ground black pepper. Secure the lid and select "Manual"; cook at HIGH pressure for 15 minutes.

Once cooking is complete, press "Cancel" and perform a natural release. Taste it for doneness and serve hot.

Mexican Chorizo Chili

(Ready in about 30 minutes | Servings 8)

Ingredients

2 tablespoons olive oil

2 cups dried pinto beans, rinsed and soaked overnight

6 cups water

12 ounces Mexican chorizo, without casing

3 garlic cloves, minced

1 red onion, chopped

1 large jalapeño, seeded and minced

1 bell pepper, chopped

1 tablespoon unsweetened cocoa powder

1 teaspoon ground cumin

1 teaspoon chili powder

1 teaspoon dried basil

1 teaspoon dried oregano

1 (14.5-ounce) can diced tomatoes with juice

1/2 teaspoon salt

1/4 teaspoon ground black pepper

Directions

Place 1 tablespoon of olive oil, beans, and water in the Instant Pot. Select "Manual" setting and cook for 13 minutes under HIGH pressure.

After that, press "Cancel". Drain the beans, reserving 2 cups of cooking liquid.

Choose "Sauté" button and add the remaining 1 tablespoon of the oil. Then, brown the chorizo, breaking up with a wooden spoon; it will take about 6 minutes.

Add the remaining ingredients. Secure the lid and press the "Manual" key. Cook at HIGH pressure for 10 minutes. Serve warm.

Lentil and Shrimp Soup with Swiss Chard

(Ready in about 30 minutes | Servings 6)

Ingredients

2 tablespoons canola oil

1 large-sized yellow onion, chopped

1 celery stalk, chopped

2 carrots, trimmed and chopped

1 parsnip, trimmed and chopped

3 garlic cloves, minced

1/2 teaspoon ground thyme

1 cup water

2 cups roasted-vegetable stock

1 cup dried lentils, rinsed and drained

3/4 teaspoon salt

1/4 teaspoon freshly cracked black pepper

12 large-sized shrimp, peeled and deveined

5 ounces Swiss chard, cut into pieces

2 tablespoons balsamic vinegar

Directions

Add all ingredients, except shrimp, chard, and vinegar, to the Instant Pot.

Now, select "Soup" button; set the timer for 20 minutes.

After that, choose "Sauté" setting. Throw in the shrimp and Swiss chard, and bring to a boil.

Turn the heat off. Allow it to stand approximately 6 minutes. Stir in the vinegar and serve in individual soup bowls. Bon appétit!

Caramelized Vidalia Onion Soup

(Ready in about 35 minutes | Servings 6)

Ingredients

2 tablespoons oil

2 pounds Vidalia onions, cut into thinly slices

1/2 teaspoon dried dill weed

3/4 teaspoon salt

1/4 teaspoon freshly cracked black pepper

1 tablespoon white sugar

1/2 cup dry white wine

6 cups vegetables stock

1 fresh thyme sprig

Toasted French bread slices, to serve

Directions

Preheat your cooker by selecting "Sauté" mode. Then, heat the oil and sauté the onions until translucent, 12 to 15 minutes.

Then, turn the heat to low. Now, add the dill weed, salt, black pepper, and white sugar. Continue stirring constantly until the onions are caramelized.

Add the wine, and scrape off any brown bits from the bottom of the Instant Pot. Now, pour in the stock and stir to combine well; add the thyme.

Secure the cooker's lid, and select "Manual"; cook at HIGH pressure for 7 minutes. Spoon the soup into individual bowls and serve with toasted French bread.

Duck with Mushrooms and Pearl Onions

(Ready in about 40 minutes | Servings 4)

Ingredients

4 duck legs

3/4 teaspoon salt

1/4 teaspoon freshly ground black pepper

1 teaspoon cayenne pepper

2 tablespoons olive oil

8 ounces small pearl onions

10 ounces sliced mushrooms

3 garlic cloves, minced

1/2 cup dry white wine

1 cup chicken stock

Directions

Preheat the Instant Pot by selecting "Sauté" function. Then, heat the oil.

Pat dry the duck and season it with salt, black pepper, and cayenne pepper. Place it in the pot and cook for about 5 minutes. Reserve.

Turn the heat down to medium. Then, warm the oil and sauté the onions, mushrooms and garlic. Cook until tender or for 3 minutes.

Add the wine and scrape up any brown bits from the bottom of the cooker. Pour in the stock and choose "Manual"; cook at HIGH pressure for 20 minutes.

Afterward, use the Quick pressure release. Serve.

Cremini Mushroom and Sausage Risotto

(Ready in about 30 minutes | Servings 6)

Ingredients

4 tablespoons olive oil

12 ounces fully cooked chicken sausage, sliced

1 pound cremini mushrooms, thinly sliced

1 medium-sized onion, chopped

3 garlic cloves, minced

2 thyme sprigs, leaves only

1 rosemary sprig, leaves only

3/4 teaspoon kosher salt

1/4 teaspoon freshly cracked black pepper

1/2 teaspoon cayenne pepper

1/2 teaspoon paprika

1/2 teaspoon fennel seeds

1 teaspoon cumin seeds

1 tablespoon tamari soy sauce

1/4 cup dry red wine

4 cups vegetable broth, preferably homemade

1 ½ cups Calrose rice

Directions

Select "Sauté" and add the oil. Now, cook the sausage for 5 minutes, stirring often, until it is browned. Reserve browned sausage.

Turn the heat to medium. Stir the mushrooms and onions into the sausage drippings; cook until tender or approximately 6 minutes. Stir in the garlic and cook for 1 minute longer. Add the seasonings.

Next, add tamari soy, followed by wine. Use wine to scrape up any brown bits off the bottom of the cooker; add the broth, and rice; stir to combine well. Secure the lid and select "Manual" setting; cook for 6 minutes using HIGH pressure.

After that, use a quick release. Stir before serving and enjoy!

Beef and Green Bean Stew

(Ready in about 20 minutes | Servings 6)

Ingredients

1 tablespoon olive oil

1 onion, chopped

2 cloves garlic, minced

1 quart roasted-vegetable broth

1 (28-ounce) can tomatoes, diced

1 pound boneless beef bottom round, diced

2 medium carrots, diced

1 parsnip, chopped

1 teaspoon cumin seeds

1 teaspoon dried marjoram

1/2 teaspoon ground black pepper

1/2 teaspoon sea salt

16 ounces green beans, trimmed and cut into small pieces

Directions

Preheat your Instant Pot by selecting the "Sauté" button. Then, heat the oil; sauté the onion and garlic until just tender.

Now, add the rest of the above ingredients, except for green beans. Click "Soup" button and cook for 15 minutes under HIGH pressure. Use the Quick-release method to drop the pressure.

Then, open the pot; throw in green beans. Seal the lid again and wait for 5 minutes to warm up and blanch the beans. Serve warm and enjoy!

Pot Roast with Root Vegetables

(Ready in about 35 minutes | Servings 8)

Ingredients

2 ½ pounds chuck roast

1/2 teaspoon dried marjoram

1 teaspoon dried thyme

1 teaspoon dried rosemary

Salt and ground black pepper, to your liking

2 tablespoons canola oil

2 green garlics, chopped

1 onion, thinly sliced

2 large-sized carrots, trimmed and thinly sliced

1 celery stalk, peeled and thinly sliced

2 large-sized parsnips, trimmed and thinly sliced

8 medium-sized potatoes, peeled and diced

1 ¼ cups vegetable stock

2 red onions, cut into rings

1/4 cup dry red wine

Directions

Rub the chuck roast with seasonings.

Add canola oil to the inner pot. Choose the "Meat" setting and sear the beef on all sides. Set aside.

Throw in the remaining ingredients and let it cook for 5 more minutes. Add the beef back to the cooker.

Choose the "Warm" setting and cook for 25 minutes longer. Carefully remove the lid and serve immediately.

Curried Okra and Chicken Soup

(Ready in about 20 minutes | Servings 4)

Ingredients

3 cups water

1 can coconut milk

1 teaspoon curry powder

6 ounces carrots

6 ounces okra, frozen

6 ounces sugar snap peas

1 cup chicken breast, chopped

Directions

Throw all ingredients into an electric pressure cooker.

Select "Soup" setting. Serve hot and enjoy!

Two-Mushroom Risotto

(Ready in about 20 minutes | Servings 6)

Ingredients

4 tablespoons vegetables oil

1 medium-sized onion, chopped

3 garlic cloves, minced

1/2 pound oyster mushrooms, thinly sliced

1/2 pound cremini mushrooms, thinly sliced

1 teaspoon fresh or dried rosemary

1 teaspoon dried basil

1/4 teaspoon freshly cracked black pepper

1/2 teaspoon red pepper flakes

1 teaspoon salt

1 teaspoon cumin seeds

1/4 cup dry red wine

4 cups roasted-vegetable stock

1 ½ cups Arborio rice

Directions

Select "Sauté" setting; heat the oil and sauté the onions, along with garlic and mushrooms. Then, cook until everything is tender and thoroughly warmed. Add all seasonings.

Next, add wine, followed by roasted-vegetable stock and Arborio rice; stir to combine well. Secure the lid and select "Manual" setting; cook for 6 minutes under HIGH pressure.

Perform a quick release. Stir before serving and enjoy!

Rich Bean and Ground Meat Soup

(Ready in about 25 minutes | Servings 4)

Ingredients

1 cup canned kidney beans

1 onion, chopped

2 cloves garlic, minced

1/2 pound lean pork, ground

1/2 pound lean beef, ground

1 turnip, finely chopped

2 potatoes, diced

2 carrots, trimmed and thinly sliced

2 celery stalks, finely chopped

4 cups beef broth

1/2 cup water

28 ounces canned tomatoes, crushed

1/2 teaspoon salt

Freshly cracked black pepper, to your liking

2 tablespoons pear cider vinegar

Directions

Add all of the above ingredients, except vinegar, to an electric pressure cooker; give it a good stir.

Seal the lid and select "Manual" setting; cook under HIGH pressure for 20 minutes.

Serve hot in individual bowls; drizzle each serving with pear cider vinegar.

Vegetarian Mushroom and Zucchini Soup

(Ready in about 25 minutes | Servings 4)

Ingredients

1 cup canned beans

1 pound mushrooms, chopped

2 cups diced zucchini

2 potatoes, diced

2 cloves garlic, minced

1 shallot, chopped

4 ½ cups vegetable stock

1/2 teaspoon dried dill weed

1/2 teaspoon sea salt

1/2 teaspoon ground black pepper

1/2 teaspoon cayenne pepper

28 ounces canned tomatoes, crushed

Grated Cheddar cheese, shredded

Directions

Add all of the above ingredients, except Cheddar cheese, to your Instant Pot; give it a good stir and seal the lid.

Select "Manual" setting. Cook for 20 minutes under HIGH pressure. Serve warm, topped with Cheddar cheese. Serve at once and enjoy!

Tender Short Ribs with Pearl Onions

(Ready in about 50 minutes | Servings 8)

Ingredients

8 short ribs, excess fat trimmed

1 teaspoon salt

1/2 teaspoon freshly cracked black pepper

1/2 teaspoon cayenne pepper

1 ½ cups pearl onions

1 cup vegetable broth

1 cup water

1 tablespoon dry red wine

2 carrot, trimmed and cut into coins

8 potatoes, quartered

2 sprigs thyme, leaves only

1 sprig rosemary, leaves only

4-5 black peppercorns

Directions

Rub the short ribs with salt, black pepper, and cayenne pepper. Choose the "Meat" setting and warm the oil; brown the ribs in hot oil. Reserve.

Stir in the pearl onions and sauté them for 5 to 6 minutes.

Add the reserved ribs back to the cooker; stir in the rest of the above items. Press the "Stew" key and cook for 40 minutes. Serve immediately.

Creamed Root Vegetable Chowder

(Ready in about 30 minutes | Servings 6)

Ingredients

1 turnip, finely chopped

1 celery stalk, thinly sliced

2 carrots, sliced

8 potatoes, peeled and diced

1 cup kale leaves, chopped

1 onion, chopped

3 cups vegetable broth

1 teaspoon sea salt

1/2 teaspoon ground black pepper

1/2 teaspoon dried dill weed

1 teaspoon red pepper flakes

Cheddar cheese, grated

Directions

Simply throw all of the above ingredients, except the cheese, into an electric pressure cooker. Now, choose the "Soup" setting; adjust the timer to 30 minutes.

Blend the soup using an immersion blender. Serve your soup topped with grated Cheddar cheese. Bon appétit!

Cheesy Creamed Cauliflower and Potato Soup

(Ready in about 30 minutes | Servings 6)

Ingredients

1 head cauliflower, chopped into florets

2 yellow potatoes, peeled and diced

2 carrots, sliced

1 parsnip, finely chopped

1 yellow onion, chopped

3 cups vegetable broth

1/2 teaspoon sea salt

1/4 teaspoon ground black pepper

1/2 teaspoon cayenne pepper

1/2 teaspoon dried marjoram

Colby cheese, grated

Directions

Place all of the above items, except the cheese, in your Instant Pot.

Next, press the "Soup" button; adjust the timer to 30 minutes.

Then, puree the soup using an immersion blender. Serve the soup in individual bowls; top each serving with grated Colby cheese. Bon appétit!

Turkey and Green Pea Soup

(Ready in about 20 minutes | Servings 6)

Ingredients

3/4 pound turkey breasts, boneless, skinless and diced

1 quart chicken stock

1 (28-ounce) can diced tomatoes

2 shallots, chopped

2 cloves garlic, minced

1 celery stalk, chopped

2 carrots, diced

1 teaspoon dried basil

1/2 teaspoon dried oregano

1/2 teaspoon dried marjoram

1/2 teaspoon ground black pepper

3/4 teaspoon kosher salt

1 tablespoon fresh parsley

16 ounces green peas

Directions

Throw all of the above ingredients, except for peas, into the inner pot. Lock the lid onto the pot.

Cook for 15 minutes using HIGH pressure. Then, perform the Quick-release method to drop the pressure.

Remove the cover and stir in the green peas. Seal the lid again and wait for 5 minutes to blanch the peas. Serve with garlic croutons, if desired.

Cheesy Broccoli and Root Vegetable Soup

(Ready in about 30 minutes | Servings 6)

Ingredients

1 head broccoli, broken into small florets

1 parsnip, finely chopped

1 celery rib, finely chopped

1 celery stalk, finely chopped

2 carrots, sliced

1 red bell pepper, seeded and chopped

1 green bell pepper, seeded and chopped

1 shallot, chopped

3 cups roasted-vegetable broth

1/2 teaspoon salt

3/4 teaspoon ground black pepper, to your liking

1/2 teaspoon cayenne pepper

Parmesan cheese, grated

Directions

Place all of the above ingredients, except the cheese, in your cooker.

Next, choose the "Soup" button; adjust the timer to 30 minutes.

Purée the soup using an immersion blender. Serve the soup topped with grated Parmesan cheese. Enjoy!

Family Cremini Mushroom and Bean Soup

(Ready in about 25 minutes | Servings 4)

Ingredients

1 onion, chopped

2 cloves garlic, minced

1 pound cremini mushrooms, thinly sliced

1 cup canned white beans

1 large-sized parsnip, chopped

1 celery stalk, finely chopped

2 carrots, trimmed and thinly sliced

4 cups roasted-vegetable, preferably homemade

2 cups crushed fresh tomatoes

1 teaspoon dried rosemary

1 teaspoon dried thyme

1 teaspoon kosher salt

1/2 teaspoon freshly cracked black pepper

1 teaspoon cayenne pepper

Directions

Throw all ingredients into your Instant Pot; stir until everything is well incorporated.

Cover with the lid according to the instructions; choose "Manual" setting, HIGH pressure and for 20-minute cook time. Bon appétit!

Chipotle and Root Vegetable Soup

(Ready in about 35 minutes | Servings 6)

Ingredients

2 tablespoons olive oil

2 carrots, chopped

1 celery stalk, chopped

2 parsnips, chopped

1 turnip, chopped

1 onion, finely chopped

1 Chipotle peppers in Adobo sauce, minced

4 cups chicken broth

3 cups water

1 teaspoon ground cumin

1 teaspoon celery seeds

1 ½ teaspoons fennel seeds

Croutons, to serve

Directions

Press "Sauté" button to preheat your cooker; now warm the oil till it is hot and smoky. Then, sauté the vegetables approximately 5 minutes.

Add the remaining ingredients, except croutons. Press "Soup" key and set the timer for 30 minutes.

Serve with croutons of choice. Bon appétit!

Easy Country Chicken Soup

(Ready in about 35 minutes | Servings 6)

Ingredients

2 chicken breasts, boneless, skinless, and chopped

3 carrots, trimmed and chopped

2 celery stalks, chopped

1 parsnip, chopped

1 yellow onion, peeled and diced

3 cups chicken broth

1 cup water

2 bay leaves

1 teaspoon dried basil

Salt and cracked black pepper, to taste

1 tablespoon fresh parsley leaves, chopped

Directions

Just throw all of the above ingredients into your Instant Pot.

Turn "Manual" mode and set the timer for 35 minutes. Serve hot.

The Best Borscht Ever

(Ready in about 25 minutes | Servings 6)

Ingredients

1 tablespoon ghee

2 cloves garlic, minced

1 shallot, diced

1/2 pound lamb, cubed

1 carrot, chopped

1 pound red beets

1 head read cabbage, shredded

1 (15-ounce) can tomatoes, diced

7 cups turkey broth

1/2 cup red wine vinegar

1 tablespoon lemon juice

3/4 teaspoon salt

1/2 teaspoon freshly cracked black pepper

Directions

Choose the "Sauté" function. Then, melt the ghee, and sauté the garlic and shallot, stirring frequently, until they are tender and fragrant.

Then, stir in the lamb and cook until just browned. Press "Cancel" button. Add the other ingredients; stir until everything is incorporated.

Close the cooker's lid and choose "Manual" function. Let it cook for 10 minutes. Remove the lid and release the pressure according to manufacturer's directions. Savor for seasoning and ladle the soup into individual bowls.

Rich and Yummy Beef Stew

(Ready in about 40 minutes | Servings 8)

Ingredients

2 ½ pounds chuck roast, cut into bite-sized chunks

3 tablespoons vegetable oil

1 teaspoon smoked cayenne pepper

1 teaspoon salt

14 ounces tomato sauce

16 ounces chicken stock

1 pound potatoes, cut into bite sized pieces

1/2 pound carrots, cut into bite sized pieces

1 onion, cut into bite sized pieces

2 garlic cloves, minced

1/2 teaspoon dried dill weed

Directions

Brown the meat chunks in the Instant Pot in hot vegetable oil. Now, add cayenne pepper, salt, tomato sauce, and chicken stock. Cook until heated through.

Next, add the rest of the above ingredients; click the "Soup" button and set the timer for 30 minutes. Eat warm.

Porcini Mushroom and Barley Soup

(Ready in about 40 minutes | Servings 6)

Ingredients

1 tablespoon corn oil

1 leek, chopped

2 cloves garlic, minced

8 ounces dried porcini mushrooms

1 medium-sized celery rib, chopped

2 medium-sized celery stalks, chopped

6 cups bone broth, preferably homemade

1 cup pearl barley

1 teaspoon fresh dill weed

1 tablespoon thyme leaves, stemmed

Sea salt and cracked black pepper, to taste

1 teaspoon dried basil

1 teaspoon cayenne pepper

Directions

Warm corn oil in an electric pressure cooker turned to the browning setting. Add the leeks, garlic, mushrooms, and celery to the cooker.

Then, sauté the vegetables, stirring continuously, until they have softened. Add the remaining ingredients. Lock the lid onto the Instant Pot.

Set the machine to cook for 40 minutes under HIGH pressure. Reduce the pressure. Unlock and open the cooker according to the manufacturer's directions. Eat warm.

The Yummiest Hamburger Soup Ever

(Ready in about 15 minutes | Servings 6)

Ingredients

2 cups bone broth, preferably homemade

1 cup water

1 (14-ounce) can tomatoes with juice, diced

2 garlic cloves, chopped

1 red onion, diced

2 medium-sized Serrano peppers, stemmed and chopped

2 medium-sized carrots, thinly sliced

1 celery stalk, thinly sliced

1 large-sized potato, peeled and diced

1/4 cup loosely packed fresh parsley leaves, chopped

1 teaspoon salt

1/4 teaspoon crushed red pepper flakes

1 ½ pounds lean ground beef

Directions

Whisk the broth, water, and canned tomatoes with juice in a mixing dish; transfer the mixture to the inner pot.

Stir in the garlic, onion, Serrano peppers, carrots, celery, and potato. Now, sprinkle parsley, salt, and red pepper over all. Crumble in the meat in small clumps.

Stir to combine well and lock the lid onto the pot.

Set the cooker to cook at HIGH pressure for 8 minutes. After that, perform the Quick-release method. Stir before serving. Spoon a little pickle relish into the middle of each bowlful and eat warm.

Two-Pepper and Pinto Bean Soup

(Ready in about 35 minutes | Servings 4)

Ingredients

2 tablespoons corn oil

1 onion, finely diced

1 Serrano pepper, finely diced

1 Poblano pepper, finely diced

1 turnip, chopped

1 parsnip, chopped

1 carrot, chopped

3 garlic cloves, minced

1 teaspoon dried marjoram

1 teaspoon ground cumin

1 bay leaf

5-6 black peppercorns

1 pound dried pinto beans, rinsed

7 cups bone broth

1/2 teaspoon cayenne pepper

1/4 teaspoon salt

Directions

Preheat your cooker by choosing "Sauté" setting. Then, heat corn oil and sauté the onion, peppers, turnip, parsnip, and carrot until they are tender; now, stir in the garlic and continue sautéing for 3 more minutes, or until it is fragrant.

Stir in the rest of the above ingredients. Secure the lid and choose the "Manual" setting; cook for 30 minutes using a HIGH pressure. After that, use the Natural pressure release.

Toss out bay leaves and serve.

Turkey Chorizo and Potato Chowder

(Ready in about 30 minutes | Servings 6)

Ingredients

2 tablespoons vegetable oil

10 ounces cooked turkey chorizo, sliced

1 onion, chopped

2 garlic cloves, minced

2 pounds yellow potatoes, peeled and cubed

6 cups turkey broth

3/4 teaspoon salt

1/2 freshly ground black pepper

1 bunch kale, stemmed and torn into pieces

Directions

Add all ingredients, except for kale, to your electric pressure cooker. Then, press the "Soup" button; set the timer for 8 minutes.

Then, mash about 1/2 of the mixture.

Next, select the "Sauté" setting and add the kale. Cook for an additional 5 minutes, until the kale is wilted. Serve at once and enjoy.

Mushroom and Barley Soup with Pancetta

(Ready in about 45 minutes | Servings 6)

Ingredients

1 tablespoon vegetable oil

4 ounces pancetta, cut into strips

2 garlic cloves, minced

1/2 cup red onion, chopped

1/2 cup carrots, trimmed and grated

1/2 cup parsnip, trimmed and grated

2 cups water

3 ½ cups beef stock

1/2 cup pearl barley

1/2 ounce porcini mushrooms, thinly sliced

Pecorino-Romano cheese, shaved

Directions

First, heat the oil in your cooker turned to the browning setting. Add the pancetta, garlic, onion, carrots, and parsnips to the cooker.

Sauté the mixture, stirring often, for 5 to 6 minutes. Add the rest of the above ingredients, except cheese. Lock the lid onto the cooker.

Set your Instant Pot to cook for 40 minutes under HIGH pressure. Reduce the pressure and open the cooker. Ladle the soup into individual bowls and top each serving with shaved cheese. Enjoy!

Smoky Broccoli and Turnip Chowder

(Ready in about 30 minutes | Servings 6)

Ingredients

1 onion, chopped

1 head broccoli, chopped into florets

1 turnip, chopped

2 carrots, sliced

2 red potatoes, peeled and diced

3 cups roasted-vegetable stock

A few drops of liquid smoke

3/4 teaspoon sea salt

1/2 teaspoon ground black pepper

1/2 teaspoon cayenne pepper

Pecorino Romano cheese, shaved

Directions

Just throw all of the above ingredients, except Pecorino Romano cheese, into the inner pot of your Instant Pot.

Next, select "Soup" setting; adjust the timer for 30 minutes.

When the cooking is finished, carefully open the cooker. Now, puree your soup using an immersion blender.

Serve the soup, topped with cheese. Bon appétit!

Beef Brisket Soup

(Ready in about 1 hour 15 minutes | Servings 8)

Ingredients

1 pound beef brisket, cut into thick slices

1 quart chicken broth

3 ½ cups canned tomatoes with juice, diced

1 (12-ounce) bottle beer

1 potato, peeled and diced

1/4 cup brown sugar

1/4 cup pear cider vinegar

3/4 teaspoon sea salt

1/4 teaspoon ground black pepper

1/2 teaspoon dry mustard

1 teaspoon ground coriander

Directions

Combine all ingredients in an electric pressure cooker; make sure to stir until the sugar dissolves completely.

Cover the cooker and set it to cook for 75 minutes under HIGH pressure. Reduce the pressure.

Turn off the cooker. Serve warm and enjoy!

Oyster Mushroom and Cabbage Soup

(Ready in about 25 minutes | Servings 4)

Ingredients

1 cup canned beans

1/2 pound oyster mushroom, chopped

4 potatoes, diced

2 carrots, chopped

1/2 small head of cabbage, shredded

1 onion, chopped

2 cloves garlic, minced

1 cup water

3 ½ cups vegetable stock

1/2 teaspoon sea salt

1/2 teaspoon ground black pepper

1/2 teaspoon cayenne pepper

28 ounces canned tomatoes, crushed

Directions

Just dump all of the above ingredients in your Instant Pot; give it a good stir.

Select "Manual" mode. Cook for 20 minutes using a HIGH pressure. Serve warm with Feta cheese on the side. Enjoy!

Creamed Cauliflower and Potato Soup

(Ready in about 20 minutes | Servings 6)

Ingredients

2 tablespoons vegetable oil

1 red onion, peeled and sliced

2 garlic cloves, smashed

1 cauliflower head, broken into florets

1 pound red potatoes, peeled and cut into ½-inch cubes

4 cups roasted-vegetable stock

3/4 teaspoon salt

1/2 freshly cracked black pepper

1 teaspoon cayenne pepper

1 cup light cream

1 cup sharp Colby cheese, shaved

Directions

Preheat the cooker by selecting "Sauté" setting. Once hot, add the oil; sauté the onion and garlic. Stir and cook for 3 to 5 minutes.

Stir in the cauliflower, red potatoes, and roasted-vegetable stock. Season with salt, black pepper, and cayenne pepper. Secure the cooker's lid.

Choose "Manual" setting and cook for 5 minutes under HIGH pressure. Press "Cancel" key; release any remaining steam.

Add the cream and stir until everything is well incorporated. Puree with an immersion blender. Serve topped with Colby cheese. Bon appétit!

Cheesy Beef and Onion Soup

(Ready in about 1 hour 5 minutes | Servings 6)

Ingredients

2 tablespoons butter	6 cups bone broth
2 tablespoons canola oil	1/2 cup dry white wine
1 pound onion, peeled and sliced	1 teaspoon salt
2 cloves garlic, minced	1/2 teaspoon freshly cracked black pepper
3 tablespoons cognac	1 tablespoon potato starch
2 beef ribs	6 ounces Gruyère cheese, shredded

Directions

Melt the butter and canola oil in an electric pressure cooker turned to the browning function. Stir in the onions and garlic, and cook, stirring often, until the onions are golden brown, about 15 minutes.

Pour in the cognac and scrape up any browned bits. Add the beef, bone broth, wine, salt, and black pepper. Lock the lid onto the cooker.

Cook for 45 minutes under HIGH pressure. Perform the Quick-release method. Uncover and transfer the beef ribs to a cutting board. Now, discard the bones; chop the meat and stir it back into the cooker.

Lock the lid back onto the pot. Continue to cook at HIGH pressure for 5 minutes. Afterward, use the Quick-release method.

Whisk the potato starch with 1 tablespoon water in a small mixing bowl. Stir the slurry into the soup until thickened. Turn off the machine. Serve warm, topped with Gruyère cheese.

Asian-Style Beef and Noodle Soup

(Ready in about 20 minutes | Servings 6)

Ingredients

6 cups turkey broth

1 ½ pounds boneless beef sirloin, trimmed and cubed

1/2 cup soy sauce

2 tablespoons dry white wine

1 onion, sliced

2 cloves garlic, minced

8 dried mushrooms, stemmed and sliced

2 tablespoons vinegar

1/4 cup mirin

4 ounces fettuccini

Directions

Combine turkey broth, beef, soy sauce, and wine in an electric pressure cooker; now, add the onion, garlic, and mushrooms.

Add the vinegar and mirin. Lock the lid onto the pot.

Set the cooker to cook at HIGH pressure for 15 minutes. Open the cooker according to manufacturer's directions and stir in the fettuccini. Cook another 2 minutes.

Use the Quick-release method and uncover the cooker. Serve warm.

Creamed Ham and Corn Chowder

(Ready in about 15 minutes | Servings 6)

Ingredients

2 ½ cups vegetable stock

3 tablespoons all-purpose flour

3 tablespoons butter

12 ounces ham, chopped

1 onion, chopped

3 cups frozen kernels, thawed

1 medium white potato, diced

1/2 teaspoon dried basil

1/2 teaspoon dried oregano

1/2 teaspoon salt

1/2 teaspoon freshly ground black pepper

3/4 cup dry white wine

1/2 cup heavy cream

Directions

Whisk the stock and flour in a mixing bowl until everything is well incorporated; set aside.

Melt the butter in your cooker turned to the browning function. Stir in the ham and cook until it is well browned, about 4 minutes.

Add the onion and corn kernels; cook, stirring often, until the onion becomes translucent. Stir in the rest of the ingredients, except for heavy cream. Pour in the wine and scrape up any browned bits.

Stir in the stock/flour mixture. Seal the cooker and set the machine to cook at HIGH pressure for 10 minutes. Turn off the machine. Then, release the pressure.

Next, stir in the cream. Stir and serve warm.

Shrimp, Scallion and Lentil Soup

(Ready in about 30 minutes | Servings 4)

Ingredients

2 tablespoons olive oil

2 garlic cloves, minced

1 cup scallions, chopped

2 carrots, trimmed and chopped

1 parsnip, trimmed and chopped

1 celery stalk, chopped

2 cups roasted-vegetable stock

1 cup water

1 cup dried lentils, rinsed and drained

1/2 teaspoon salt

1/2 teaspoon freshly cracked black pepper

5 ounces kale, cut into pieces

12 large-sized shrimp, peeled and deveined

2 tablespoons fresh lemon juice

Directions

Add all ingredients, except kale, shrimp and lemon, to the Instant Pot.

Now, choose "Soup" setting and set the timer for 20 minutes.

Then, add the kale and shrimp and bring it to a boil.

Turn the heat off; wait for 6 minutes. Drizzle fresh lemon juice over all. Bon appétit!

Nutty Sweet Potato Soup

(Ready in about 15 minutes | Servings 4)

Ingredients

1 tablespoon corn oil

1 cup green onions, chopped

2 cloves garlic, finely chopped

4 large-sized sweet potatoes, cubed

2 Roma tomatoes, seeded and chopped

1 ½ cups non-dairy milk

2 cups vegetable broth

1 tablespoon vinegar

1/2 cup almond butter

Sea salt and black pepper, to taste

Fresh chopped chives, for garnish

Directions

Select "Sauté" setting. Heat corn oil, and sauté green onions and garlic, stirring constantly, until they are softened. Press "Cancel" button.

Stir in the other ingredients, except for chives. Cover the cooker and choose "Manual" mode. Let it cook about 5 minutes. Uncover and release the pressure.

Puree the soup to your desired consistency, and serve warm, garnished with chives. Bon appétit!

Easy Two-Bean Chili

(Ready in about 25 minutes | Servings 8)

Ingredients

2 tablespoons olive oil

1 onion, thinly sliced

2 cloves garlic, minced

3 ½ cups bone broth

1/2 cup dried pinto beans, soaked, drained and rinsed

1/2 cup dried cannellini beans, soaked, drained and rinsed

1 carrot, chopped into sticks

1 red bell pepper, de-seeded and thinly sliced

1 jalapeño pepper, finely minced

1 teaspoon celery seeds

1 teaspoon fennel seeds

1 teaspoon sea salt, to taste

3/4 teaspoon ground black pepper

2 bay leaves

2 (14.5-ounce) cans diced tomatoes

Directions

Select "Sauté" button and warm the oil until it is hot; sauté the onion and garlic for 4 to 5 minutes.

Now, stir in the other ingredients, except the tomatoes. Select "Manual" setting; cook under HIGH pressure for 12 minutes.

Stir in the tomatoes; stir until they are thoroughly warmed. Serve warm.

Rich Country Stew

(Ready in about 45 minutes | Servings 8)

Ingredients

16 ounces stew meat

2 large-sized onions, chopped

3 garlic cloves, minced

1 green bell pepper, seeded and coarsely chopped

1 red bell pepper, seeded and coarsely chopped

2 carrots, chopped

1 celery stalk, chopped

3 potatoes, chopped

2 cups bone broth

1 tablespoon olive oil

1 tablespoon sea salt

1/2 teaspoon ground black pepper

1 teaspoon crushed red pepper flakes

2 bay leaves

1 teaspoon fennel seeds

2 tablespoons tomato ketchup

2 tablespoons arrowroot flour

Directions

Press the "Sauté" button on your cooker. Now, sauté stew meat, onion and garlic until the meat is no longer pink.

Add the other ingredients, except arrowroot flour. Cover and select "Meat/Stew" setting.

Cook for 35 minutes using a HIGH pressure.

Meanwhile make the slurry; whisk the arrowroot flour with 1/4 of the cooking liquid. Slowly add the slurry back to the pot. Serve right away.

Squash and Red Lentils with Garam Masala

(Ready in about 20 minutes | Servings 6)

Ingredients

2 tablespoons olive oil

1 large-sized leek, chopped

3 cloves garlic, minced

1 ½ pounds butternut squash, roughly chopped

1 teaspoon Garam masala

Salt and freshly cracked black pepper, to taste

4 cups roasted-vegetable stock

1 cup red lentils, rinsed

1 can tomatoes, diced

Fresh chopped parsley, for garnish

Directions

Select the "Sauté" setting and heat the oil. Sauté the leek and garlic about 5 minutes.

Then, stir in the butternut squash, Garam masala, salt, and black pepper. Continue to cook for about 5 minutes.

Add the stock and lentils. Seal the lid and push the "Manual" button; adjust the timer to 6 minutes; cook under HIGH pressure. Stir in the canned tomatoes.

Puree the soup using an immersion blender. Serve topped with fresh parsley.

Spicy Pork and Mushroom Stew

(Ready in about 45 minutes | Servings 6)

Ingredients

10 ounces porcini mushrooms, thinly sliced

1 pound pork side rib

1 cup carrots coins

1/2 cup parsnip, thinly sliced

2 bay leaves

1/2 teaspoon marjoram

3/4 teaspoon sea salt

1/2 teaspoon black pepper, preferably freshly ground

1 teaspoon smoked cayenne pepper

1 teaspoon mustard seeds

6 cups of water

Directions

Just throw all ingredients into the inner pot of your Instant Pot.

Press the "Meat/Stew" button; cook 40 minutes.

Release the pressure and serve warm. Bon appétit!

Root Vegetable Stew with Green Beans

(Ready in about 50 minutes | Servings 6)

Ingredients

1 pound pork side rib

1 celery stalk, chopped

1 celery rib, chopped

2 yellow potatoes, peeled and diced

2 carrots, trimmed and sliced

1 bell pepper, seeded and chopped

1/2 tablespoon sea salt

1/4 teaspoon black pepper, ground

1 teaspoon cayenne pepper

3 cups vegetable stock

3 cups water

1 cup green beans, diced

Directions

Add all ingredients, except for green beans, to the inner pot of your Instant Pot.

Choose "Meat/Stew" setting, and cook approximately 40 minutes.

Throw in green beans; cover again and let it sit for 5 to 7 minutes. Serve warm.

Flavorful Beef and Turkey Stew

(Ready in about 25 minutes | Servings 8)

Ingredients

2 tablespoons canola oil

1 onion, chopped

2 cloves garlic, smashed

1/2 pound lean ground beef

1 pound ground turkey

2 large-sized tomatoes

2 cups chicken broth

2 (14-ounce) cans beans, drained and rinsed well

1 teaspoon cumin powder

1 teaspoon fennel seeds

2 bay leaves

1 ½ cups water

Colby cheese, shaved

Directions

Melt canola oil in an electric pressure cooker. Then, sauté the onion for 5 minutes or until tender and translucent. Add the garlic, ground beef, and turkey; cook until the meat turns brown.

Stir in the rest of the above ingredients, except Colby cheese. Cover and cook under HIGH pressure for 15 minutes.

Ladle the stew into individual bowls; serve topped with Colby cheese. Enjoy!

Barley with Pork and Mushrooms

(Ready in about 20 minutes | Servings 6)

Ingredients

1/2 pound lean ground pork

1/2 pound mushroom, thinly sliced

1 medium-sized onion, finely chopped

2 garlic cloves, minced

3 cups vegetable stock

3 cups water

2 Roma tomatoes, seeded and chopped

1 cup quick barley

3 carrots, peeled and sliced

4 cups cabbage, chopped

1 teaspoon dried marjoram

1/2 teaspoon salt

1/4 teaspoon freshly cracked black pepper

1/2 teaspoon cayenne pepper

Directions

Select "Sauté" setting and cook the pork and mushrooms until the mushrooms are just tender. Now, stir in the onion and garlic; continue to sauté for 3 to 5 minutes.

Next, add the vegetable stock, water, tomatoes, and barley. Choose "Soup" mode; cook for 10 minutes under HIGH pressure.

After that, perform the Quick pressure release; add the rest of the above ingredients. Put the cooker's lid on; choose "Soup" setting and bring to HIGH pressure. Eat warm.

Two-Mushroom Zucchini Stew

(Ready in about 45 minutes | Servings 6)

Ingredients

6 ounces button mushrooms, thinly sliced

6 ounces porcini mushrooms, thinly sliced

4 cloves garlic, peeled and smashed

1/2 pound zucchini, thinly sliced

1 bell pepper, seeded and chopped

2 carrots, thinly sliced

2 parsnips, thinly sliced

2 bay leaves

2 medium-sized tomatoes, chopped

1/2 teaspoon thyme

3/4 teaspoon kosher salt

1/2 teaspoon freshly cracked black pepper

1 teaspoon paprika

1 teaspoon mustard seeds

6 cups of water

Directions

Add all ingredients to the inner pot of your Instant Pot.

Choose the "Soup" button and cook for 40 minutes using a HIGH pressure. Release the pressure and serve at once.

Broccoli Chowder with Velveeta Cheese

(Ready in about 15 minutes | Servings 8)

Ingredients

8 cups broccoli florets

1 carrot, chopped

4 cups vegetable broth

1 shallot, chopped

1/2 teaspoon kosher salt

1/4 teaspoon ground black pepper, or to your taste

1 teaspoon dried basil

1/2 teaspoon dried oregano

1/2 teaspoon dried dill weed

1 cup Velveeta cheese

Directions

Add all ingredients, except Velveeta cheese, to the inner pot of your Instant Pot.

Place the lid on; press "Manual" key and cook for 6 minutes. Remove the lid.

Puree the soup using an immersion blender. Fold in Velveeta cheese and choose "Sauté" setting; stir until the cheese is completely melted. Serve and enjoy!

Winter Potato and Parsnip Soup

(Ready in about 45 minutes | Servings 6)

Ingredients

1 tablespoon oil

2 garlic cloves, smashed

2 onions, peeled and diced

2 medium-sized potatoes, peeled and diced

2 parsnips, trimmed and diced

1 apple, cored, peeled and diced

2 cups vegetable stock

1 teaspoon dried dill weed

3/4 teaspoon salt

1/4 teaspoon ground black pepper

2 heaping tablespoons fresh parsley, roughly chopped

Directions

Add all ingredients, except fresh parsley, to the inner pot of your Instant Pot.

Choose the "Soup" button and cook for 40 minutes using a HIGH pressure. Afterward, release the pressure.

Purée the soup using an immersion blender or process it in a blender, working with batches.

Divide the soup among six serving bowls; top each serving with parsley. Enjoy!

Summer Squashes and Vidalia Onion Soup

(Ready in about 25 minutes | Servings 8)

Ingredients

1 tablespoon butter, melted

2 Vidalia onions, chopped

1 green bell pepper, chopped

1 red bell pepper, chopped

4 yellow summer squashes, shredded

2 large-sized carrots, chopped

1 (12-ounce) package silken tofu, pressed

1 cup boiling water

1 cup vegetable stock

1 teaspoon cayenne pepper

Directions

Choose the "Sauté" mode and melt the butter; then, sauté Vidalia onions and bell peppers until just tender.

Add the rest of the above ingredients and choose the "Soup" function.

Remove the lid; purée the mixture with an immersion blender.

Caramelized Scallion Soup

(Ready in about 25 minutes | Servings 4)

Ingredients

2 tablespoons olive oil

1 pound scallions, sliced

3/4 teaspoon salt

1/4 teaspoon ground black pepper

1 tablespoon white sugar

1/2 cup Chardonnay

6 cups vegetables stock

1 bay leaf

1 fresh rosemary sprig

Toasted bread slices, to serve

Directions

Preheat your Instant Pot by choosing "Sauté" setting. Heat olive oil; sauté the scallions in hot oil until just tender.

Next, turn the heat to low. Now, add the salt, black pepper, and sugar. Continue stirring until the onions are caramelized.

Add the wine to scrape off any brown bits from the bottom of the Instant Pot. Now, pour in the stock and stir to combine well; add the bay leaf and rosemary sprig.

Secure the cooker's lid, and press "Manual" button; cook for 8 minutes under HIGH pressure. Divide the soup among individual bowls; serve with toasted bread and enjoy.

Turkey Stew with Spinach and Noodles

(Ready in about 25 minutes | Servings 8)

Ingredients

2 tablespoons corn oil

1/2 pound ground turkey

1/2 teaspoon dried thyme

1 rosemary sprig, leaves only

1 teaspoon paprika

3/4 teaspoon salt

1/2 teaspoon ground black pepper, or to taste

1 shallot, diced

1 celery rib, chopped

1 celery stalk, chopped

2 Roma tomatoes, seeded and chopped

1/2 cup dry white wine

8 cups chicken broth, preferably homemade

1 large bunch spinach leaves, chopped

8 ounces noodles, cooked

Directions

Set your Instant Pot to "Sauté" function. Now, warm corn oil; then, add the ground turkey and all seasonings. Cook, stirring continuously, until the meat has browned.

Stir in the shallot, celery, and tomatoes and continue to cook for 7 to 9 minutes or until it is thoroughly heated. Add dry white wine to deglaze the pot.

Add the broth and spinach; put the lid back on. Serve garnished with cooked noodles.

Mediterranean Chicken and Zucchini Soup

(Ready in about 35 minutes | Servings 6)

Ingredients

2 chicken breasts, boneless and skinless

2 zucchinis, diced

2 carrots, trimmed and chopped

4 baking potatoes, diced

1/2 cup shallots, peeled and diced

2 garlic cloves, finely minced

4 cups chicken stock

1 teaspoon dried basil

1/2 teaspoon dried oregano

1 rosemary sprig, leaves only

1 teaspoon hot paprika

3/4 teaspoon sea salt

1/4 teaspoon cracked black pepper, or to taste

Feta cheese, to serve

Directions

Simply throw all of the above ingredients, except Feta cheese, into the inner pot of your Instant Pot.

Turn "Manual" setting and set the timer for 35 minutes. Serve at once with Feta cheese on the side. Enjoy!

Lentil and Roasted Vegetable Soup

(Ready in about 20 minutes | Servings 6)

Ingredients

1 leek, rinsed and chopped (white and green parts)

2 cloves garlic, minced

Seasoned salt and ground black pepper, to taste

3/4 teaspoon paprika

1/4 teaspoon marjoram

2 roasted bell peppers, cut into strips

1 pound Yukon Gold potatoes, diced

1 parsnip, trimmed and thinly sliced

2 carrots, trimmed and thinly sliced

2 cups red lentils, rinsed

1 bay leaf

4 cups roasted-vegetable broth

4 cups water

Directions

Preheat your Instant Pot by choosing "Sauté" function. Now, sauté the leeks, and garlic until just tender.

Now, add all seasonings, followed by roasted pepper, potatoes, parsnips, and carrots. Continue sautéing for 5 to 6 minutes; make sure to stir continuously.

Next, add the lentils, bay leaves, roasted-vegetable broth, and water.

Cover the cooker and bring to HIGH pressure. After that, perform the Quick-release method to release the pressure and open the lid. Serve at once.

Hearty Red Lentil and Butternut Squash Soup

(Ready in about 20 minutes | Servings 6)

Ingredients

2 tablespoons olive oil

2 cloves garlic, minced

1 shallot, diced

1 ½ pounds butternut squash, roughly chopped

1 teaspoon cumin powder

Salt and ground black pepper, to taste

1 teaspoon celery seeds

2 cups vegetable broth

2 cups water

1 cup red lentils, rinsed

1 cup canned tomatoes, diced

Fresh chopped cilantro leaves, for garnish

Directions

Choose the "Sauté" function and heat the oil. Sauté the garlic and shallot for 5 minutes or until tender.

Stir in the butternut squash, cumin powder, salt, ground black pepper, and celery seeds. Continue cooking for 3 to 4 minutes.

Add the broth, water, and red lentils. Secure the lid and push the "Manual" button; adjust the timer to 6 minutes and use a HIGH pressure. Stir in the tomatoes.

Purée the soup using your immersion blender. Serve topped with fresh cilantro. Serve warm.

Harvest Potato and Squash Soup

(Ready in about 40 minutes | Servings 4)

Ingredients

2 tablespoons butter

2 cloves garlic, minced

2 large leeks, chopped (white and pale green parts only)

1/2 teaspoon salt

Freshly ground black pepper, to taste

Cayenne pepper, to taste

1 teaspoon cumin seeds

2 potatoes, peeled, and diced

2 cups butternut squash, cubed

1 quart chicken stock

2 tablespoons vermouth

1/2 cup light cream

Fresh chopped parsley leaves, for garnish

Directions

Add all ingredients, except for cream and parsley, to the inner pot of your Instant Pot.

Choose the "Soup" button and cook for 40 minutes under HIGH pressure.

Release the pressure according to manufacturer's instructions.

Add the cream, put the lid back on the cooker and let the mixture stand about 5 minutes; serve at once, garnished with fresh parsley.

Curried Butternut Squash Soup

(Ready in about 20 minutes | Servings 6)

Ingredients

2 tablespoons corn oil

1 yellow onion, finely chopped

2 cloves garlic, minced

1 ½ pounds butternut squash, roughly chopped

Salt and ground black pepper, to taste

1 teaspoon fennel seeds

1-inch fresh ginger, finely minced

1/2 teaspoon turmeric powder

3 ½ cups roasted-vegetable stock

1 cup split lentils, rinsed

1 cup tomato purée, diced

Curry leaves, for serving

Directions

Preheat your cooker by selecting the "Sauté" function; now, heat the oil and sauté the onion and garlic until just tender and fragrant.

Stir in the squash and all seasonings. Continue cooking for 4 minutes more.

Add the stock and lentils. Secure the lid and choose the "Manual" button; cook for 6 minutes under HIGH pressure. Stir in the tomato purée.

After that, purée the soup using an immersion blender or process it in a blender, working with batches. Afterward, garnish with some curry leaves, serve in individual bowls, and enjoy!

Carrot and Sweet Potato Soup

(Ready in about 15 minutes | Servings 6)

Ingredients

1 tablespoon corn oil

1 yellow onion, roughly chopped

2 cloves garlic, finely chopped

4 large-sized sweet potatoes, cubed

1/2 carrots, chopped

2 ripe tomatoes, seeded and chopped

1 (14-ounce) can coconut milk

1/2 teaspoon ground allspice or pumpkin pie spice

2 cups vegetable stock

1/2 cup nut butter

1/2 teaspoon sea salt

1/4 teaspoon black pepper, preferably freshly ground

1 tablespoon fresh lime juice

Directions

Start by preheating your Instant Pot on the "Sauté" setting. Then, heat the oil; now, cook the onions and garlic, stirring often, until they are softened. Press "Cancel" button.

Stir in the other ingredients, excluding the lime juice; give it a good stir.

Close the lid and choose "Manual" function. Let the soup cook for 5 minutes. Release the pressure and remove the lid.

Puree the soup to your desired consistency. Divide the soup among 6 individual bowls; drizzle lime juice over each serving and enjoy!

Two-Bean Vegan Chili

(Ready in about 25 minutes | Servings 8)

Ingredients

2 tablespoons olive oil

2 cups leeks, chopped

4 cloves garlic, minced

2/3 cup dried red beans, soaked, drained and rinsed

1 1/3 cups dried black beans, soaked, drained and rinsed

3 ½ cups boiling water

2 celery stalks, chopped

2 carrots, chopped into sticks

1 red bell pepper, de-seeded and thinly sliced

1 red chili pepper, minced

2 tablespoons chili powder

1 teaspoon smoked cayenne pepper

1 large bay leaf

4-5 black peppercorns

Salt and black pepper, to taste

2 (14.5-ounce) cans diced tomatoes

Directions

Preheat your Instant Pot by choosing "Sauté" mode. Now, heat the olive oil.

Then, sauté the leeks and garlic for 4 to 5 minutes, until they are tender and fragrant.

Add the rest of the above ingredients, except for canned tomatoes. Give it a good stir.

Set the Instant Pot to "Manual" function, and cook under HIGH pressure for 12 minutes.

Stir in the tomatoes and cover the cooker again; serve hot and enjoy!

Easy One-Pot Stew

(Ready in about 45 minutes | Servings 8)

Ingredients

1 tablespoon olive oil

16 ounces stew meat

1 onion, finely chopped

2 garlic cloves, minced

2 celery stalks, chopped

2 carrots, chopped

1 red bell pepper, seeded and thinly sliced

2 cups beef bone broth

1 teaspoon smoked cayenne pepper

1 tablespoon sea salt

1/2 teaspoon black pepper, ground

2 bay leaves

1 teaspoon celery seeds

2 tablespoons tomato ketchup

2 tablespoons arrowroot flour

Directions

Preheat your Instant Pot by selecting "Sauté" mode. Heat the oil and add the meat. Then, brown stew meat, along with onion and garlic.

Add the rest of the above ingredients, except the arrowroot flour. Now place the lid on your Instant Pot and select "Meat/ Stew" function.

Cook for 35 minutes using a HIGH pressure.

To make the slurry, in a small-sized mixing bowl, whisk together the arrowroot flour with 1/4 cup of the cooking liquid. Add the slurry back to the pot. Stir until everything is well combined. Serve warm.

Pork Rib and Potato Soup

(Ready in about 45 minutes | Servings 6)

Ingredients

4 beef bouillon cubes

1 pound pork side rib

4 Yukon Gold potatoes, peeled and diced

1 tablespoon sea salt

1/2 teaspoon black pepper, ground

1 teaspoon sweet paprika

3 cups of water

Directions

Dissolve bouillon cubes in water (1 cube in 1 cup of water); add the mixture to the inner pot of your electric pressure cooker.

Simply throw all remaining ingredients into the pot.

Choose "Soup" function and cook for 40 minutes. Serve warm and enjoy!

Vegan Red Lentil and Cabbage Stew

(Ready in about 25 minutes | Servings 8)

Ingredients

1 tablespoon olive oil

1 red onion, chopped

4 cloves garlic, minced

1/2 teaspoon curry powder

1 teaspoon smoked paprika

Kosher salt, to taste

1/2 teaspoon black pepper

1/4 teaspoon chili flakes

1 small-sized head of red cabbage, peeled and cubed

1 stalk celery, chopped

1 large-sized carrot, trimmed and diced

1 ½ cups red lentils

2 cups vegetable broth

1 cup tomato purée

Directions

Begin by preheating your cooker on "Sauté" function. Then, warm the oil and sauté the onions and garlic for 3 to 4 minutes.

Add the remaining ingredients, except canned tomato purée. Cover the cooker and set it to "Manual" mode and 10-minute pressure.

Now, allow pressure to come down naturally.

Next, stir in tomato purée, and cook an additional 5 minutes, stirring frequently. Taste and adjust the seasonings. Stir before serving and enjoy!

Hungarian Stew with Pork (Pörkölt)

(Ready in about 40 minutes | Servings 6)

Ingredients

2 tablespoons sunflower oil

1 onion, peeled and diced

2 garlic cloves, minced

1 bell pepper, seeded and diced

4 potatoes peeled and diced

3 strips bacon, cut into pieces

1 tablespoon Hungarian paprika

2 pounds boneless pork chops, trimmed and cut into bite-sized chunks

2 cups vegetable broth

1 (15) ounce can tomatoes with juice, diced

Reduced-fat sour cream, to serve

Directions

Preheat your Instant Pot by selecting "Sauté" function. Heat the oil and sauté the onion and garlic.

Stir in the rest of the above ingredients, except the canned tomatoes and sour cream. Place the lid on your cooker, and select "Meat/ Stew" mode. Cook for 35 minutes using a HIGH pressure.

Release the pressure. Now, add the tomatoes and stir until everything is well combined. Serve warm, garnished with sour cream.

Corny Bacon and Potato Chowder

(Ready in about 25 minutes | Servings 4)

Ingredients

1 tablespoon sunflower oil

1 onion, peeled and diced

4 potatoes diced

4 cups chicken stock

1 teaspoon caraway seeds

3/4 teaspoon salt

1/2 teaspoon freshly cracked black pepper, or to taste

6 cups fresh corn kernels

1 cup heavy cream

1/2 pound of bacon, cut into small pieces and cooked

Directions

Click "Sauté" button and heat the oil. Then, sauté the onion until just tender. Now, add the diced potatoes.

Continue to cook, adding a splash of chicken stock if needed.

Now, add the stock, caraway seeds, salt, and black pepper. Select the "Manual" button; cook for 10 minutes under HIGH pressure. Once pressure has been released, carefully open the lid.

Stir in the corn kernels, cream, and bacon. Simmer uncovered for 3 more minutes or until everything is thoroughly warmed. Serve warm and enjoy!

Pork and Mushroom Goulash

(Ready in about 45 minutes | Servings 6)

Ingredients

3 beef bouillon cubes

1 pound pork fillet, cubed

1 tablespoon sunflower oil

2 garlic cloves, minced

1 onion, peeled and sliced

8 ounces mushrooms, chopped

2 cups water

1 ½ tablespoons tomato purée

1 tablespoon corn flour

Directions

First of all, dissolve bouillon cubes in water (1 cube in 1 cup of water); add dissolved cubes to the electric pressure cooker.

Next, add all remaining ingredients, except corn flour, to the pot.

Then, press the "Soup" button and cook for 40 minutes. Mix the corn flour to a smooth paste with a little water; add it to the cooker and simmer, uncovered, for 4 minutes, till the sauce has thickened.

Serve warm with egg noodles.

Swiss-Style Pork Chowder

(Ready in about 45 minutes | Servings 6)

Ingredients

1 pound pork side rib

1 turnip, peeled and sliced

2 carrots, peeled and sliced

1 parsnip, chopped

1 celery stalk, chopped

1 celery rib, chopped

3/4 tablespoon seasoned salt

1/2 teaspoon black pepper, ground

1 teaspoon granulated garlic

1 teaspoon sweet paprika

6 cups vegetable stock

1 cup Swiss chard, diced

1 cup Swiss cheese, shaved

Directions

Simply throw all ingredients, except Swiss chard and Swiss cheese, into your electric pressure cooker.

Choose "Soup" setting; cook it for 40 minutes using a HIGH pressure. Uncover, add Swiss chard, and stir until it is completely wilted. Serve warm, topped with cheese.

Bean and Farro with Porcini Mushrooms

(Ready in about 35 minutes | Servings 4)

Ingredients

1 cup dried pinto beans, soaked overnight

1/2 cup farro

1 cup water

2 cups porcini mushrooms, thinly sliced

4 cloves garlic, finely chopped

1 cup scallions, chopped

1 small-sized Serrano pepper, finely chopped

1 tablespoon turmeric powder

2 ripe Roma tomatoes, diced

Directions

Throw all of the above ingredients, except the tomatoes, into the cooker. Then, select the "Soup" button and cook 30 minutes under HIGH pressure.

Release the pressure and uncover your cooker. Now, add the diced tomatoes. Stir until everything is combined well. Serve at once.

Mushroom and Kale Pilaf

(Ready in about 15 minutes | Servings 8)

Ingredients

2 ½ cups vegetable stock

2 cups Arborio rice, rinsed

2 tablespoons olive oil

1 cup leftover meat, chopped

1 celery stalk, chopped

1 celery rib, chopped

2 carrots, chopped

1 ½ pounds cremini mushrooms, halved

3 cups fresh kale leaves, chopped

1 tablespoon oyster sauce

Fresh chopped chives, for garnish

Directions

Combine the stock, rice, and olive oil in the inner pot of your Instant Pot.

Add all remaining ingredients, except chives, to the pot.

Cover and choose "Bean/Chili". Cook for 8 minutes under HIGH pressure.

Then, allow the pressure to release naturally. Gently stir to combine. Serve warm, garnished with fresh chopped chives.

Sausage and Black Eyed Pea Soup

(Ready in about 15 minutes | Servings 6)

Ingredients

1/2 pound bacon, cut into chunks

2 tablespoons garlic, minced

1 onion, minced

2 cups dried black-eyed peas, soaked overnight and rinsed

1 cup water

6 cups chicken broth

1/4 cup tomato puree

1 teaspoon basil

1 teaspoon oregano

2 bay leaves

3/4 teaspoon salt

1/4 ground black pepper, or to your taste

1 teaspoon cayenne pepper

2 tablespoons brown sugar

1/2 pound kielbasa sausage, cut into bite-sized chunks

1/3 cup fresh parsley leaves, chopped

Directions

Add the bacon, garlic, and onion, to the electric pressure cooker; cook until the onion turns tender.

Throw all remaining ingredients into the cooker; stir to combine.

Cook under HIGH pressure for 5 minutes. Now, use the Natural pressure release. Spoon the soup into individual bowls and enjoy.

Hungarian Beef Stew

(Ready in about 40 minutes | Servings 6)

Ingredients

2 tablespoons corn oil

1 red onion, peeled and diced

2 garlic cloves, minced

1 red bell pepper, seeded and diced

1 green bell pepper, seeded and diced

3 potatoes peeled and diced

3 strips bacon, cut into pieces

1 teaspoon hot paprika

1 teaspoon sweet paprika

1 teaspoon caraway seeds

1 tablespoon soy sauce

1 ½ pounds chuck steak, cut into bite-sized chunks

2 cups roasted-vegetable stock, preferably homemade

1 (15) ounce can tomatoes with juice, diced

Directions

Start by preheating your Instant Pot using the "Sauté" function. Heat corn oil and sauté the onion and garlic.

Stir in the rest of the above ingredients, except the canned tomatoes. Cover according to manufacturer's instructions and select "Meat/ Stew" setting. Cook for 35 minutes using a HIGH pressure.

Release the pressure and uncover the pot. Afterward, stir in the canned tomatoes; stir until well combined. Serve hot.

Sunday Beef Stew

(Ready in about 45 minutes | Servings 6)

Ingredients

3 pounds beef chuck roast, cubed

2 cups roasted-vegetable broth

1 shallot, chopped

3 cloves garlic, minced

2 tablespoons olive oil

2 carrots, chopped

1 parsnip, chopped

4 potatoes, diced

1 bell pepper, sliced

1 cup water

1 (8-ounce) can tomato sauce

1 tablespoon soy sauce

2 tablespoons cornstarch

1 teaspoon dried thyme

1 teaspoon cayenne pepper

Kosher salt and ground black pepper, to taste

Directions

Sear the meat in the oil using "Sauté" setting. Deglaze the pot with a splash of roasted-vegetable broth. Add the shallot and garlic, and continue sautéing for 2 minutes longer. Turn off your cooker.

Add all remaining ingredients. Now, seal the lid and cook under HIGH pressure for 35 minutes.

Afterward, use the Natural pressure release. Serve warm.

Refreshing Tomato and Rice Soup

(Ready in about 15 minutes | Servings 4)

Ingredients

1/2 cup white rice

1 tablespoon olive oil

1 yellow onion, chopped

2 cups canned tomatoes with juices

4 cups water

Salt and ground black pepper, to taste

Paprika, to your liking

1 teaspoon cayenne pepper

Directions

Put all ingredients into your cooker; cook under HIGH pressure for 7 minutes; allow the Natural pressure release.

After the pressure has been released, carefully open the cooker's lid. Ladle the soup into individual soup bowls and serve. Enjoy!

Turkey and Vegetable Risotto

(Ready in about 15 minutes | Servings 8)

Ingredients

2 cups long grain rice, rinsed

2 ½ cups turkey broth

2 tablespoons canola oil

1 cup cooked turkey, chopped

1 celery stalk, chopped

2 carrots, chopped

1 turnip, chopped

3 cups fresh spinach leaves, chopped

1 tablespoon oyster sauce

Directions

Combine the rice, turkey broth, and canola oil in the inner pot of the electric pressure cooker. Stir to combine well.

Add the rest of the above ingredients to the pot. Seal the cooker's lid.

Now, select "Bean/Chili" setting. Cook for 10 minutes under HIGH pressure.

Release the pressure and serve warm.

Hearty Chicken and Turkey Chili

(Ready in about 25 minutes | Servings 8)

Ingredients

2 tablespoons corn oil

3-4 garlic cloves, finely minced

1 onion, finely chopped

1 green bell pepper, chopped

1 red bell pepper, chopped

1/2 pound ground chicken

1 pound ground turkey

2 cups chicken broth

1 ½ cups water

1/2 teaspoon dried marjoram

2 (14-ounce) cans beans, drained and rinsed

2 (14-ounce) cans diced tomatoes with green chilies

Sour cream, to serve

Directions

Select "Sauté" function and warm corn oil; now, cook garlic, onion, and bell peppers for about 6 minutes. Stir in the ground chicken and turkey; cook until they have browned.

Add the remaining ingredients, except for sour cream. Put the lid on, and cook for 7 minutes under HIGH pressure.

Divide your chili among eight serving bowl. Add a dollop of sour cream to each serving. Enjoy!

Beef Smoked Sausage Pilaf

(Ready in about 15 minutes | Servings 8)

Ingredients

2 tablespoons olive oil

1 shallot, finely chopped

2 cups brown rice, rinsed

2 ½ cups beef bone broth

1 cup beef smoked sausage, chopped

2 bell peppers, seeded and chopped

2 carrots, chopped

2 parsnips, chopped

1 celery stalk, chopped

1 teaspoon garlic powder

1 teaspoon chipotle powder

3 cups greens of choice, torn into pieces

1 tablespoon soy sauce

Mustard, for garnish

Directions

Preheat your cooker by selecting the "Sauté" function and heat the oil. Now, sauté the shallots until just tender.

Next, add the remaining ingredients; give it a good stir. Seal the cooker's lid.

Press "Bean/Chili" button. Cook for 10 minutes using a HIGH pressure. Once the pressure has been released, open the lid according to manufacturer's directions. Serve at once. Bon appétit!

DINNER

Quinoa Sloppy Joes

(Ready in about 15 minutes | Servings 8)

Ingredients

1/2 cup red quinoa

2 tablespoons canola oil

1 large-sized onion, chopped

3 garlic cloves, finely minced

1 large-sized bell pepper, seeded and chopped

2 pounds lean ground beef

1 (28-ounce) can tomatoes, crushed

1/2 cup old-fashioned rolled oats

1/4 cup packed dark brown sugar

2 tablespoons Dijon mustard

2 tablespoons apple cider vinegar

Salt and cracked black pepper, to taste

Directions

Add the quinoa to an electric pressure cooker; fill the cooker with water until the quinoa are submerged.

Cover and set the pot to cook for 3 minutes under HIGH pressure. Use the Quick-release method. Unlock and open the cooker. Drain the quinoa.

Heat the oil in the cooker turned to "Sauté" function. Now, cook the onion, garlic, and pepper about 4 minutes. Crumble in the ground beef and cook, stirring frequently, until the beef is no longer pink.

Stir in the tomatoes, oats, sugar, mustard, and vinegar. Season with salt and black pepper; now, add the drained quinoa; give it a good stir. Lock the lid onto the pot according to manufacturer's directions.

Set the machine to cook for 8 minutes under HIGH pressure. Then, perform the Quick-release method. Eat warm.

Beef and Sour Cream Curry

(Ready in about 25 minutes | Servings 4)

Ingredients

1 cup beef, cut into bite-sized chunks

1 tablespoon red curry paste

1 cup vegetable broth

1 red onion, finely chopped

4 cloves garlic, peeled and minced

1 parsnip, chopped

2 carrots, chopped

1 tablespoon balsamic vinegar

1 zucchini, peeled and diced

Salt and black pepper, to your liking

1 teaspoon grated nutmeg

Sour cream, to serve

Directions

Just throw the ingredients, except sour cream, into the pressure cooker.

Cover and choose "Meat" function; cook for 20 minutes.

While it is still hot, stir in sour cream. Stir until everything is well combined. Enjoy!

Chili Mac and Cheese Casserole

(Ready in about 20 minutes | Servings 8)

Ingredients

2 tablespoons corn oil

2 onions, chopped

2 (4½-ounce) canned mild green chilies, chopped

2 garlic cloves, minced

1 ½ pounds lean ground beef

1 teaspoon chili powder

1 teaspoon salt

1 (28-ounce) can tomatoes, crushed

2 (15-ounce) cans small red beans, drained and rinsed

2 cups chicken stock

8 ounces dried pasta

1 cup Cheddar cheese, shredded

Directions

Heat the oil in an electric pressure cooker turned to the "Sauté" function. Add the onion, chilies, and garlic; cook, stirring periodically, until the onions soften, about 5 minutes.

Stir in the ground beef and cook an additional 3 minutes or until slightly browned.

Stir in the chili powder, salt, tomatoes, red beans, chicken stock, and dried pasta. Lock the lid onto the pot.

Set the machine to cook under HIGH pressure for 8 minutes. Reduce the pressure. Turn off the machine. Use the Quick-release method. Afterward, stir before serving and serve topped with Cheddar cheese.

Cauliflower Risotto with Pineapple

(Ready in about 30 minutes | Servings 6)

Ingredients

2 cups Arborio rice

1/2 pineapple, cut into chunks

1 head cauliflower, minced

2 teaspoons sunflower oil

1 teaspoon salt

1/4 teaspoon red pepper flakes

Directions

Pour the water to the level 2 mark on the inner pot. Now, throw all ingredients into the cooker.

Choose the "Rice" setting. Serve warm, garnished with sour cream. Bon appétit!

Sweet Potato and Beef Dinner

(Ready in about 15 minutes | Servings 4)

Ingredients

2 tablespoons olive oil

1½ pounds lean ground beef

1 large-sized onion, chopped

1 pound sweet potatoes, peeled and shredded

1 teaspoon ground allspice

1/2 teaspoon dried sage

1/2 teaspoon garlic powder

1/2 teaspoon salt

1/4 teaspoon ground black pepper

2 tablespoons yellow cornmeal

2 tablespoons maple syrup

2 ½ cups roasted-vegetable broth, preferably homemade

Directions

Heat the oil in your Instant Pot turned to the browning function. Stir in the ground beef and cook about 5 minutes. Add the onion and cook until softened, about 5 minutes.

Stir in the sweet potato, allspice, sage, garlic powder, salt, and ground black pepper. Cook for 1 to 2 minutes, stirring frequently.

Stir in the cornmeal and maple syrup, and cook for an additional 2 minutes. Pour in the broth. Lock the lid onto the pot.

Now, cook under HIGH pressure for 5 minutes. Perform the Quick-release method and uncover the cooker. Serve warm.

Rice with Apple and Broccoli

(Ready in about 30 minutes | Servings 6)

Ingredients

4 cups water

2 cups long-grain rice

1 apple, cored and cut into chunks

1 head broccoli, minced

1 tablespoon butter, melted

1 teaspoon salt

1/4 teaspoon white pepper

1 teaspoon ground allspice

Yogurt, for garnish

Fresh sage leaves, for garnish

Directions

Simply add all ingredients, except the yogurt and sage, to your Instant Pot.

Select the "Rice" mode. Perform the Quick-release method and uncover the cooker. Pour in the yogurt and stir until everything is well incorporated.

Serve warm, garnished with fresh sage leaves. Bon appétit!

Cheesy Penne with Sausage and Bacon

(Ready in about 20 minutes | Servings 6)

Ingredients

4 slices bacon

1 pound pork sausage

1 onion, finely chopped

2 cloves garlic, minced

2 cups tomato purée

1/2 teaspoon salt

1/4 teaspoon ground black pepper

1 pound penne pasta

1 teaspoon dried basil

1 teaspoon dried rosemary

1/4 cup Parmigiano-Reggiano cheese, grated

Directions

Set the cooker to "Sauté" mode. Then, fry the bacon until crisp. Add the sausage and brown it until cooked through.

Stir in the onion and garlic and continue to sauté them for 4 minutes, or until they're tender. Add the rest of the ingredients, except cheese.

Choose "Manual" mode and cook for 5 minutes using a LOW pressure. Stir in Parmigiano-Reggiano and serve at once. Bon appétit!

Home-Style Sunday Meatloaf

(Ready in about 8 hours | Servings 10)

Ingredients

For the Meatloaf:

Nonstick cooking spray

1 onion, finely chopped

2 garlic cloves, minced

1/2 pound ground beef

1/2 pound ground pork

1 large-sized egg

3/4 cup brown rice, cooked

1 teaspoon turmeric powder

1 teaspoon dried marjoram

1 cup whole milk

Salt and freshly cracked black pepper, to your liking

1 teaspoon cayenne pepper

For the Topping:

1 tablespoon brown sugar

3/4 cup tomato paste

Directions

First, lightly oil the inner pot with a nonstick cooking spray.

Then, combine all ingredients for the meatloaf. Form your mixture into a round meatloaf; lay it in the pot.

Now, mix the ingredients for the topping. Spread the topping over the meatloaf.

Cover the cooker and select the "Slow Cook" function; cook for 6 to 8 hours on LOW. Bon appétit!

Tender Pork with Sweet Onions

(Ready in about 35 minutes | Servings 6)

Ingredients

2 pounds pork belly, sliced

1/4 cup dry red wine

1/4 cup tamari soy sauce

1 tablespoon maple syrup

2 cups beef bone broth

4 slices fresh ginger

4 sweet onions, peeled and thinly sliced

6 cloves garlic, sliced

Directions

Select "Sauté" setting; now, sear the pork on both sides. Add the rest of the above ingredients. Gently stir to combine.

Press "Meat/Stew" key and cook for 30 minutes or so, until the pork is almost falling apart. Serve at once and enjoy!

Ziti with Pork sausage and Ricotta Cheese

(Ready in about 20 minutes | Servings 6)

Ingredients

1 teaspoon lard, at room temperature

1 onion, finely chopped

2 cloves garlic, minced

1 pound pork sausage

2 cups tomato purée

Salt and ground black pepper, to taste

1 pound dry ziti

1 teaspoon marjoram

1 teaspoon dried basil

1 teaspoon dried rosemary

1 teaspoon Dijon mustard

1/4 cup Ricotta cheese, crumbled

Directions

Set the cooker to "Sauté" mode. Then, melt the lard, and cook the onion, garlic, and sausage about 5 minutes.

Stir in the remaining ingredients, except cheese.

Press "Manual" button and cook for 5 minutes under LOW pressure. Stir in Ricotta and serve at once. Enjoy!

Light and Easy Peanut Salad

(Ready in about 25 minutes | Servings 4)

Ingredients

1 pound raw peanuts, shelled

2 cups water

2 ripe tomatoes, chopped

2 sweet onions, peeled and diced

1 cucumber, diced

2 carrots, trimmed and chopped

1 red bell pepper, seeded and thinly sliced

2 tablespoons olive oil

1 tablespoon fresh lemon juice

1 teaspoon dried dill weed

1/4 teaspoon freshly ground black pepper

3/4 teaspoon sea salt

Directions

Blanch your peanuts in boiling salted water for 1 minute; drain them and discard the skins.

Add peanuts and 2 cups of water to the Instant Pot; cook for 20 minutes under HIGH pressure. Let the peanuts cool slightly.

Transfer prepared peanuts to a salad bowl. Stir in the rest of the above ingredients and toss to coat.

Fall-Apart-Tender Pork

(Ready in about 1 hour | Servings 16)

Ingredients

4 pounds pork butt roast

1 ¼ cups unsweetened apple juice

1/4 cup Worcestershire sauce

4 cloves garlic, finely minced

1 teaspoon onion powder

1 teaspoon cumin powder

1 teaspoon mustard seeds

3/4 teaspoon sea salt

1/4 teaspoon ground black pepper, to taste

Directions

Add all of the above ingredients to the inner pot of your cooker. Add enough water to cover the pork.

Close the lid and choose "Meat/Stew" button; cook for 1 hour.

Serve at once.

Pasta with Meat and Tomato Sauce

(Ready in about 10 minutes | Servings 6)

Ingredients

1 tablespoon olive oil

1/2 pound lean ground pork

1/2 pound lean ground beef

1 ½ pounds tomato paste

1 onion, finely minced

2 garlic cloves, minced

Sea salt and ground black pepper, to taste

1/2 teaspoon dried oregano

1 teaspoon dried rosemary

1/2 teaspoon dried basil

1 pound dried egg noodles

Directions

Press "Sauté" button and heat olive oil; then, brown the pork and beef until they are no longer pink.

Add the remaining ingredients and cook for 7 minutes. Serve at once and enjoy!

Fish Fillets with Mayo Sauce

(Ready in about 15 minutes | Servings 4)

Ingredients

4 fish fillets

1/2 teaspoon sea salt

1/4 teaspoon ground black pepper

1 teaspoon cayenne pepper

1 tablespoon lemon juice

1 tablespoon balsamic vinegar

3 tablespoons mayonnaise

1 teaspoon dried dill weed

2 tablespoons olive oil

1 tablespoon fresh cilantro

Directions

Season fish fillets with sea salt, ground black pepper, and cayenne pepper. Press the "Sauté" button and brown the fish on both sides.

Add 3/4 cup of water to the pot. Place browned fish on a rack. Seal the cooker's lid according to manufacturer's instructions; press the "Steam" button and cook for 5 minutes.

Meanwhile, make the sauce by mixing the remaining ingredients. Then, pour the sauce over the fish fillets. Serve and enjoy!

Sunday BBQ Pork Ribs

(Ready in about 40 minutes | Servings 4)

Ingredients

2 pork ribs

1 cup water

2 cups barbecue sauce

2 medium-sized shallots, slice into rings

2 carrots, thinly sliced

2 red potatoes, peeled and diced

Salt and ground black pepper, to your liking

1 teaspoon sweet or hot paprika

Directions

Lay pork ribs in your Instant Pot. Add the water along with 1 cup of barbecue sauce.

Next, select the "Meat/Stew" button. Add the remaining ingredients. Cover and choose "Manual" setting; set the timer for 40 minutes.

Transfer the content of the cooker to the serving platter. Drizzle the remaining barbecue sauce over all and serve right away.

Barbecue Juicy Pork Butt

(Ready in about 1 hour | Servings 16)

Ingredients

6 pounds pork butt roast

4 cloves garlic, halved

1 teaspoon shallot powder

1 teaspoon turmeric powder

1 teaspoon fennel seeds

3/4 teaspoon sea salt

1/4 teaspoon ground black pepper

1/4 cup Worcestershire sauce

2 tablespoons tomato puree

2 (12-ounce) bottles barbecue sauce

Directions

Rub the pork with garlic; now, sprinkle it with all seasonings.

Next, add Worcestershire sauce and tomato puree. Add enough water to cover the pork.

Close the lid according to the manufacturer's directions, and select "Meat/Stew" setting; cook for 1 hour. Serve warm, drizzled with barbecue sauce.

Fettuccine with Sweet Italian Sausage Sauce

(Ready in about 10 minutes | Servings 6)

Ingredients

1 tablespoon olive oil

1 onion, finely minced

2 garlic cloves, minced

1 teaspoon white sugar

1 pound sweet Italian sausage, coarsely chopped

1/2 teaspoon sea salt

1/4 teaspoon freshly ground black pepper, or to taste

Cayenne pepper, to taste

1/2 teaspoon dried basil

1/2 teaspoon dried oregano

1 teaspoon dried thyme

1 ½ pounds tomato puree

1 pound dried Fettuccine

Directions

Begin by selecting the "Sauté" mode; warm the oil; then, cook the onion and garlic in hot oil until just tender and fragrant.

Stir in the chopped Italian sausage. Cook for 3 more minutes, stirring constantly; throw in the rest of the above ingredients.

Now, cook for 7 minutes using a HIGH pressure. Then, perform 5-minute natural release. Serve at once and enjoy!

Garlic and Lemon Tilapia Fillets

(Ready in about 10 minutes | Servings 4)

Ingredients

4 tilapia fillets

1 teaspoon dried dill weed

1 teaspoon dried rosemary, crushed

1 teaspoon dried thyme, crushed

1/2 teaspoon sea salt

1/4 teaspoon freshly cracked black pepper

1 teaspoon cayenne pepper

4 small-sized cloves garlic, minced

2 lemons, sliced

2 tablespoons extra-virgin olive oil

1 tablespoon fresh cilantro

Directions

Sprinkle the seasonings over tilapia fillets. Place tilapia fillets on the stainless steel steam rack.

Add 3/4 cup of water to the pot. Sprinkle minced garlic over the fish fillets; top them with lemon slices.

Select "Manual" setting and set the timer for 5 minutes using [+-] button. After that, manually release the pressure.

Drizzle olive oil over warm fish and serve garnished with fresh cilantro. Enjoy!

Summer Brown Rice Salad with Sage

(Ready in about 30 minutes | Servings 4)

Ingredients

2 ½ cups water

2 cups brown rice

4 tomatoes, diced

1 cucumber, cored and diced

1 red bell pepper, sliced

1 green bell pepper, sliced

1 cup red onions, chopped

1 teaspoon dried oregano

1/2 teaspoon salt

1/4 teaspoon ground black pepper

Fresh sage leaves, coarsely chopped

Directions

Add the water and brown rice to the inner pot of your Instant Pot. Close and lock the lid according to the manufacturer's directions. Press the "Manual" button and set the timer for 22 minutes using [+-] key.

After that, open the cooker by using the Natural pressure release. Transfer the rice to a salad bowl.

Add the remaining ingredients and toss to combine. Serve well chilled.

Rice Noodles with Mushroom Sauce

(Ready in about 20 minutes | Servings 6)

Ingredients

2 tablespoons olive oil

1 onion, finely chopped

2 garlic cloves, minced

1 pound cremini mushrooms, coarsely chopped

3/4 teaspoon sea salt

1/2 teaspoon freshly ground black pepper, or to taste

1/4 teaspoon crushed red pepper flakes

1 teaspoon dried oregano

1 teaspoon dried dill

1 ½ pounds tomato puree

1 pound dried rice noodles

Directions

Begin by selecting the "Sauté" button; heat olive oil; then, cook the onion and garlic until just tender.

Stir in cremini mushrooms. Cook for 3 more minutes or until they are fragrant; throw in the remaining items.

Now, cook for 7 minutes using a HIGH pressure. Afterward, perform 5-minute natural release. Serve warm and enjoy!

Spring Black Bean Salad

(Ready in about 15 minutes | Servings 4)

Ingredients

4 cups water

1 cup black beans, soaked overnight

4 spring onions, chopped

2 garlic cloves, chopped

1 red bell pepper, seeded and thinly sliced

1 yellow or orange bell pepper, seeded and thinly sliced

2 tablespoons extra-virgin olive oil

1 tablespoon red wine vinegar

1/2 teaspoon kosher salt

1/4 teaspoon freshly cracked black pepper

Red pepper flakes, to your liking

Directions

Add the water and beans to the inner pot. Choose "Manual" mode and 8-minute pressure cooking time.

Drain your beans and transfer them to a large-sized salad bowl. Now, add the remaining ingredients and toss to combine. Serve well-chilled and enjoy!

Tuna and Rice Salad

(Ready in about 30 minutes | Servings 4)

Ingredients

2 ½ cups lightly salted water

2 cups brown rice

2 cups canned tuna

1 red onion, peeled and thinly sliced

1 red bell pepper, thinly sliced

1 green bell pepper, thinly sliced

1 large-sized tomato, diced

2 tablespoons extra-virgin olive oil

1/2 teaspoon dried dill weed

1/2 teaspoon sea salt

Freshly ground black pepper, to your liking

1 bunch flat-leaf parsley, roughly chopped

Directions

Add the water and rice to the inner pot. Close and lock the lid according to the manufacturer's instructions. Choose "Manual" mode and set the timer for 22 minutes using [+-] button.

After that, open the cooker with the Natural pressure release. Allow your rice to cool completely.

Throw in the remaining ingredients. Toss to combine and serve well-chilled.

Hot Bean Purée

(Ready in about 20 minutes | Servings 6)

Ingredients

2 tablespoons sunflower oil

1 medium-sized onion, peeled and chopped

2 garlic cloves, finely minced

1/2 teaspoon chipotle powder

1 teaspoon cumin powder

2 cups dry white beans, soaked

2 cups water

1 teaspoon sea salt

1/2 teaspoon black pepper

1 teaspoon dried dill weed

1 teaspoon hot paprika

Directions

Press "Sauté" button to preheat the Instant Pot. Now, heat the oil and add the onion, followed by garlic, chipotle powder, and cumin powder.

Next, stir in dry beans and water. Close and lock the lid and select "Manual" setting; cook for 10 minutes.

Afterward, purée the mixture with an immersion blender or potato masher. Season with salt, black pepper, dill, and hot paprika. Garnish with fresh cilantro leaves, if desired. Enjoy!

Spaghetti with Mushroom Sauce

(Ready in about 20 minutes | Servings 4)

Ingredients

2 tablespoons olive oil

1 shallot, finely chopped

2 garlic cloves, minced

1/2 pound porcini mushrooms, coarsely chopped

1/2 pound cremini mushrooms, coarsely chopped

1/4 teaspoon smoked cayenne pepper

3/4 teaspoon salt

1/2 teaspoon freshly ground black pepper, or to taste

1 teaspoon dried oregano

1 ½ pounds tomato puree

1 pound dry spaghetti

Directions

Start by selecting the "Sauté" mode; now, heat olive oil and sauté the shallot and garlic until the shallot turns tender and the garlic turns slightly brown.

Stir in the mushrooms and continue sautéing another 4 minutes or until they are fragrant; throw in the rest of the above items.

Set the machine to cook for 7 minutes under HIGH pressure. Lastly, perform 5-minute natural release. Bon appétit!

Pilaf with Turkey Sausage

(Ready in about 20 minutes | Servings 8)

Ingredients

2 tablespoons canola oil

1 red onion, finely chopped

2 green garlics, chopped

2 cups long-grain rice, rinsed

2 ½ cups roasted-vegetable broth

1 cup Italian turkey sausage, sliced

1 bell pepper, seeded and thinly sliced

1 celery stalk, chopped

2 carrots, chopped

1 teaspoon chipotle powder

3 cups kale, torn into pieces

1/4 cup red wine

Salt and ground black pepper, to your liking

Mustard, for garnish

Directions

Preheat your Instant Pot by selecting the "Sauté" button; now, warm the oil. When the oil is hot, throw in the onion. Sauté the onion until just tender. Throw in the garlic and continue sautéing for 1 to 2 minutes longer or until it's fragrant.

Next, add the rest of the above ingredients; give it a good stir. Seal the cooker's lid according to the manufacturer's directions.

Press the "Bean/Chili" button; allow it to cook for 10 minutes using a HIGH pressure. Once the pressure has been released, open the lid. Bon appétit!

Cheesy Risotto with Tomatoes

(Ready in about 20 minutes | Servings 6)

Ingredients

1 tablespoon sunflower oil

1 large-sized white onion, thinly sliced

3 celery ribs, coarsely chopped

1 1/3 cups long-grain rice

2 medium-sized ripe tomatoes, chopped

3 cups bone stock, preferably homemade

Cheddar cheese, grated

Directions

Heat the sunflower oil in the pressure cooker turned to "Sauté" function; brown the onion and celery for a couple of minutes.

Stir in the rice and tomatoes; cook for 3 to 4 minutes.

Pour in bone stock; close the lid properly and cook under HIGH pressure for 7 minutes. Afterward, lower the pressure.

Once the pressure has been released, open the lid. Divide your risotto among individual serving plates; top with grated Cheddar cheese and enjoy!

Quick and Easy Curried Rice

(Ready in about 15 minutes | Servings 4)

Ingredients

1 tablespoon olive oil

1 cup Arborio rice

1 ½ cups vegetable stock, preferably homemade

1 teaspoon curry powder

1 tablespoon soy sauce

1 tablespoon ghee, melted

Fresh parsley, for garnish

Directions

Put the oil, rice and stock into the inner pot of your cooker.

Cook under HIGH pressure for 7 minutes. Then, perform 5-minute natural release.

Add the curry powder, soy sauce, and ghee to the rice; stir to combine well. Serve at once, garnished with fresh parsley. Enjoy!

Garam Masala Potatoes with Mushrooms

(Ready in about 20 minutes | Servings 4)

Ingredients

1 tablespoon sunflower oil

1/2 pound mushrooms, thinly sliced

1/2 cup scallions, chopped

1/2 teaspoon sea salt

1/4 teaspoon ground black pepper

1/2 teaspoon dried dill weed

1 teaspoon garlic powder

1/2 cup chicken broth

1 teaspoon Garam masala

4 potatoes, peeled and sliced

Directions

Heat the oil in your cooker turned to "Sauté" function; sauté the mushrooms and scallions until just tender.

Now, add all remaining ingredients to the cooker; stir to mix well.

Cook under HIGH pressure for 4 minutes; after that, use the Natural pressure release. Carefully open the lid. Serve warm.

Easy Festive Chicken Breasts

(Ready in about 15 minutes | Servings 4)

Ingredients

4 medium-sized chicken breast, skinless and boneless

1 ½ cups chicken stock

2 garlic cloves, minced

1 teaspoon sea salt

1/2 teaspoon freshly ground black pepper

1 teaspoon cayenne pepper

Directions

Add all ingredients to the Instant Pot; cook for 15 minutes under HIGH pressure.

Perform the Natural pressure release; remove the chicken breasts.

Yummy Chicken with Coleslaw Mix

(Ready in about 15 minutes | Servings 4)

Ingredients

1 tablespoon sunflower oil

2 chicken breasts, skinless, boneless and cubed

1/4 cup onions, peeled and diced

1 package coleslaw mix

1/4 cup canned bamboo shoots

1/2 cup white mushrooms, sliced

3/4 teaspoon sea salt

1/2 teaspoon ground black pepper

1 teaspoon cayenne pepper

1 ½ cups chicken broth

Directions

Preheat your cooker on "Sauté" function. Then, heat the oil and brown the chicken on all sides, along with diced onion.

Stir in all remaining ingredients; cook under HIGH pressure for 5 minutes. Perform the Natural pressure release; then, open the lid.

Stir before serving and enjoy!

Chicken Breasts with Tomato Sauce

(Ready in about 15 minutes | Servings 6)

Ingredients

1/4 cup canola oil

1 pound chicken breasts, cut up in pieces

1 onion, peeled and thinly sliced

2 (14.5-ounce) cans tomato sauce

2 cloves garlic, minced

1/2 teaspoon salt

1/2 teaspoon freshly ground black pepper

1/2 teaspoon red pepper flakes

Directions

Press "Sauté" button and heat the oil in the cooker; gently brown the chicken pieces on all sides.

Then, throw in the onion and cook until it is translucent. Add the remaining ingredients to the Instant Pot.

Cook under HIGH pressure for 10 minutes; use the Natural pressure release. Once the pressure has been released, carefully open the lid.

You can thicken the sauce, if desired. Serve at once.

Tender Mediterranean Turkey Breasts

(Ready in about 20 minutes | Servings 4)

Ingredients

1 pound turkey breasts, skinless and boneless

1 ½ cups turkey stock, preferably homemade

2 garlic cloves, minced

1 teaspoon dried rosemary, crushed

1 teaspoon dried marjoram

1 thyme sprig, leaves only

Sea salt and freshly ground black pepper

1 teaspoon cayenne pepper

Directions

Add all ingredients to the inner pot; cook for 15 minutes using a HIGH pressure.

Afterward, use the Natural pressure release. Serve warm.

Tangy Chicken Breasts with Mango

(Ready in about 20 minutes | Servings 6)

Ingredients

6 small-sized chicken breasts, skinless and boneless

1 teaspoon garlic powder

1 teaspoon cayenne pepper

1/2 teaspoon sea salt

White pepper, to taste

1 tablespoon sugar

1 tablespoon Worcestershire sauce

1 (15-ounce) can sliced mango in syrup

Directions

Rub the chicken with all seasonings. Lightly grease the inner pot of your cooker and brown the chicken on all sides.

Sprinkle the sugar over the top of the chicken; drizzle Worcestershire sauce over all. Add the mango along with syrup.

Cook under HIGH pressure for 8 minutes; use the Natural pressure release. Once the pressure has been released, open the cooker's lid.

Transfer everything to a serving platter and serve at once.

Spicy Mustard Pork Chops

(Ready in about 20 minutes | Servings 4)

Ingredients

1 tablespoon spicy brown mustard

4 pork chops, trimmed of excess fats

1/2 teaspoon salt

1/4 teaspoon ground black pepper

2 tablespoons all-purpose flour

1 tablespoon coconut butter

Directions

Spread the mustard over the pork chops.

Now, mix all remaining ingredients in a bowl. Spread the mixture over the pork chops. Arrange the pork chops on the trivet. Add 3/4 cup of water.

Now, cook at HIGH pressure for 12 minutes; use the Natural pressure release. Afterward, open the lid according to the manufacturer's directions. Serve warm.

Pulled Pork Sandwiches

(Ready in about 50 minutes | Servings 12)

Ingredients

1 boneless pork loin roast

1 tablespoon brown sugar

3/4 teaspoon sea salt

1/2 teaspoon ground black pepper

1/2 teaspoon red pepper flakes, crushed

1 cup dry red wine

1 cup barbecue sauce

Hamburger buns

Directions

Sprinkle the pork with the sugar, salt, black pepper, and red pepper flakes. Place the pork in the inner pot. Add dry red wine.

Cook under HIGH pressure for 45 minutes; use the Natural pressure release.

Next, shred the meat with two forks. Add barbecue sauce. Serve prepared pork on hamburger buns.

Colorful Broccoli and Pepper Salad

(Ready in about 10 minutes | Servings 6)

Ingredients

For the Salad:

1 head broccoli, broken into florets

2 carrots, thinly sliced

1 large-sized parsnip, chopped

1 cup water

1 yellow bell pepper, peeled and sliced thinly

1 red bell pepper, peeled and sliced thinly

1 shallot, thinly sliced

For the Vinaigrette:

4 tablespoons extra-virgin olive oil

1 orange, zested and squeezed

2 cloves garlic, smashed

Freshly ground black pepper, to taste

Salt, to taste

1/2 teaspoon red pepper flakes

1 tablespoon fresh basil, roughly chopped

1 tablespoon fresh parsley, roughly chopped

Directions

In the inner pot of your electric pressure cooker, place the broccoli, carrots, parsnip, and water. Lock the cooker's lid and choose "Manual" setting and 7-minute pressure cooking time.

Transfer prepared vegetables to a salad bowl. Throw in bell peppers and shallots.

To make the vinaigrette: thoroughly whisk all the vinaigrette ingredients.

Lastly, open the Instant Pot according to manufacturer's directions. Dress the salad and serve chilled.

One-Pot Mushroom Curry

(Ready in about 15 minutes | Servings 4)

Ingredients

1 tablespoon olive oil

2 cloves garlic, peeled and minced

1 shallot, diced

2 tablespoons curry paste

1 cup white mushrooms, thinly sliced

2 cups coconut milk

2 cups vegetable stock, preferably homemade

1 ½ cups lentils

1/2 teaspoon celery seeds

1/2 teaspoon dried basil

1/4 teaspoon dried rosemary

1/2 teaspoon dried oregano

Cayenne pepper, to taste

Salt and ground black pepper, to taste

Directions

Choose the "Sauté" setting on your Instant Pot. Heat the oil; now, sauté the garlic and shallot until just tender.

Next, choose the "Cancel" button. Add the curry paste and white mushrooms; give it a good stir.

Add the coconut milk, followed with the rest of the ingredients.

Close the lid and press "Manual" button; set the timer for 6 minutes. Serve warm.

Chicken, Sausage and Rice Casserole

(Ready in about 25 minutes | Servings 6)

Ingredients

2 tablespoons canola oil

1/2 pound chicken sausage, cut into pieces

6 chicken thighs, boneless and skinless

1 leek, chopped

1 yellow bell pepper, stemmed, cored, and chopped

1 green bell pepper, stemmed, cored, and chopped

2 cloves garlic, finely minced

1/2 cup rosé wine

2 ripe tomatoes, roughly chopped

1 ¼ cups chicken or vegetable broth

1 ¼ cups long-grain white rice

1 tablespoon smoked cayenne pepper

3/4 teaspoon salt

1/2 teaspoon ground black pepper

Directions

Heat canola oil using "Sauté" function on your Instant Pot. Then, brown the sausage, turning them occasionally, 4 to 5 minutes. Reserve.

Now, throw in the chicken wings; brown them approximately 6 minutes. Add them to the reserved sausage.

Stir in the leeks, peppers, and minced garlic; cook, stirring continuously, until they are tender.

Pour in the wine and bring it to a simmer. Let it simmer until the wine has reduced to a thick glaze. Stir in the remaining ingredients.

Return the reserved meat to the cooker. Stir until everything is well combined. Lock the lid onto the cooker and let it cook for 15 minutes under HIGH pressure.

Use the Quick-release method. Serve warm.

Chicken Thighs with Potatoes

(Ready in about 30 minutes | Servings 6)

Ingredients

2 tablespoons corn oil

6 chicken thighs, boneless, skinless and halved

2 green garlics, finely minced

1 shallot, finely chopped

6 small potatoes, quartered

1 large-sized carrot, chopped

1 ½ cups canned mild green chilies, chopped

1/2 tablespoon mustard seeds

1 teaspoon dried basil

1 teaspoon dried rosemary

1 cup chicken stock

Directions

Heat the oil in an electric pressure cooker turned to the "Sauté" mode. Add the chicken thighs; cook approximately 6 minutes, turning once. Set them aside, keeping warm.

Sauté the garlic and shallot until softened, about 3 minutes. Stir in the rest of the above ingredients. Now, add reserved chicken thighs. Lock the lid onto the cooker.

Set the machine to cook for 15 minutes under HIGH pressure. Afterward, use the Quick-release function. Serve at once. Bon appétit!

Savoy Cabbage and Apple Delight

(Ready in about 30 minutes | Servings 4)

Ingredients

2 tablespoons butter, room temperature

1 yellow onion, peeled and diced

2 tart apples, peeled, cored and diced

1 head savoy cabbage, shredded and stems removed

1 cup rosé wine

1 cup roasted-vegetable stock, preferably homemade

Salt and ground black pepper, to your liking

1/8 teaspoon freshly grated nutmeg

1/4 teaspoon brown sugar

A slurry (2 tablespoons cornstarch dissolved in 5 tablespoons water)

Directions

Set your Instant Pot to "Sauté" mode. Warm the butter until it's completely melted. Then, sauté the onion and apples approximately 8 minutes.

Add the rest of the above components, except the cornstarch slurry.

Select "Manual" setting and cook for 10 minutes. Perform the Quick-release and carefully open the cooker.

Select "Sauté" setting and bring the mixture to a boil. Now, add the cornstarch slurry; boil for 5 minutes or until liquid has thickened. Stir before serving and enjoy!

Rigatoni with Turkey and Avocado

(Ready in about 20 minutes | Servings 4)

Ingredients

1 tablespoon avocado oil

1 pound turkey breasts, skinless and chopped

4 cloves garlic, finely minced

1 medium-sized onion, chopped

2 cups tomato purée

1 tablespoon fresh sage

1 tablespoon fresh basil, chopped

Salt and ground black pepper, to taste

1 pound dried rigatoni pasta

Avocado slices, to garnish

Directions

Press "Sauté" button and heat avocado oil. Now, brown the turkey breasts for 5 minutes. Add the garlic and onion, and cook an additional 5 minutes.

Add the remaining ingredients, except the slices of avocado. Close and lock the lid. Press the "Manual" button, and choose LOW pressure and 5-minute cook time.

Next, release the pressure and carefully open the cooker. Serve and enjoy!

Chicken Thighs with Pears and Scallions

(Ready in about 25 minutes | Servings 8)

Ingredients

2 tablespoons olive oil

2 pounds chicken thighs, boneless, skinless, halved

3/4 teaspoon cayenne pepper

1/2 teaspoon salt

1/4 teaspoon ground black pepper

1 cup scallions, chopped

2 firm pears, peeled, cored, and sliced

A pinch of grated nutmeg

1/4 cup dry red wine

2/3 cup vegetable stock

Directions

Warm the oil in a cooker turned to the browning function. Sprinkle the chicken thighs with cayenne pepper, salt, and ground black pepper. Now, brown them on both sides, turning once or twice. Reserve.

Add the rest of the above items. Nestle the browned chicken into the scallion mixture. Choose "Poultry" setting and cook until tender, about 15 minutes.

Unlock and open the pot according to the manufacturer's directions. Stir before serving and enjoy.

Risotto with Pears and Cauliflower

(Ready in about 30 minutes | Servings 6)

Ingredients

2 cooking pears, peeled, cored and diced

2 cups jasmine rice

1 small-sized head cauliflower, chopped into florets

2 tablespoons butter, softened

3/4 teaspoon salt

1/4 teaspoon red pepper, crushed

A pinch of grated nutmeg

Directions

Add the water to the level 2 mark on the inner pot.

Now, add all ingredients and stir to combine well. Select the "Rice" setting.

Release the pressure and carefully open the pot. Transfer everything to a serving platter. Bon appétit!

Macaroni with Sausage and Cottage Cheese

(Ready in about 20 minutes | Servings 6)

Ingredients

1 pound sausage meat

2 cloves garlic, minced

1 cup onions, finely chopped

2 cups tomato puree

1 tablespoon tomato ketchup

1 tablespoon soy sauce

Salt and ground black pepper, to taste

1 pound dry macaroni

1 teaspoon dried oregano

1/4 teaspoon dried dill weed

1/4 cup Cottage cheese, crumbled

Directions

Set your Instant Pot to "Sauté" mode. Cook the sausage for 4 to 5 minutes or until they are browned.

Add the garlic and onions, and continue sautéing them for an additional 4 minutes or until tender. Add the remaining ingredients, except for cheese.

Select "Manual" setting and cook under LOW pressure for 5 minutes. Divide the macaroni mixture among 6 serving plates and serve garnished with Cottage cheese.

The Best Beef Sandwiches Ever

(Ready in about 1 hour 10 minutes | Servings 6)

Ingredients

1 tablespoon lard, melted

1 1/3 pounds frozen beef roast

1 cup beef bone stock

For the Sauce:

1/2 teaspoon salt

1/4 teaspoon ground black pepper

1 teaspoon cayenne pepper

1/2 cup tomato paste

2 teaspoons honey

1/4 cup water

Directions

Grease the Instant Pot with melted lard. Add the beef and bone stock. Now, select the "Meat/Stew" setting; adjust the time to 70 minutes.

Meanwhile, thoroughly combine all sauce ingredients.

Turn the machine off and use the Quick pressure release. Pull the cooked beef apart into the chunks. Afterward, pour the sauce over the beef. Assemble the sandwiches and enjoy!

Pasta with Ground Turkey Sauce

(Ready in about 10 minutes | Servings 6)

Ingredients

1/2 pound ground turkey

2 cups tomato puree

1 shallot, peeled and chopped

2 garlic cloves, peeled and finely minced

1/2 teaspoon sea salt

1/2 teaspoon ground black pepper

1/2 teaspoon dried basil

1/4 teaspoon dried marjoram

1/2 teaspoon dried basil

1 teaspoon mustard seeds

1 teaspoon fennel seeds

1 pound dried egg noodles

Directions

Preheat your Instant Pot by selecting the "Sauté" setting; now, cook the turkey until it is browned; make sure to stir constantly.

Add the rest of the above ingredients. Set the timer for 8 minutes and cook under HIGH pressure.

Divide your pasta among 6 individual serving dishes and serve right away.

Barbecue Pork Ribs with Carrots

(Ready in about 20 minutes | Servings 6)

Ingredients

2 pork ribs, cut for serving

1 ½ cups beef bone broth

1 ½ cups barbecue sauce

1 red onion, cut into rings

2 cloves garlic, peeled and crushed

2 carrots, thinly sliced

1 teaspoon sea salt

1/4 teaspoon ground black pepper

1 teaspoon caraway seeds

Directions

Arrange pork ribs on the bottom of your cooker. Now, pour in the broth and barbecue sauce. Close the lid according to the manufacturer's directions. Choose the "Meat/Stew" setting. Press the "Cancel" button.

Add the remaining ingredients. Then, select "Manual" function; set the timer for 5 minutes. Serve right away.

Barbecue Pork with Root Vegetables

(Ready in about 40 minutes | Servings 4)

Ingredients

2 pork ribs

1 cup water

2 cups barbecue sauce

2 onions, sliced into thin rings

2 parsnips, thinly sliced

2 carrots, thinly sliced

4 potatoes, peeled and diced

2 cloves garlic, peeled and crushed

1 teaspoon dried dill weed

Salt and ground black pepper, to your liking

Cayenne pepper, to your liking

Directions

Arrange the ribs on the bottom of the cooker. Pour in the water and 1 cup of the sauce. Close the lid and select "Meat/Stew" setting.

Add the vegetables. Sprinkle with dill, salt, black pepper, and cayenne pepper. Cover and select "Manual" setting; set the timer for 2 minutes.

Drizzle the remaining barbecue sauce over all and serve at once.

Winter Risotto with Savoy Cabbage

(Ready in about 30 minutes | Servings 6)

Ingredients

2 cups rice

1 cup savoy cabbage, shredded

1 carrot, grated

1 parsnip, roughly chopped

1 bay leaf

1/4 cup tomato purée

2 tablespoons canola oil

3/4 teaspoon salt

4-5 black peppercorns

1/4 teaspoon cayenne pepper

Directions

Add the water to the level 2 mark on the inner pot. Throw all ingredients into the inner pot.

Give it a good stir. Select the "Rice" setting.

Serve warm and enjoy!

Juicy Chicken Breasts with Prunes

(Ready in about 25 minutes | Servings 8)

Ingredients

2 tablespoons corn oil

2 pounds chicken breasts, boneless, skinless and cut into cubes

1/2 teaspoon salt

1/4 teaspoon ground black pepper

1/2 cup green onions, chopped

2 carrots, trimmed and thinly sliced

1/2 cup prunes, pitted and halved

1/4 cup dry red wine

2/3 cup chicken broth

Directions

Heat the oil in a cooker turned to the browning function. Sprinkle the chicken breasts with salt and ground black pepper. Now, brown them for 5 minutes on each side. Set aside.

Next, stir in the remaining ingredients. Nestle the chicken breasts into the mixture. Choose "Poultry" mode and set the timer for 15 minutes.

Release the pressure and carefully open the pot. Serve and enjoy!

Farfalle with Sausage and Ham

(Ready in about 20 minutes | Servings 8)

Ingredients

2 tablespoons sunflower oil

1 red onion, peeled and chopped

4 garlic cloves, peeled and crushed

2 slices ham, chopped

1/2 pound sausage meat

2 pounds pasta sauce of choice

1 teaspoon spicy brown mustard

1/2 teaspoon sea salt

1/4 teaspoon ground black pepper

1 teaspoon dried oregano

1 pound dried farfalle

Directions

Preheat your Instant Pot by selecting the "Sauté" setting; then, melt the oil and sauté the onion, garlic, ham and sausage meat. Cook, stirring frequently, for 4 to 5 minutes.

Add the rest of the above items. Cook another 10 minutes. Serve warm and enjoy!

Chicken Thighs with Pearl Onions

(Ready in about 40 minutes | Servings 4)

Ingredients

1 pound bone-in chicken thighs, halved

1 cup chicken broth

2 cups tomato sauce

2 cups pearl onions

2 cloves garlic, peeled and crushed

1 teaspoon kosher salt

1/2 teaspoon freshly ground black pepper, or to taste

1/4 cup fresh basil leaves, chiffonade

Directions

Lay the chicken thighs on the bottom of your cooker. Pour in the broth and tomato sauce. Close the lid according to the manufacturer's instructions. Choose the "Meat/Stew" function.

Stir in the rest of the above ingredients, except basil leaves. Cover, and choose "Manual" mode; set the timer for 2 minutes. Serve warm, garnished with basil, and enjoy!

Buttery Chicken Thighs with Mushrooms and Spinach

(Ready in about 30 minutes | Servings 6)

Ingredients

2 tablespoons butter, melted

10 bone-in, skin-on chicken thighs

1 cup onion, thinly sliced

1 cup button mushrooms

2 cloves garlic, peeled and crushed

1 teaspoon paprika

1/4 teaspoon freshly ground black pepper

1 teaspoon kosher salt

1 cup roasted-vegetable stock

2 cups tomato puree

2 cups baby spinach, torn into pieces

Directions

Click the "Sauté" button to preheat the cooker. Melt the butter and brown chicken thighs, along with the onions and mushrooms; cook about 7 minutes. Stir in the minced garlic; sauté an additional 2 minutes.

Next, just throw the remaining ingredients, except the spinach, into the electric pressure cooker.

Cover and choose "Meat/Stew" mode; set the timer for 20 minutes.

While the mixture is still hot, stir in the spinach; stir until it is wilted. Serve and enjoy!

Saucy Cod Fillets with Mushrooms

(Ready in about 15 minutes | Servings 4)

Ingredients

1 tablespoon ghee, melted

4 cod fillets

Salt and ground black pepper, to taste

1/2 teaspoon dried rosemary

1 teaspoon paprika

1 cup red onions, chopped

2 garlic cloves, finely minced

1 carrot, chopped

1 cup white mushrooms, chopped

1 teaspoon celery seeds

2 tablespoons dry white wine

2 tablespoons extra-virgin olive oil

1 tablespoon fresh parsley

Directions

Drizzle the melted ghee over the fish fillets. Then, coat the filets with seasonings. Press the "Sauté" button and brown cod fillets.

Pour approximately 3/4 cup of water into the inner pot. Lower the fish fillets onto a metal rack. Place the onions, garlic, carrot, and mushrooms over the fish fillets. Seal the lid; choose "Steam" setting and 5-minute cook time.

To make the sauce, whisk the remaining ingredients in a bowl. Serve fish with vegetables and sauce on the side.

Greek-Style Brown Rice Salad

(Ready in about 30 minutes + chilling time | Servings 4)

Ingredients

2 ½ cups water

2 cups brown rice

1 green bell pepper, thinly sliced

1 carrot, thinly sliced

2 ripe tomatoes, diced

1 cucumber, cored and diced

1 cup green onions, chopped

Salt and white pepper, to your liking

1/2 cup Feta cheese, crumbled

1/4 cup Kalamata olives, pitted and halved

Directions

Pour the water into the cooker. Stir in the rice; close and lock the lid. Select "Manual" setting and 22-minute cook time.

Open the cooker using the Natural pressure release. Let the rice cool completely.

Add the rest of the above items. Give it a gentle stir and serve chilled. Enjoy!

Refreshing Pinto Bean Salad

(Ready in about 15 minutes | Servings 4)

Ingredients

1 cup pinto beans, soaked overnight

4 cups water

4 garlic cloves, smashed

1 tablespoon fresh sage, finely chopped

1 red onion, chopped

2 tablespoons extra-virgin olive oil

1 tablespoon red wine vinegar

1/2 teaspoon dried basil

1 teaspoon sea salt

Freshly cracked black pepper, to taste

Directions

Stir the beans, water, and garlic into the inner pot. Select "Manual" setting and 8-minute pressure cooking time.

Drain cooked beans and allow them to cool completely; add the other ingredients.

Toss until everything is well combined. Serve chilled and enjoy.

Beef Brisket in Tomatillo Sauce

(Ready in about 1 hour 15 minutes | Servings 6)

Ingredients

1 (8 ounce) can tomato sauce

2 (11-ounce) cans whole tomatillos, drained

1 cup water

1/2 teaspoon ground black pepper

1/2 teaspoon red pepper flakes

1 teaspoon salt

1 teaspoon sugar

2 tablespoons corn oil

1 onion, chopped

4 cloves garlic, chopped

3 pounds beef brisket

Directions

Add the tomatillos, tomato sauce, water, black pepper, red pepper, salt, and sugar to a food processor; blend until creamy, uniform and smooth. Set aside.

Heat the oil using "Sauté" setting; sauté the onion and garlic until the onions are translucent. Add the beef brisket to the pressure cooker; now, sear it on all sides.

Pour the tomatillo mixture over the brisket, and stir, bringing to a boil. Cook for 1 hour and 15 minutes.

Allow the Instant Pot to release pressure on its own. Serve at once.

Lima Beans and Bacon

(Ready in about 50 minutes | Servings 8)

Ingredients

1 pound bacon, sliced

1 onion, chopped

1 pound dried large lima beans, soaked overnight

4 cups water

1 (12-ounce) can beer

1/2 teaspoon ground cumin

1 chipotle pepper, finely minced

2 garlic cloves, minced

Directions

Set your cooker to "Sauté" function and 10-minute cook time. Fry the bacon slices until crisp, reserving the bacon grease. Now, sauté the onion until tender and translucent.

Add the beans, followed by the water, beer, cumin, chipotle, and minced garlic. Place the lid on the cooker and secure it tightly. Cook under HIGH pressure for 30 minutes;

Now, release the pressure and crumble reserved bacon over beans. Close the cooker and cook until it is heated through; turn off heat. Release the pressure. Serve warm.

Prosecco Risotto with Mozzarella Cheese

(Ready in about 20 minutes | Servings 6)

Ingredients

2 tablespoons butter

2/3 cup scallions, finely chopped

3 garlic cloves, minced

1 1/3 cups medium-grain rice, uncooked

1 cup prosecco

Salt and freshly ground black pepper, to taste

3 cups roasted-vegetable stock

1 teaspoon grated lemon rind

2 ounces Mozzarella cheese

Directions

Heat your cooker using "Sauté" mode. Now, swirl butter until it's melted. Stir in the scallions and sauté for 2 to 3 minutes. Stir in the garlic and sauté for 30 seconds to 1 minute more, stirring frequently.

Add the rice and 1/2 cup of prosecco; cook about 2 minutes, stirring frequently. Stir in the remaining 1/2 cup of prosecco along with the salt, black pepper, stock, and lemon rind.

Close the lid securely and bring to HIGH pressure. Cook for 8 minutes. After that, release the pressure. Serve warm, topped with Mozzarella cheese. Enjoy!

Pineapple and Scallion Rice Salad

(Ready in about 20 minutes + chilling time | Servings 6)

Ingredients

3 cups jasmine rice, rinsed

3 cups water

1 cup scallions, chopped

1 green bell pepper, cut into thin strips

1/2 cup pineapple, diced

3 tablespoons extra-virgin olive oil

1/4 cup fresh mint, torn into small pieces

Directions

Stir jasmine rice into the cooker. Pour in the water and lock the lid according to the manufacturer's directions.

Select "Manual" setting; use the [+ -] button and set 4-minute cook time.

Let the rice cool completely in a salad bowl. Add the rest of the above ingredients. Serve chilled.

Garden Vegetables with Walnuts

(Ready in about 40 minutes | Servings 4)

Ingredients

1 teaspoon sea salt

1 medium-sized eggplant, peeled and cubed

1/4 cup olive oil

1 celery stalk, thinly sliced

1 parsnip, thinly sliced

2 carrots, thinly sliced

1 onion, thinly sliced

2 potatoes, peeled and cubed

1/4 cup almonds, toasted and coarsely chopped

Directions

Coat the eggplant with the salt and transfer it to a strainer; let it stand for 30 minutes.

Press the "Sauté" button and warm the oil. Now, cook the celery, parsnip, carrots, onion, and the potatoes until they have softened.

Now, choose the "Manual" mode and use 6-minute cook time. Serve topped with almonds. Enjoy!

Green Bean and Potato Dinner

(Ready in about 10 minutes | Servings 4)

Ingredients

4 potatoes, peeled and cubed

3/4 pounds green beans

2 tablespoons butter, melted

2 garlic cloves, minced

1 carrot, chopped

1 onion, minced

1 tablespoon parsley, minced

Salt and freshly ground black pepper

1/2 cup chicken stock

Directions

In the cooker, combine together all ingredients. Lock the lid in place and bring to pressure; cook for 5 minutes under HIGH pressure.

Then, use the Quick release method and carefully remove the lid. Serve warm.

Sesame Zucchini and Broccoli Salad

(Ready in about 10 minutes + chilling time | Servings 6)

Ingredients

For the Salad:

2 zucchinis, sliced

2 carrots, thinly sliced

1/2 head broccoli, broken into florets

1 cup water

1 shallot, thinly sliced

2 garlic cloves, minced

1 tablespoon toasted sesame seeds, for garnish

For the Vinaigrette:

4 tablespoons extra-virgin olive oil

2 cloves garlic, smashed

Salt, to taste

Freshly ground black pepper, to taste

1/2 teaspoon red pepper flakes

1 tablespoon fresh cilantro, roughly chopped

Directions

In the inner pot, combine the zucchini, carrots, broccoli, and water. Lock the lid and press the "Manual" button; cook for 7 minutes under HIGH pressure.

Remove the vegetables to a salad bowl. Add the shallot and garlic; toss to combine.

Make the vinaigrette by mixing all the vinaigrette ingredients. Place the salad in the refrigerator for a few hours.

Dress the salad and serve sprinkled with toasted sesame seeds. Enjoy!

Mom's Pinto Bean Salad

(Ready in about 15 minutes | Servings 6)

Ingredients

4 cups water

1 ½ cups pinto beans, soaked overnight

3 large-sized garlic cloves, smashed

1 leek, peeled and coarsely chopped

1 red bell pepper, seeded and chopped

1/4 cup extra-virgin olive oil

1 tablespoon red wine vinegar

1/2 tablespoon cumin seeds

1/2 teaspoon dried dill weed

1/2 teaspoon salt

1/2 teaspoon freshly cracked black pepper

2 tablespoons fresh parsley, chiffonade

2 tablespoons fresh cilantro, chiffonade

Directions

Simply throw the water and beans into the inner pot of the electric pressure cooker.

Choose "Manual" mode and set the timer for 10 minutes.

Drain the beans and let them cool completely; stir in the rest of the above ingredients. Then, refrigerate for a couple of hours. Bon appétit!

Sausage and Green Bean Casserole

(Ready in about 15 minutes | Servings 4)

Ingredients

1 tablespoon lard, melted

1/2 pound Italian sausage, sliced

3/4 pound green beans

3 potatoes, peeled and diced

1 carrot, chopped

1 onion, minced

2 garlic cloves, minced

1 Serrano pepper, diced

1 Poblano pepper, finely minced

1 tablespoon fresh cilantro, finely chopped

1 teaspoon sea salt

1/4 teaspoon freshly ground black pepper

1/2 cup chicken broth

Directions

Mix all ingredients in the inner pot of your Instant Pot. Lock the lid in place and bring to pressure; cook for 10 minutes.

Afterward, perform the Quick release method and remove the lid according to manufacturer's directions. Serve warm.

Winter Cauliflower and Carrot Salad

(Ready in about 10 minutes + chilling time | Servings 4)

Ingredients

1 cup water

1 head cauliflower, trimmed and broken into florets

2 carrots, julienned

1 cup leeks, thinly sliced

2 garlic cloves, minced

1/4 cup dill pickles, chopped

3/4 cup mayonnaise

Kosher salt and ground black pepper, to taste

Directions

Place the water, cauliflower, and carrots in the inner pot. Lock the lid and select "Manual" setting; cook under HIGH pressure for 8 minutes.

Add the rest of the above ingredients. Cover and refrigerate at least 3 hours or overnight. Serve well chilled and enjoy!

Cannellini Bean Salad with Avocado

(Ready in about 15 minutes | Servings 6)

Ingredients

1 ½ cups cannellini beans, soaked overnight

4 cups water

1/2 lime, juiced

1/4 teaspoon chili powder

3 large-sized garlic cloves, smashed

1 small-sized red onion, peeled and coarsely chopped

1/4 cup extra-virgin olive oil

1/2 teaspoon dried dill weed

1/2 teaspoon salt

Freshly ground black pepper, to taste

1 avocado, halved, pitted and diced

2 tablespoons fresh cilantro, chiffonade

Directions

Add the beans and water to the inner pot of your cooker.

Choose "Manual" setting and set the timer for 10 minutes.

Drain cannellini beans and let them cool completely; add the rest of the above ingredients to the cooled beans.

Then, refrigerate at least 4 hours. Bon appétit!

Mandarin Chicken with Egg Noodles

(Ready in about 35 minutes | Servings 4)

Ingredients

3/4 pound chicken breasts, boneless, skinless and cubed

1 tablespoon white vinegar

2 cups chicken broth

1 shallot, cut into thin wedges

1 (11-ounce) can mandarin oranges, drained

1 tablespoon tamari soy sauce

4 tablespoons cornstarch

1/4 cup water

Sea salt and freshly ground black pepper, to taste

8 ounces egg noodles, cooked

Directions

In the pressure cooker, combine the chicken, white vinegar, chicken broth, and shallots.

Lock the cooker's lid in place and bring to pressure; now, set the timer for 15 minutes. Use the Natural release method for 10 minutes. Now, carefully remove the lid.

Transfer the chicken to a serving platter.

Then, add the remaining ingredients, except for noodles, to the cooking liquid. Cook, uncovered, until the sauce has thickened. Pour the sauce over the chicken and serve with cooked noodles.

Sage and Mandarin Turkey in Sauce

(Ready in about 35 minutes | Servings 4)

Ingredients

1 pound turkey breasts, boneless, skinless and cubed

2 cups chicken broth

1 cup scallions, chopped

4 tablespoons cornstarch

1/4 cup water

1 (11-ounce) can mandarin oranges, drained

1 tablespoon fresh sage, chopped

Sea salt and freshly ground black pepper, to taste

Directions

Throw the turkey, chicken broth, and scallion into your inner pot.

Lock the cooker's lid in place and bring to pressure; cook for 15 minutes under HIGH pressure. Afterward, perform the Natural release method for 10 minutes.

Now, remove the lid according to the manufacturer's directions. Transfer the turkey to a serving platter.

In a small-sized mixing bowl, combine the cornstarch and water until it is dissolved. Add the slurry to the cooker; stir in the oranges, sage, salt, and black pepper; stir to combine.

Then, cook the mixture, uncovered, until the sauce has thickened. Pour the sauce over the turkey and serve with hot rice.

Chorizo and Garbanzo Bean Delight

(Ready in about 1 hour | Servings 8)

Ingredients

2 tablespoons sunflower oil

1 white onion, chopped

2 garlic cloves, minced

4 ounces Spanish chorizo, diced

2 cups water

3 cups roasted-vegetable stock, preferably homemade

1 ½ cups garbanzo beans, dried

1 bay leaf

6 cups lettuce, chopped

1 tablespoon fresh lemon juice

1/2 teaspoon kosher salt

1/2 teaspoon freshly ground black pepper

Directions

Select "Sauté" function and heat the oil. Sauté the onion, garlic and chorizo until the onion is translucent.

Add the water, stock, beans, and bay leaf. Close the lid securely and bring to HIGH pressure; set the timer for 1 hour.

Next, release the pressure. Add the remaining ingredients; toss to combine. Serve and enjoy!

Garlicky Chicken in Sauce

(Ready in about 30 minutes | Servings 8)

Ingredients

1 tablespoon butter, melted

1 onion, diced

2 pounds chicken breasts

1 garlic head, peeled and minced

3/4 teaspoon sea salt

1/2 cup roasted-vegetable stock

1/2 teaspoon paprika

1/4 cup white wine

2 tablespoons arrowroot flour

Directions

Turn the cooker to the "Sauté" mode. Melt the butter and sauté the onions for 10 minutes.

Stir in the rest of the above ingredients, except the arrowroot flour.

Secure the lid on the cooker. Select the "Poultry" setting.

In the meantime, make a slurry by mixing 1/4 cup of cooking juice with the arrowroot flour.

Once the cooking is done, release the pressure and carefully open the pot. Add the slurry to the pot and stir to combine. Serve at once and enjoy!

Chicken and Pineapple in Mayo Sauce

(Ready in about 20 minutes | Servings 8)

Ingredients

2 pounds chicken breasts, boneless and cubed

2 cups chicken stock

1 yellow onion, quartered

1 parsnip, thinly sliced

2 celery stalks, diced

1/2 pound carrot coins

2 tablespoons fresh cilantro leaves, chopped

2 tablespoons fresh parsley leaves, chopped

1 ½ cups pineapple chunks

2 tablespoons yogurt

2 cups mayonnaise

1 teaspoon spicy brown mustard

Directions

Place the chicken, stock, onion, parsnip, celery, and carrot in the inner pot. Now, add the cilantro and parsley to the cooker.

Lock the lid in place and bring to pressure; cook for 10 minutes under HIGH pressure.

Allow pressure to drop by using the Quick release method. Take the chicken breasts out of the cooker; allow them to cool completely. Stir in the pineapple chunks and toss to combine.

In a separate mixing dish, combine the yogurt, mayonnaise, and mustard. Add the dressing to the chicken and serve at once.

Lamb with Cannellini Beans

(Ready in about 40 minutes | Servings 8)

Ingredients

4 shoulder lamb chops, trimmed

1 ½ cups dry cannellini beans, washed and soaked

2 cups canned tomatoes, diced

2 medium-sized leeks, chopped

4 tablespoons garlic, coarsely chopped

1 sprig fresh thyme, leaves only

1 sprig fresh rosemary, leaves only

1 teaspoon salt

1/2 teaspoon ground black pepper

2 teaspoons Worcestershire sauce

1 cup water

1 cup beef bone broth

Directions

Throw all ingredients into your cooker. Click the "Bean/Chili" button and cook 40 minutes under HIGH pressure.

Now, allow pressure to drop by using the Quick release method. Carefully remove the lid following the manufacturer's directions. Serve warm and enjoy!

Fall-Apart-Tender Pork Ribs with Cauliflower

(Ready in about 25 minutes | Servings 4)

Ingredients

2 pork ribs

1 cup cauliflower, chopped into bite-sized florets

1 cup beef bone broth

1/2 cup rosé wine

1 cup green onions, sliced

2 cloves garlic, peeled and crushed

1 celery stalk, coarsely chopped

1 celery rib, coarsely chopped

1/2 teaspoon kosher salt

1/4 teaspoon ground black pepper, or to your liking

1 teaspoon paprika

1 teaspoon spicy brown mustard

Directions

Arrange the pork ribs on the bottom of the Instant Pot. Now, lay the cauliflower florets over the ribs.

Pour in the broth and wine. Close the lid and choose the "Meat/Stew" setting.

Stir in the rest of the above ingredients. Next, choose the "Manual" setting and cook for 3 minutes longer. Bon appétit!

Tangy Red Bean and Rice Salad

(Ready in about 20 minutes+ chilling time | Servings 6)

Ingredients

4 cups water

1 ½ cups dried red beans, soaked overnight and rinsed

2 bay leaves

4-5 black peppercorns

1 red onion, peeled and coarsely chopped

2 garlic cloves, smashed

2 tablespoons sunflower or corn oil

1 teaspoon fresh orange juice

1 teaspoon orange zest, grated

1 cup arugula leaves

1/2 teaspoon dried marjoram

Freshly cracked black pepper, to your liking

Cayenne pepper, to your liking

1/2 teaspoon sea salt

1/4 cup fresh cilantro, chopped

1 ½ cups white rice, cooked

Directions

Place the water, soaked beans, bay leaves, and black peppercorns in the inner pot of your cooker. Next, select "Manual" setting and cook for 10 minutes.

After that, add the remaining ingredients. Serve well-chilled and enjoy!

Broccoli and Anchovy Salad

(Ready in about 20 minutes | Servings 6)

Ingredients

4 cups broccoli florets

1/2 teaspoon salt

1 cup water

2 cloves garlic, peeled and minced

2 canned anchovies, rinsed and drained

1 red onion, peeled and thinly sliced

1 tablespoon fresh lemon juice

1 teaspoon Dijon mustard

2 tablespoons mayonnaise

2 tablespoons Parmesan cheese, freshly grated

1/4 cup extra-virgin olive oil

1 teaspoon cayenne pepper

Salt and ground black pepper, to savor

Directions

Place the broccoli, salt, and water in the cooker. Choose "Manual" setting and set the timer for 3 minutes. Lock the lid into place. Cook under HIGH pressure until the broccoli is just tender.

Transfer the broccoli to a salad bowl. Add the garlic, anchovies, and red onion, and gently stir to combine.

In a mixing dish, combine all remaining ingredients. Pour the mixture over all. Toss to combine. Serve and enjoy!

Black Bean and Quinoa Salad

(Ready in about 20 minutes + chilling time | Servings 6)

Ingredients

1 ½ cups black beans, soaked overnight

4 cups water

1 bay leaf

1 cup green onions, chopped

4 garlic cloves, smashed

1 tablespoon red wine vinegar

2 tablespoons extra-virgin olive oil

1 teaspoon lime juice

Salt and freshly cracked black pepper, to your liking

1 teaspoon cumin powder

1/4 cup fresh cilantro, chopped

1 ½ cups quinoa, cooked

Directions

Add the beans, water, and bay leaf to the inner pot. Click the "Manual" button and cook for 15 minutes.

Drain cooked black beans; toss with the other ingredients. Toss until everything is well combined and serve well chilled.

Colorful Quinoa Salad

(Ready in about 5 minutes + chilling time | Servings 4)

Ingredients

2 ¼ cups water

1 ½ cups uncooked quinoa, well rinsed

1 teaspoon cayenne pepper

Sea salt and ground black pepper, to taste

1/2 teaspoon dried oregano

1 teaspoon dried basil

1/2 teaspoon dried rosemary

1 cup tomatoes, diced

1 cucumber, thinly sliced

1 red bell pepper, thinly sliced

1 yellow bell pepper, thinly sliced

Directions

Add all ingredients to the inner pot of the cooker.

Choose HIGH pressure and 1-minute cook time. Now, use the Quick pressure release; carefully remove the cooker's lid.

Stir in the remaining ingredients. Serve well chilled.

Quinoa with Pumpkin and Kale

(Ready in about 10 minutes | Servings 4)

Ingredients

2 ¼ cups water

1 ½ cups uncooked quinoa, well rinsed

1/2 teaspoon ground allspice

1/4 teaspoon salt

1 cup canned pumpkin puree

1 tablespoon Moroccan seasoning

2 cups kale leaves, trimmed and torn into pieces

Directions

Throw all components, except the kale, into the inner pot.

Choose HIGH pressure and 1-minute cook time. Now, use the Quick pressure release; carefully remove the lid.

Add the kale and stir until it is wilted. Serve at once.

Broccoli and Chicken in Yogurt/Mayo Sauce

(Ready in about 10 minutes | Servings 6)

Ingredients

4 cups broccoli florets

1 cup salted water

3 cloves garlic, peeled and minced

1 cup chicken, skinless, boneless and cubed

1 red onion, peeled and thinly sliced

1 tablespoon fresh lemon juice

2 tablespoons yogurt

1/4 cup mayonnaise

1 teaspoon spicy brown mustard

2 tablespoons olive oil

1 teaspoon cayenne pepper

Salt and ground black pepper, to savor

2 tablespoons cream cheese, freshly grated

Directions

Select "Manual" setting, 3-minute cook time and HIGH pressure. Cook broccoli florets in a salted water until fork tender. Allow it to cool slightly.

In a salad bowl, combine cooled broccoli florets with garlic, chicken, and onion.

In a medium-sized mixing dish, whisk the rest of the above ingredients. Pour the yogurt/mayo mixture over all. Toss to combine and serve chilled.

Adzuki Bean and Rice Salad

(Ready in about 10 minutes + chilling time | Servings 6)

Ingredients

1 ½ cups Adzuki beans, soaked overnight

4 cups water

2 bay leaves

5-6 black peppercorns

4-5 green peppercorns

3 garlic cloves, smashed

1 cup leeks, chopped

2 tablespoons extra-virgin olive oil

1 tablespoon red wine vinegar

1 teaspoon fennel seeds

1/2 teaspoon sea salt

1/2 teaspoon freshly ground black pepper

2 tablespoons fresh cilantro, chopped

2 tablespoons fresh parsley, chopped

1 ½ cups rice, cooked

Directions

Throw Adzuki beans, water, bay leaves, black peppercorns, green peppercorns into the inner pot. Select "Manual" setting and cook for 10 minutes.

Drain cooked Adzuki beans; add all remaining ingredients. Toss until everything is well combined; serve chilled and enjoy!

Rice and Pineapple Salad with Walnuts

(Ready in about 10 minutes | Servings 4)

Ingredients

3 cups Arborio rice, rinsed

3 cups water

1/2 teaspoon turmeric powder

1 cup sweet onion, chopped

1/2 can pineapple chunks

3 tablespoons corn oil

1/4 cup walnuts, coarsely crushed

1/2 cup cucumber, chopped

1/4 cup fresh cilantro, roughly chopped

Directions

Add the rice and water to the Instant Pot.

Cover with the lid and select "Manual" button; use the [+ -] key to choose 5-minute cook time.

Transfer the rice to the salad bowl and let it cool completely. Add the other ingredients. Serve well-chilled.

Chicken Breasts with Potatoes and Baby Carrots

(Ready in about 30 minutes | Servings 4)

Ingredients

2 medium-sized chicken breasts, halved

1/2 pound baby carrots, thinly sliced

4 red potatoes, peeled and diced

1 cup chicken broth

1/2 cup dry red wine

1 cup scallions, chopped

2 cloves garlic, peeled and crushed

1 celery rib, chopped

1 celery stalk, chopped

Salt and ground black pepper, to your liking

1 teaspoon cayenne pepper

1 teaspoon fennel seeds

Directions

Place the chicken breasts on the bottom of the Instant Pot. Then, place the potatoes and baby carrots over the chicken breasts.

Pour in the broth and red wine. Close the lid and select the "Poultry" setting.

Stir in the rest of the above ingredients. Choose the "Manual" setting and cook for 3 minutes longer. Bon appétit!

Green Lentils with Garden Vegetables

(Ready in about 25 minutes | Servings 6)

Ingredients

1 shallot, chopped

3 cloves garlic, minced

1/2 teaspoon salt

1/2 teaspoon ground black pepper

1 teaspoon sweet paprika

1/2 teaspoon chili flakes

1 bell pepper, thinly sliced

1 stalk celery, chopped

2 potatoes, peeled and cubed

1 carrot, chopped

1 ½ cups green lentils

2 cups vegetable broth

2 ripe tomatoes, crushed

Directions

Click "Sauté" button on your Instant Pot. Then, sauté the shallot and garlic for 3 to 4 minutes, adding a splash of vegetable broth as needed.

Add the other ingredients, except the tomatoes. Cover and set the cooker to "Manual" function; use 10-minute pressure cooking time.

Then, allow pressure to come down naturally. Add the tomatoes to the cooker and continue to cook, uncovered, for 5 to 6 minutes. Serve warm.

Chicken with Lemon Sauce

(Ready in about 20 minutes | Servings 6)

Ingredients

Juice of 3 lemons

4 garlic cloves, minced

2 sprigs fresh thyme, leaves only

2 sprigs fresh rosemary, leaves only

4 tablespoons olive oil

1/2 teaspoon sea salt

1/4 teaspoon ground black pepper

1 whole chicken, cut into pieces

1/2 cup dry white wine

1 cup chicken broth, preferably homemade

Directions

First, make the marinade by whisking the first seven ingredients; whisk thoroughly until everything is well combined.

Place the chicken pieces in the marinade; let it stand at least 3 hours in the refrigerator.

Press the "Sauté" button to preheat your Instant Pot. Set the timer for 5 minutes.

Deglaze the cooker with white wine; cook until the liquid has evaporated. Add the chicken back to the pot along with the marinade. Pour in the chicken broth.

Select "Manual" setting and cook for 12 minutes longer. Discard the chicken. Choose "Sauté" setting and cook for a few minutes more to thicken the sauce. Serve and enjoy!

Navy Beans with Bacon

(Ready in about 30 minutes | Servings 6)

Ingredients

3 cups Navy beans, soaked overnight

3 cups roasted-vegetable stock

2 cups water

1 onion, diced

1/2 cup cooked bacon bits

2 tablespoons tomato puree

1/2 teaspoon sea salt

1/2 teaspoon ground black pepper, or to taste

1 teaspoon cayenne pepper

1 teaspoon molasses

Directions

Add all of the above ingredients to your Instant Pot.

Stir to combine and select "Bean/Chili" function. Serve warm.

Black Rice and Lentils with Garden Vegetables

(Ready in about 25 minutes | Servings 4)

Ingredients

1/2 cup black rice

1/2 cup black lentils

1 medium-sized red onion, finely chopped

3 cloves garlic, pressed

1 carrot, chopped

1 zucchini, diced

1 stalk celery, chopped

1 teaspoon fennel seeds

1 teaspoon dried coriander

1/2 teaspoon ground black pepper

1/2 teaspoon seasoned salt

2 cups roasted-vegetable broth

Directions

Place the rice and lentils in a bowl and cover them with water. Let them soak about 1 hour.

Meanwhile, choose "Sauté" setting and cook all vegetables for 5 minutes; add a splash of broth to prevent burning, as needed.

Stir in the soaked rice and lentils along with the rest of the above ingredients. Cover and cook for 9 minutes. Now, release the pressure naturally. Enjoy!

The Best Spring Grits Ever

(Ready in about 15 minutes | Servings 4)

Ingredients

1 cup green onions, chopped

2 green garlic, chopped

2 cups vegetable broth

2 cups boiling water

1 cup grits

1 teaspoon dried basil

1/2 teaspoon dried oregano

1/2 teaspoon paprika

Directions

Press the "Sauté" button and add green onions and garlic; cook, stirring periodically until they are just tender.

Add the broth, boiling water, and grits. Season with basil, oregano, and paprika. Lock the cooker's lid in place.

Next, select "Manual" function, and cook for 5 minutes under HIGH pressure.

Use the Quick pressure release and serve immediately. Enjoy!

Delicious Pizza Beans

(Ready in about 30 minutes | Servings 6)

Ingredients

3 cups Great Northern beans, soaked overnight

3 cups beef bone broth

1 onion, diced

1/2 pound mild Italian sausage, ground

6 ounces sliced pepperoni, cut into quarters

2 tablespoons tomato puree

1/2 teaspoon sea salt

1/2 teaspoon ground black pepper, or to taste

1 teaspoon cayenne pepper

1 teaspoon dried oregano

Shredded mozzarella, for topping

Fresh basil leaves, for garnish

Directions

Add all of the above ingredients, except for Mozzarella and basil leaves, to your Instant Pot.

Stir to combine and select "Bean/Chili" function. Serve warm, topped with Mozzarella and fresh basil leaves. Enjoy!

Mushroom and Veggie Spread

(Ready in about 15 minutes | Servings 4)

Ingredients

2 tablespoons corn oil

1 medium-sized onion, chopped

2 cloves garlic, minced

2 stalks celery, finely chopped

1 celery rib, chopped

2 carrots, finely chopped

1 bell pepper, finely chopped

1 cup Porcini mushrooms, chopped

2 cups vegetable broth

1 (27-ounce) can tomatoes, chopped

1/2 teaspoon salt

1/2 teaspoon ground black pepper

Directions

Select "Sauté" setting and heat the oil. Now, sauté the onions, garlic, celery, carrots, and bell pepper for 5 minutes.

Then, add the mushrooms and cook, stirring periodically, for an additional 3 minutes.

Stir in the remaining ingredients. Select "Manual" setting and set the timer for 7 minutes. Serve warm with your favorite crusty bread.

Zingy Ginger and Honey Chicken

(Ready in about 35 minutes | Servings 6)

Ingredients

1 medium-sized chicken

1 teaspoon salt

1/2 teaspoon ground black pepper

2 tablespoons honey

1 thumb-size piece of fresh ginger, peeled and minced

1 tablespoon soy sauce

1/4 cup dry white wine

1 lime, cut into wedges

Directions

Season the chicken with salt and ground black pepper. Then, spread the honey over the chicken.

Place the chicken in the inner pot of your cooker. Now, add ginger, soy sauce, and wine.

Choose the "Poultry" function. Serve your chicken with lime slices.

Winter Beans with Bacon

(Ready in about 35 minutes | Servings 8)

Ingredients

3 tablespoons corn oil

1 leek, chopped

3 cloves garlic, minced

4 bacon slices, chopped

1 cup water

1 pound cannellini beans, soaked overnight

1 teaspoon mustard seeds

1 teaspoon fennel seeds

Directions

Select "Sauté" setting and warm the oil; sauté the leeks, garlic, and bacon about 5 minutes.

Add the water and select "Sauté" setting; cook for 5 minutes. Now, stir in cannellini beans and 4 cups of the water.

Stir in the mustard and fennel seeds; close the cooker's lid according to the manufacturer's directions. Select "Bean/Chili" setting. Perform the Quick release method and serve right away.

Multigrain and Vegetable Dinner

(Ready in about 30 minutes | Servings 6)

Ingredients

3 cups water

3 cups multi-grain rice

1 cup chicken breasts, chopped

1/4 cup shallots, chopped

1 green bell pepper, seeded and thinly sliced

1 red bell pepper, seeded and thinly sliced

1 zucchini, diced

1 tablespoon apple cider vinegar

1/2 teaspoon sea salt

1/2 teaspoon ground black pepper, or to taste

1 teaspoon cayenne pepper

1/2 teaspoon dried oregano

1/2 teaspoon dried basil

Directions

Add all of the above ingredients to the inner pot of your Instant Pot.

Use the "Multigrain" mode. Perform the Quick release method.

Serve immediately and enjoy!

Easy Farfalle with Mushrooms and Sausage

(Ready in about 20 minutes | Servings 4)

Ingredients

1 pound Italian sausage

1 onion, diced

2 cloves garlic, minced

1 cup white mushrooms, thinly sliced

1 box farfalle

1 jar marinara sauce

2 cups water

3/4 cup Cheddar cheese, shredded

Directions

Preheat the cooker by using the "Sauté" mode. Now, brown the sausage, onion, garlic, and mushrooms until they have softened.

Add the farfalle, marinara sauce, and water. Use "Meat/Stew" setting and cook for 6 minutes under HIGH pressure.

Perform the Quick release method. Serve topped with Cheddar cheese.

Sticky Sesame Chicken with Scallions

(Ready in about 35 minutes | Servings 6)

Ingredients

1 small-sized chicken, cut into pieces

1 teaspoon salt

1 teaspoon smoked cayenne pepper

1/2 teaspoon ground black pepper

1/4 cup brown sugar

1 thumb-size piece of fresh ginger, peeled and minced

2 tablespoons soy sauce

1 cup scallions, chopped

1 tablespoon sesame seeds, toasted

Directions

Season your chicken with salt, cayenne pepper, and black pepper. Then, sprinkle the sugar over the chicken.

Next, lay the chicken on the bottom of the inner pot. Now, stir in minced ginger, soy sauce, and scallions.

Then, select the "Poultry" setting. Serve your chicken immediately, sprinkled with toasted sesame seeds.

Country Noodles with Ground Meat

(Ready in about 20 minutes | Servings 4)

Ingredients

1 tablespoon corn oil

1/2 pound lean ground beef

1/2 pound lean ground pork

1 onion, chopped

2 garlic cloves, minced

1 carrot, chopped

2 pounds tomato puree

1 teaspoon dried basil leaves

1/2 teaspoon dried thyme

1 teaspoon dried marjoram

1/2 teaspoon salt

1/4 teaspoon black pepper, ground

1 cup dried egg noodles

Directions

Preheat your cooker on "Sauté" mode. Heat the oil; brown ground meat in hot oil, stirring constantly. Then, add the onions, garlic, and carrots; continue sautéing until they're tender.

Add the remaining items. Pressure cook for 7 minutes. Serve right away.

Easy Barley with Sausage

(Ready in about 30 minutes | Servings 6)

Ingredients

3 cups water

3 cups pearl barley

1 cup sausage, cut into chunks

1 onion, chopped

1 celery stalk, thinly sliced

2 tablespoons corn oil

1 teaspoon mustard seeds

1 teaspoon salt

1/2 ground black pepper, or to taste

1/2 teaspoon cayenne pepper

Directions

Just throw the ingredients into the inner pot.

Select "Rice" setting. Afterward, perform the Natural release method.

Serve warm and enjoy!

Mandarin and Soy Short Ribs

(Ready in about 45 minutes | Servings 4)

Ingredients

1 cup water

3/4 cup tamari soy sauce

2 tablespoons honey

1 mandarin orange, freshly squeezed

1 cup scallions, chopped

2 garlic cloves, minced

1/2 teaspoon smoked salt

1/4 teaspoon ground black pepper

1/2 teaspoon dried dill weed

4 beef short ribs

2 tablespoons corn oil

Directions

In a mixing bowl, place the water, soy sauce, honey, and fresh orange juice; whisk to combine well.

Add the scallions, garlic, smoked salt, black pepper, and dill; stir thoroughly until everything is well combined. Place short ribs in the bowl; let short ribs marinate at least 3 hours.

Heat corn oil in a cast-iron skillet. Sear the marinated ribs 3 minutes per side. Transfer the ribs to the inner pot of your Instant Pot.

Select "Meat\Stew" mode, and cook 30 minutes. Afterward, perform the Natural release method. Serve warm and enjoy!

Chinese-Style Fried Rice and Chicken

(Ready in about 30 minutes | Servings 6)

Ingredients

3 cups medium grain rice

3 cups water

1 cup chicken, chopped

4 green onions, chopped

1/2 cup carrots, chopped

1 cup bean sprouts

2 tablespoons sesame oil

Salt and ground black pepper, to taste

2 tablespoons light soy sauce

1/2 cup frozen peas, thawed

Directions

Stir the rice, water, chicken, onions, carrots, and bean sprouts into your Instant Pot. Stir to combine well.

Now, add the oil, salt, black pepper, and soy sauce.

Select the "Multigrain" function. After that, add frozen peas and gently stir until heated through. Serve right away.

Spicy Ginger Glazed Pork Ribs

(Ready in about 45 minutes | Servings 4)

Ingredients

3/4 cup soy sauce

1 cup water

2 tablespoons light brown sugar

1/4 cup dry sherry

1 cup leeks, chopped

2 garlic cloves, minced

1 (1-inch) piece fresh ginger, peeled and minced

1 dried chili de Arbol pepper

1/2 teaspoon orange zest

1 teaspoon dried rosemary

1/2 teaspoon dried thyme

1/2 teaspoon sea salt

1/4 teaspoon ground black pepper

1 pound pork ribs

2 tablespoons olive oil

Directions

In a mixing dish, thoroughly combine soy sauce, water, sugar, and dry sherry.

Throw in the leeks, garlic, ginger, dried chili, orange zest, and all seasonings. Place the pork in the mixing dish; let the pork marinate about 3 hours in the refrigerator.

Heat olive oil in a pan. Sear pork ribs 3 to 4 minutes on each side. Transfer seared pork ribs to the inner pot of your cooker.

Press the "Meat\Stew" button and cook 30 minutes. After that, use the Natural release method. Serve at once.

FAST SNACKS

Hot Ginger Chicken Wings

(Ready in about 15 minutes | Servings 8)

Ingredients

1 tablespoon coconut butter, melted

3/4 cup hot sauce

2 tablespoons fresh ginger, minced

1 teaspoon Garam masala

4 pounds chicken wings, frozen

Smoked salt and ground black pepper, to taste

Directions

Pour the coconut butter and hot sauce into the inner pot. Stir in the ginger and Garam masala.

Add the wings and gently stir to coat. Season the wings with smoked salt and ground black pepper to taste.

Place and lock the cooker's lid. Select "Soup" setting. Serve warm with a dipping sauce such as barbecue sauce or orange-glazed sauce.

Beet Appetizer with Slivered Almonds

(Ready in about 25 minutes | Servings 8)

Ingredients

2 ½ cups water

2 pounds beets

2 tablespoons red wine vinegar

1 teaspoon honey

1/2 teaspoon kosher salt

1/4 teaspoon freshly ground black pepper

2 tablespoons olive oil

2 tablespoons almonds, slivered

Directions

Add the water and beets to your inner pot. Close cooker's lid securely.

Choose "Manual" setting and cook for 25 minutes. Uncover, drain and rinse the beets.

Now, rub off skins and cut the beets into wedges. Transfer them to a serving bowl.

In a bowl, combine the wine vinegar, honey, salt, black pepper, and olive oil. Drizzle the vinaigrette over prepared beets and toss to coat. Serve sprinkled with slivered almonds.

Herbed Fingerling Potatoes

(Ready in about 30 minutes | Servings 6)

Ingredients

4 tablespoons butter, melted

2 pounds fingerling potatoes

1 sprig rosemary, leaves only

1 teaspoon dried dill weed

3 garlic cloves, with outer skin

1 cup roasted-vegetable broth, preferably homemade

1 teaspoon seasoned salt

1/2 teaspoon ground black pepper, or to your liking

Directions

First, press the "Sauté" button in order to preheat the electric pressure cooker. Warm the butter and stir in fingerling potatoes, rosemary, dill, and garlic.

Cook the potatoes, turning once or twice, for 10 minutes. Add the broth, salt and black pepper.

Next, choose "Manual" mode and cook an additional 11 minutes. Perform the Quick pressure release. Serve immediately.

Orange Wings with Dried Cherries

(Ready in about 35 minutes | Servings 4)

Ingredients

4 tablespoons butter, at room temperature

4 chicken wings

1 teaspoon smoked paprika

1 teaspoon garlic powder

1 teaspoon onion powder

Sea salt and ground black pepper, to taste

1 ½ cups dried cherries

2 tablespoons orange juice

1/4 cup white wine

1 ½ cups vegetable broth

Directions

Use "Sauté" setting and melt the butter. Brown the wings on all sides. Sprinkle smoked paprika, garlic powder, onion powder, salt, and black pepper over all.

Now add dried cherries. Pour the orange juice, wine, and vegetable broth over all. Close the cooker's lid and select "Manual"; cook for 20 minutes under HIGH pressure.

Next, preheat a broiler and place chicken wings under the broiler for 5-6 minutes or until crisp.

Meanwhile, choose "Sauté" setting and cook the cooking liquid until it has thickened. To serve: arrange chicken wings on a serving platter. Spoon the sauce over the wings. Enjoy!

Party Potato Snack

(Ready in about 20 minutes | Servings 8)

Ingredients

1/4 cup butter, melted

1 ½ pounds russet potatoes, cut into thick slices

1/2 teaspoon red pepper flakes, crushed

1 teaspoon sea salt

1/2 teaspoon ground black pepper, or to taste

1 teaspoon cumin powder

1/4 teaspoon grated nutmeg

1 cup chicken broth

Directions

Select "Sauté" function; heat the butter and throw in the potatoes. Continue to cook for 8 to 9 minutes, stirring periodically.

Add the remaining ingredients. Secure the cooker's lid; choose "Manual" setting. Cook for 7 minutes and open the cooker according to the manufacturer's directions. Serve warm and enjoy!

Lime and Parsley Steamed Artichokes

(Ready in about 25 minutes | Servings 2)

Ingredients

2 whole artichokes, rinsed

1 small-sized lime

2 sprigs parsley, chopped

1 cup water

Directions

First, remove any outer leaves from artichokes. Trim the artichoke and cut off the sharp tips with kitchen shears. Drizzle them with lime juice. Add the parsley.

Set a steamer basket into the Instant Pot. Pour 1 cup of water into the cooker. Lay the artichokes on the steamer basket.

Close the lid and select "Manual" setting; adjust the time to 20 minutes. Enjoy!

Buttery Lemon Fingerling Potatoes

(Ready in about 30 minutes | Servings 6)

Ingredients

4 tablespoons butter, melted

1 teaspoon granulated garlic

2 pounds fingerling potatoes

A few sage leaves, chopped

1 sprig rosemary, leaves only

1 teaspoon finely grated lemon zest

1 cup vegetable stock, preferably homemade

1 teaspoon cayenne pepper

1 teaspoon seasoned salt

1/2 teaspoon ground black pepper, or to your liking

Directions

Choose "Sauté" setting to preheat the cooker. Warm the butter and add granulated garlic, fingerling potatoes, sage, rosemary, and grated lemon zest.

Cook fingerling potatoes, turning periodically, for 10 minutes. Add the stock, cayenne pepper, seasoned salt, and black pepper.

Select "Manual" mode and cook 12 minutes longer. Use the Quick pressure release. Serve warm and enjoy!

Balsamic Baby Carrots

(Ready in about 20 minutes | Servings 6)

Ingredients

1 tablespoon butter

2 tablespoons olive oil

2 tablespoons balsamic vinegar

1 tablespoon brown sugar

1/2 cup water

1/4 teaspoon coarse salt

1 pound baby carrots

Directions

Put all ingredients, except baby carrots, into your cooker. Select "Sauté" setting and cook for 30 seconds; make sure to stir frequently. Throw in the carrots.

Then, select "Steam" setting and set the timer for 15 minutes.

Remove the lid and select "Sauté" setting. Cook until all cooking liquid has evaporated. Serve at room temperature.

Parsnip and Carrot Sticks

(Ready in about 10 minutes | Servings 8)

Ingredients

2 tablespoons corn oil

1/2 pound parsnips, peeled and halved lengthwise

1 pound carrots, cut into matchsticks

1/4 teaspoon baking soda

2 tablespoons honey

1/2 teaspoon coarse salt

1/2 teaspoon grated orange peel

Directions

Click the "Sauté" button and heat the oil. Add the parsnips and carrots along with the rest of the above ingredients.

Pressure cook for 4 minutes. Serve warm or at room temperature.

Sugar Snap Peas Appetizer

(Ready in about 10 minutes | Servings 8)

Ingredients

2 tablespoons butter

2 ½ cups frozen sugar snap peas

3 carrots, cut into matchsticks

1/2 teaspoon kosher salt

3 tablespoons lemon marmalade

Directions

Simply throw all ingredients into your cooker.

Set the timer for 4 minutes. Transfer everything to a serving dish. Enjoy!

Italian Sausage and Tomato Dip

(Ready in about 15 minutes | Servings 10)

Ingredients

1 tablespoon olive oil

1/2 pound ground Italian sausage

1 (28-ounce) can tomatoes, crushed

2 cloves garlic, sliced

1 shallot, chopped

1 teaspoon dried basil

2 tablespoons flour

1/2 teaspoon salt

1/2 teaspoon ground black pepper, or to taste

1/2 teaspoon cayenne pepper

Directions

Heat the oil in your cooker. Add ground Italian sausage and cook until it is browned. Add the rest of the above items.

Close and lock the lid according to the manufacturer's instructions; set the timer for 15 minutes.

Release pressure naturally. Serve with dippers such as chips or veggie sticks. Enjoy!

Cocktail Meatballs with Marinara

(Ready in about 25 minutes | Servings 10)

Ingredients

1 tablespoon canola oil

40 frozen meatballs

2 (16-ounce) jars marinara sauce

1 cup beef bone stock

1/2 teaspoon sea salt

1/2 teaspoon ground black pepper

1/4 cup fresh parsley, chopped

1 tablespoon rosemary, chopped

Directions

Warm the oil on "Sauté" setting. Throw in the meatballs; cook until they are just browned, or 2 to 3 minutes.

Add marinara sauce and beef bone stock. Season with salt, black pepper, parsley, and rosemary. Close and lock the lid.

Then, set the timer for 20 minutes. Afterward, release the pressure manually. Enjoy!

Sesame Bok Choy Appetizer

(Ready in about 10 minutes | Servings 4)

Ingredients

1 cup water

1 medium head Bok choy, leaves separated

1 teaspoon sesame oil

2 tablespoons sesame seeds

1 tablespoon oyster sauce

1/2 teaspoon seasoned salt

1/4 teaspoon freshly ground black pepper

1/2 teaspoon cayenne pepper

1/2 teaspoon red pepper flakes

Directions

Pour the water into the inner pot of the Instant Pot; place the steamer basket on top. Place the Bok choy in the steamer basket, and secure the lid.

Select "Manual" mode and cook for 4 minutes under HIGH pressure. Then, use the Quick pressure release.

Transfer the Bok choy to a bowl and toss with the remaining ingredients.

Great Northern Bean Dip

(Ready in about 55 minutes | Servings 16)

Ingredients

8 ounces dried Great Northern beans, rinsed and soaked overnight

4 cups water

2 garlic cloves, minced

2 tablespoons extra-virgin olive oil

1/2 teaspoon ground black pepper

1 teaspoon sea salt

Juice of 1/2 lemon

Directions

Stir the beans, water, garlic, olive oil, black pepper, and salt into the inner pot. Secure the lid.

Select "Manual" setting and cook under HIGH pressure for 30 minutes. Press the "Cancel" button. Now, use the Natural pressure release for 15 minutes.

Next, drain the beans, reserving 1 cup of cooking liquid. Purée the beans in a food processor until creamy. You can add cooking liquid, 1 tablespoon at a time.

Drizzle the lemon juice over all, taste, and adjust the seasonings. Serve and enjoy.

Balsamic Cipollini Onions

(Ready in about 15 minutes | Servings 4)

Ingredients

1 pound Cipollini onions, outer layer eliminated

1/2 cup water

1 teaspoon white pepper

1/2 teaspoon salt

1 bay leaf

1 tablespoon balsamic vinegar

1 tablespoon honey

1 tablespoon flour

Directions

Add all ingredients to the cooker. Press "Steam" button and cook for 10 minutes.

Then, use the Quick pressure release.

Uncover the cooker according to the manufacturer's directions. Transfer pearl onions to a serving platter and serve warm.

Peppery Sausage Dip

(Ready in about 15 minutes | Servings 10)

Ingredients

1 tablespoon lard

2 cloves garlic, sliced

1 onion, chopped

2 bell peppers, seeded and diced

1 jalapeño pepper, minced

1 carrot, chopped

1/2 pound ground Italian sausage

1 (28-ounce) can tomatoes, crushed

1/2 teaspoon red pepper flakes, crushed

Salt and ground black pepper, to taste

Directions

Preheat your cooker on "Sauté" function and melt the lard. Now, sauté the garlic, onion, bell peppers, jalapeño pepper, and carrot for several minutes.

Stir in Italian sausage and cook until they have browned.

Add the rest of the above ingredients and cover the pot.

Set the timer for 15 minutes. Afterward, release pressure naturally. Serve warm or at room temperature.

Cheesy Black Bean Dip

(Ready in about 45 minutes | Servings 16)

Ingredients

1 cup dried black beans

2 cups water

1 tablespoon olive oil

1 small-sized red onion, peeled & diced

4 cloves garlic, peeled and minced

14 ounces canned tomatoes, diced

1 teaspoon chili powder

1/4 cup fresh cilantro, finely chopped

Salt and ground black pepper, to taste

1 cup Colby jack cheese, grated

Directions

Throw the beans and water into the Instant Pot. Secure the lid.

Press the "Manual" button and cook under HIGH pressure for 30 minutes. After that, use the Natural pressure release.

Next, drain the beans, and purée them in a food processor until creamy. You can add some cooking liquid if needed.

Add the remaining ingredients, except Colby cheese. Toss to combine and top with cheese. Serve and enjoy.

Hot Bacon and Chicken Dipping Sauce

(Ready in about 15 minutes | Servings 10)

Ingredients

1 tablespoon canola oil

3 slices bacon, diced

1 medium-sized onion, peeled and chopped

2 cloves garlic, peeled and minced

A splash of dry red wine

1/3 cup salsa

1 cup chook broth

1 teaspoon chili powder

1 pound chicken breast, finely diced

Salt and freshly ground black pepper, to savor

Cayenne pepper, to savor

Directions

Set your Instant Pot to "Sauté" mode; then, warm the oil and fry the bacon until crisp. Reserve 1 tablespoon of bacon drippings.

Throw in the onion and garlic and cook about 2 minutes, stirring frequently. Deglaze the bottom of your cooker with a splash of wine. Add the remaining ingredients and cook the mixture for 8 minutes more. Bon appétit!

Extra Yummy Potato Bites

(Ready in about 15 minutes | Servings 8)

Ingredients

8 russet potatoes, peeled and diced

3 tablespoons butter

1 teaspoon granulated garlic

1 teaspoon shallot powder

1/2 teaspoon coarse salt

1/2 teaspoon ground black pepper

1 tablespoon coriander, ground

1 tablespoon fresh lime juice

Directions

Put a metal rack into the bottom of your Instant Pot; pour in 1/2 cup of the water.

Throw in the potatoes and close the lid; set the timer for 8 minutes. Uncover and taste the potatoes for the doneness.

Transfer warm potatoes to a serving dish. Toss them with the other ingredients. Bon appétit!

Yummy Steamed Brussels Sprouts

(Ready in about 15 minutes | Servings 6)

Ingredients

2 pounds Brussels sprouts, trimmed

1/2 stick butter, melted

1 cup spring onions, finely chopped

1 teaspoon granulated garlic

Salt and freshly ground black pepper, to your liking

1/2 cup Parmesan cheese, grated

Directions

Place the steamer basket on the bottom of your cooker. Pour in 1 cup of water. Lay Brussels sprouts in the steamer basket. Cover and set the timer for 7 minutes.

Next, carefully open the cooker. While Brussels sprouts are still hot, add the butter, spring onions, granulated garlic, salt, black pepper, and Parmesan cheese; toss to coat well.

Transfer Brussels sprouts to a serving platter and enjoy!

Hot Artichoke and Spinach Dip

(Ready in about 20 minutes | Servings 12)

Ingredients

1 package (10-ounce) frozen spinach, thawed, drained and chopped

1 can (14-ounce) artichoke hearts, drained and roughly chopped

1/2 cup sour cream

1 cup Pepper Jack cheese, shredded

1/2 cup light mayonnaise

2/3 cup sour cream

1 teaspoon garlic powder

1/2 teaspoon salt

1/4 teaspoon ground black pepper

Directions

Set a wire rack in your Instant Pot. Place all ingredients in a baking dish; stir to combine thoroughly. Then, cover the baking dish with an aluminum foil.

Make a foil sling and lay it on the rack. Place the baking dish on top of the foil. Secure the cooker's lid and set the timer for 10 minutes.

Serve with pita wedges. Enjoy!

Delicious Broccoli Appetizer

(Ready in about 10 minutes | Servings 6)

Ingredients

2 pounds broccoli, trimmed and torn into florets

1/2 stick butter, melted

1 teaspoon garlic, minced

1/4 cup apple cider vinegar

Salt and freshly ground black pepper, to your liking

1/2 cup sunflower kernels

Directions

Place the steamer basket on the bottom of your Instant Pot. Pour in 1 cup of water. Place broccoli florets in the steamer basket. Cover and set the timer for 7 minutes.

Carefully open the cooker. While the broccoli is still hot, add the remaining ingredients; toss to coat. Enjoy!

Mom's Spicy Hummus

(Ready in about 30 minutes | Servings 12)

Ingredients

4 cups water

1 cup chickpeas

2 tablespoons fresh lime juice

1 green Serrano chili, minced

1 tablespoon salt

1 teaspoon onion powder

1 teaspoon paprika

1 teaspoon celery seeds

2 garlic cloves, minced

1/3 cup tahini

3 tablespoons olive oil, preferably extra-virgin

Directions

Add the water and chickpeas to your Instant Pot and drizzle with some olive oil. Use "Manual" mode. Cover and cook for 25 minutes under HIGH pressure.

Turn off the heat. Carefully open the lid; drain the chickpeas. Place chickpeas in a bowl of your food processor, followed by fresh lime juice, Serrano chili, salt, onion powder, paprika, celery seeds, and garlic and salt; blitz the mixture into a smooth purée.

While the machine is still running, slowly and gradually add the oil. Enjoy!

Turkey and Tomato Dip

(Ready in about 15 minutes | Servings 10)

Ingredients

1 tablespoon olive oil

1 ½ pounds turkey, ground

1 cup leeks, chopped

2 cloves garlic, minced

1 teaspoon fennel seeds

1/2 cup prosecco

2 (28-ounce) cans tomatoes, chopped

1 (14-ounce) can chicken broth

1 teaspoon oregano

1/4 cup heavy cream

Directions

Set the cooker on "Sauté" function; then, warm the oil and brown the turkey. Reserve 1 tablespoon of pan drippings.

Stir in the leeks, garlic, and fennel seeds; now, sauté for 1 to 2 minutes, stirring frequently. Deglaze the bottom of your cooker with prosecco. Throw in the tomatoes, chicken broth, and oregano.

Cover with the lid and set the timer for 8 minutes. While the mixture is still hot, stir in the heavy cream. Serve with favorite dippers.

Chipotle Potato Bites

(Ready in about 15 minutes | Servings 8)

Ingredients

8 red potatoes, peeled and diced

3 tablespoons butter

1 teaspoon chili powder

1 teaspoon chipotle powder

Salt and freshly ground black pepper, to taste

Fresh chopped chives, for garnish

Directions

Lower a metal rack onto the bottom of your Instant Pot; pour in 1/2 cup of water.

Throw in the potatoes and close the lid; set the timer for 8 minutes. Lastly, remove the lid according to the manufacturer's directions.

Transfer prepared potatoes to a large-sized serving dish. Toss them with the other ingredients. Bon appétit!

The Easiest Hummus Ever

(Ready in about 30 minutes | Servings 12)

Ingredients

1 cup chickpeas

4 cups water

2 tablespoons fresh lemon juice

1 tablespoon salt

1 teaspoon sumac

1/2 teaspoon cumin powder

1/3 cup tahini

3 tablespoons olive oil, preferably extra-virgin

Directions

Cook the chickpeas in water for 25 minutes under HIGH pressure.

Carefully open the lid according to the manufacturer's directions; drain your chickpeas. Add the chickpeas to a food processor.

Throw in the remaining ingredients, except for olive oil, and purée until everything is well blended.

While the machine is still running, slowly and gradually add the oil. Process until the mixture is uniform and creamy. Serve with toasted pita chips and veggie sticks.

Green Beans with Pine Nuts

(Ready in about 10 minutes | Servings 6)

Ingredients

1 ½ pounds green beans

2 garlic cloves, minced

1 cup scallions, minced

1 cup vegetable soup

1 tablespoon extra-virgin oil

Toasted pine nuts, for garnish

Directions

Add all ingredients, except pine nuts, to the cooker. Select "Manual" setting; set the timer for 4 minutes.

After that, carefully remove the lid according to the manufacturer's directions. Transfer green beans to a large serving platter; sprinkle toasted pine nuts over all.

Indian Red Bean Dip

(Ready in about 20 minutes | Servings 12)

Ingredients

1 pound red beans, soaked overnight

3 tablespoons corn oil

2 garlic cloves, minced

1 yellow onion, finely chopped

1 (1-inch) piece fresh ginger, grated

2 ripe tomatoes, chopped

1 tablespoon Garam masala

1 teaspoon fennel seeds

A pinch of cardamom

1 teaspoon capers

2 sprigs coriander leaves, finely minced

1/4 teaspoon salt

Directions

Add red beans to the inner pot; add enough water to cover the beans. Choose "Bean/Chili" mode; let it cook until tender.

In the meantime, heat corn oil in a saucepan. Then, sauté the garlic, onion, ginger, and tomatoes. Now, add the Garam masala, fennel seeds, cardamom, capers.

Next, open the lid according to the manufacturer's directions; add the sautéed mixture to the inner pot. Add the coriander and salt; stir to combine.

Next, puree the mixture in a food processor; you can work with batches. Serve and enjoy!

Yellow Beans with Pecans

(Ready in about 10 minutes | Servings 6)

Ingredients

1 ½ pounds yellow beans, trimmed

2 garlic cloves, minced

1 cup vegetable soup

2 tablespoons Dijon mustard

1 tablespoon pure maple syrup

1 tablespoon extra-virgin oil

Chopped pecans, for garnish

Directions

Add all ingredients, except chopped pecans, to the inner pot. Choose "Manual" setting; set the timer for 5 minutes.

Next, remove the lid according to the manufacturer's instructions. Transfer yellow beans to a serving dish; scatter chopped pecans over all.

Healthy Pumpkin Hummus with Pepitas

(Ready in about 30 minutes | Servings 12)

Ingredients

1 cup chickpeas

4 cups water

3/4 cup pumpkin puree

5 tablespoons tahini paste

2 tablespoons fresh lemon juice

1 tablespoon salt

1/2 teaspoon ground black pepper

1/3 cup tahini

3 tablespoons olive oil, preferably extra-virgin

Pepitas, for garnish

Directions

Select "Manual" setting and cook the chickpeas in water for 25 minutes under HIGH pressure.

Uncover and drain your chickpeas. Transfer the chickpeas to a bowl of your food processor. You can use an immersion blender.

Throw in the other ingredients, except the oil and pepitas; purée until everything is well blended.

While the machine is still running, gradually add olive oil. Process until the mixture is creamy. Serve garnished with pepitas. Bon appétit!

Thai Chicken Dip

(Ready in about 30 minutes | Servings 12)

Ingredients

1 tablespoon olive oil

1 ½ pounds ground chicken

3/4 cup scallions, chopped

4 cloves garlic, minced

2 Thai bird chilies, minced

1 ½ cups chicken broth

2 (28-ounce) cans tomatoes, chopped

1/2 teaspoon salt

1/4 teaspoon coarsely ground black pepper

1 bunch Thai basil leaves

Directions

Preheat the cooker on "Sauté" function; then, warm olive oil and brown the meat, reserving 1 tablespoon of pan drippings.

Stir in the scallions, garlic, and 2 Thai bird chilies. Sauté the mixture approximately 2 minutes, stirring frequently.

Deglaze the bottom of your cooker with a splash of chicken broth. Throw in the remaining ingredients; stir thoroughly

Lock the lid into place and set the timer for 8 minutes. Serve with favorite dippers.

Green Bean Appetizer with Cranberries

(Ready in about 15 minutes | Servings 6)

Ingredients

1 ½ pounds green beans, trimmed

2 garlic cloves, minced

1 cup vegetable broth

1 tablespoon agave nectar

1 tablespoon extra-virgin oil

1/4 cup dried cranberries

Directions

Add green beans, garlic, and broth to the inner pot. Choose "Manual" setting; set the timer for 5 minutes.

In the meantime, mix the other ingredients.

Take away the lid. Transfer the beans to a serving dish. Pour the cranberry sauce over all. Enjoy!

Harvest Bean and Corn Dip

(Ready in about 20 minutes | Servings 16)

Ingredients

1 (15-ounce) can black beans, rinsed and drained

2 tablespoons corn oil

1 red onion, finely chopped

2 garlic cloves, minced

1/2 cup fresh corn kernels

1 pickled jalapeño, finely minced

1/2 cup mild Picante sauce

1 teaspoon fennel seeds

1 teaspoon caraway seeds

Sea salt and ground black pepper, to your liking

2 tablespoons fresh cilantro

Directions

Empty the can of beans into the inner pot and select "Bean" setting.

In the meantime, heat corn oil in a saucepan; cook the remaining ingredients, except fresh cilantro.

Next, open the cooker by releasing pressure; add the sautéed mixture to the cooker with beans. Give it a good stir.

Now, switch the mixture to a food processor or blender; add the cilantro and blend it, working with batches. Serve with veggie sticks, if desired. Enjoy!

Chickpea Mint Dip

(Ready in about 20 minutes | Servings 16)

Ingredients

1 cup chickpeas

4 cups water

1 red bell pepper, seeded and finely chopped

1 tablespoon lemon juice

1/2 tablespoon fresh dill, chopped

1 tablespoon salt

1 teaspoon garlic powder

1/3 cup tahini

3 tablespoons olive oil, preferably extra-virgin

Directions

Stir the chickpeas and water into the inner pot. Use "Manual" mode, cover and cook for 25 minutes using a HIGH pressure.

Next, open the cooker by releasing pressure and drain the chickpeas. Switch the chickpeas to a food processor; add the remaining ingredients, except the oil; blitz the mixture into a smooth purée.

While the machine is still running, gradually add olive oil. Process until it's creamy. Enjoy!

Finger Lickin' Spring Appetizer

(Ready in about 10 minutes | Servings 6)

Ingredients

1/2 cup spring onions, finely chopped

1 cup spring garlic, finely chopped

1 ½ pounds green beans

1 cup vegetable broth, preferably homemade

1/2 cup spring radishes, chopped

1 tablespoon sesame oil

1 tablespoon balsamic vinegar

3 tablespoons hoisin sauce

Directions

Fill the inner pot with spring onions, spring garlic, green beans, and vegetable broth. Choose "Manual" setting; set the timer for 5 minutes.

Take away the lid. Replace prepared mixture to a serving dish. Add the other ingredients. Serve at room temperature.

Thyme Fingerling Potatoes with Chives

(Ready in about 35 minutes | Servings 4)

Ingredients

2 tablespoons butter

1 ½ pounds small fingerling potatoes, each pricked twice with a small knife

1/2 cup roasted-vegetable broth

1 teaspoon seasoned salt

Freshly ground black pepper

2 fresh thyme sprigs, leaves only

1 cup fresh chives, chopped

Directions

Preheat the Instant Pot by selecting "Sauté" and HIGH heat.

Once hot, melt the butter; stir in the potatoes. Stir until the potatoes are coated; cook for 10 to 12 minutes.

Pour in the broth and secure the lid. Now, select "Manual" setting and cook under HIGH pressure for 7 minutes.

Afterward, use the Natural pressure release for 10 minutes. Season with salt, black pepper, and thyme. Serve topped with fresh chives. Enjoy!

Nana's Winter Applesauce

(Ready in about 30 minutes | Servings 16)

Ingredients

12 medium-sized tart apples, peeled, cored, and roughly diced

1/2 cup apple cider

1 vanilla bean

1 cinnamon stick, broken in half

4-5 whole cloves

1/4 cup honey

1 tablespoon lemon juice, freshly squeezed

Directions

Add the apples, apple cider and spices to the inner pot. Secure the lid.

Select "Manual" setting and cook under HIGH pressure for 4 minutes. After that, perform the Natural pressure release.

Now, add the honey and lemon juice. You can use an immersion blender to puree the sauce if desired.

Sweet and Tangy Corn Appetizer

(Ready in about 10 minutes | Servings 8)

Ingredients

8 ears of corn, shucked

1/2 stick butter, melted

1 teaspoon brown sugar

1 tablespoon lime juice

1 tablespoon fresh coriander, finely chopped

Salt and ground black pepper, to your liking

Red pepper flakes, to your liking

Directions

Lay a metal rack on the bottom of your Instant Pot; then pour in 1 cup of water. Arrange the ears of corn on the rack. Seal the lid.

Next, select "Manual" setting; let it cook for 8 minutes. Use the Quick pressure release.

In the meantime, in a mixing dish, whisk the remaining ingredients; mix well to combine. For more flavor, drizzle the mixture over the corn and serve.

Quick and Easy Steamed Sweet Potatoes

(Ready in about 15 minutes | Servings 6)

Ingredients

1 cup boiling water

6 sweet potatoes

2 tablespoons extra-virgin olive oil

1/4 teaspoon grated nutmeg

1 teaspoon ground cinnamon

1/4 teaspoon ground cloves

Directions

Set a trivet on the bottom of your cooker. Pour in boiling water.

Scrub sweet potatoes and drizzle them with extra-virgin olive oil; wrap them in aluminum foil.

Place sweet potatoes on the trivet. Cover and select "Steam" setting; set the timer for 15 minutes. While sweet potatoes are still hot, add the nutmeg, cinnamon, and cloves. Enjoy!

Pear and Apple Sauce

(Ready in about 30 minutes | Servings 16)

Ingredients

6 pears, peeled, cored, and diced

6 tart apples, peeled, cored, and diced

1/2 cup apple juice

1 cinnamon stick, broken in half

1 teaspoon grated nutmeg

1/2 teaspoon ground anise star

1 teaspoon ground cloves

1/2 teaspoon cardamom

1/4 cup honey

Directions

Throw the pears, apples, apple juice, and spices into the inner pot. Secure the lid.

Select "Manual" mode and cook for 4 minutes under HIGH pressure. After that, use the Natural pressure release for about 15 minutes.

Lastly, stir in the honey. Refrigerate up to 4 days. Enjoy!

Corn on the Cob with Adobo Sauce

(Ready in about 10 minutes | Servings 8)

Ingredients

8 ears of corn, shucked

1/2 stick butter, melted

1 tablespoon lemon juice

1 tablespoon fresh cilantro, finely chopped

1 teaspoon seasoned salt

1/2 teaspoon ground black pepper, or to taste

Adobo sauce, to serve

Directions

Lower a metal rack onto the bottom of an electric pressure cooker; then, pour in 1 cup of water. Arrange the ears of corn on the metal rack. Seal the lid according to the manufacturer's directions.

Next, select the "Manual" mode and cook for 8 minutes using HIGH pressure. Lastly, use the Quick pressure release.

Meanwhile, in a mixing bowl, whisk the remaining ingredients. Drizzle the mixture over the corn and serve.

Yummy and Crispy Brussels Sprouts

(Ready in about 10 minutes | Servings 4)

Ingredients

2 teaspoons avocado oil

1 cup shallots, diced

1/2 cup water

1 tablespoon maple syrup

1 teaspoon apple cider vinegar

16 Brussels sprouts, cut in half

Red pepper flakes, to your liking

Sea salt and freshly ground black pepper, to your liking

Directions

Set an electric pressure cooker to "Sauté" function; warm the oil and sauté shallots for 2 minutes, stirring periodically.

In a mixing dish, whisk water with maple syrup and vinegar; add your Brussels sprouts to the cooker. Drizzle maple/vinegar mixture over them and sprinkle with all seasonings.

Cover and bring it to HIGH pressure for 2 minutes. Open the cooker by releasing the pressure and serve immediately.

5-Minute Cauliflower Appetizer

(Ready in about 5 minutes | Servings 6)

Ingredients

3 cups cauliflower florets

4 tablespoons roasted-vegetable broth

1/4 teaspoon seasoned salt

1/2 teaspoon freshly ground black pepper

1/2 teaspoon dried rosemary

1 teaspoon dried thyme

1 tablespoon fresh coriander

Directions

Put all ingredients into an electric pressure cooker.

Bring to HIGH pressure for 1 minute. Afterward, use the Quick pressure release. Bon appétit!

Jalapeño and Tomatillo Dipping Sauce

(Ready in about 15 minutes | Servings 12)

Ingredients

1 cup canned beans

1 pound tomatillos, chopped

1 teaspoon jalapeño pepper, seeded and finely chopped

1 red onion, finely chopped

2 cloves garlic, minced

2 heaping tablespoons fresh cilantro leaves, chopped

Fresh juice of 1 lime

Salt and ground black pepper, to taste

1 teaspoon cayenne pepper

Directions

Throw the beans, tomatillos, jalapeño pepper, onion, and garlic into your Instant Pot. Then, choose "Bean/Chili" mode; set the timer for 10 minutes.

Carefully open the cooker. Mash the bean mixture with a fork.

Add the other ingredients and stir to combine well. Serve with pitas and enjoy.

Asparagus and Mushroom Appetizer

(Ready in about 10 minutes | Servings 6)

Ingredients

1 cup white mushrooms, sliced

1 cup onions, chopped

1 cup asparagus, chopped

1 teaspoon garlic powder

1 teaspoon shallot powder

2 tablespoons water

1 teaspoon sea salt

1/4 teaspoon ground black pepper, to taste

Directions

Select "Sauté" setting and cook the mushrooms and onions until tender.

Add the other ingredients. Lock the lid and cook at HIGH pressure for 2 minutes. Then, use the Quick release pressure.

Transfer everything to a serving dish and enjoy!

Herby Polenta Bites

(Ready in about 30 minutes | Servings 6)

Ingredients

2 cups water

2 cups non-dairy milk

1 tablespoon butter, room temperature

1/2 teaspoon salt

1/4 teaspoon black pepper

1/2 teaspoon paprika

1 teaspoon dried rosemary, crushed

1 teaspoon garlic powder

1 cup dry polenta

Parmesan cheese, for garnish

Directions

First, fill your cooker with the water, milk, butter, salt, black pepper, paprika, rosemary, and garlic powder.

Slowly stir the polenta into the boiling liquid; make sure to stir constantly. Cover and choose "Manual" setting; set the timer for 7 minutes.

Allow the pressure to come down naturally and remove the lid. Spread the mixture over a cookie sheet and refrigerate it for 20 minutes. Cut into squares and serve topped with Parmesan cheese.

Tarragon Baby Carrots

(Ready in about 10 minutes | Servings 4)

Ingredients

3 cups baby carrots

4 tablespoons water

1/2 teaspoon seasoned salt

1/4 teaspoon freshly cracked black pepper

1/2 teaspoon dried rosemary

1/2 teaspoon dried thyme

Directions

Simply throw all ingredients into your cooker.

Select "Steam" setting and cook for 3 minutes.

Bring the pressure down by natural pressure release method and remove the lid. Serve warm.

Creamy Corn Dip

(Ready in about 10 minutes | Servings 12)

Ingredients

4 cups corn kernels, frozen

1/2 cup scallions, finely chopped

3/4 cup mayonnaise

1/2 cup sour cream

1/2 cup cream cheese

1 teaspoon salt

1/2 teaspoon ground black pepper

1/2 teaspoon cayenne pepper

10 ounces Cheddar cheese, shaved

Directions

Add corn kernels to your cooker. Select "Steam" setting; adjust the timer for 3 minutes. Transfer the steamed corn to a dish; allow it to cool.

Add the rest of the above ingredients; stir to combine well. Cover the bowl and refrigerate your dip until ready to serve.

Pumpkin and Cheese Dip

(Ready in about 15 minutes + chilling time | Servings 12)

Ingredients

1/2 cup pumpkin, cut into chunks

1 cup cream cheese, room temperature

1 tablespoon sunflower oil

1/2 teaspoon ground allspice

1/2 teaspoon kosher salt

1/4 teaspoon red pepper flakes

Toasted pumpkin seeds, for garnish

Directions

Add pumpkin chunks to the inner pot. Select "Steam" setting and cook for 10 to 12 minutes; drain the pumpkin.

Fold in the cheese; beat until it is combined. Add the oil, allspice, kosher salt, and red pepper flakes; beat until creamy.

Sprinkle with pumpkin seeds and serve chilled.

Artichoke with Mayonnaise Sauce

(Ready in about 20 minutes | Servings 12)

Ingrediens

2 large-sized artichokes

1 lemon, halved

1 cup water

2 tablespoons sour cream

1 teaspoon Dijon mustard

3 tablespoons mayonnaise

1 teaspoon smoked paprika

Directions

Discard the damaged leaves of the artichokes. Trim the bottoms; rub with 1 half of lemon.

Pour the water into the cooker; set a steamer basket. Place the artichokes in the steamer basket.

Secure the lid and press "Manual" button. Cook for 14 minutes under HIGH pressure. Once pressure cooking is complete, use the Natural pressure release.

In a bowl, combine together the sour cream, mustard, mayonnaise, and smoked paprika. Add the juice of the remaining 1/2 lemon. Serve the artichokes warm with the mayo sauce on the side.

Pumpkin and Cottage Dip

(Ready in about 25 minutes | Servings 12)

Ingredients

3/4 cup frozen pumpkin chunks

1 cup Cottage cheese, softened

1/4 teaspoon ground black pepper

1/2 teaspoon salt

1 teaspoon cayenne pepper

1 teaspoon pumpkin pie spice

1/2 cup onions, chopped

4 slices bacon, chopped

1/4 cup walnuts, toasted and roughly chopped

Directions

Throw pumpkin chunks into the inner pot. Select "Steam" setting and cook 15 minutes.

Drain the pumpkin and beat it with an electric mixer along with Cottage cheese, black pepper, salt, cayenne pepper, and pumpkin pie spice.

Next, stir the onions and bacon into the cooker. Select "Sauté" setting and cook until the onions are tender; crumble the bacon.

Add onion/bacon mixture to the pumpkin mixture. Stir until everything is well combined. Serve garnished with toasted walnuts and enjoy!

Harissa and Parmesan Corn

(Ready in about 25 minutes | Servings 8)

Ingredients

8 ears of corn, cut in half

Sea salt flakes, to your liking

Freshly ground black pepper, to your liking

1 teaspoon bourbon smoked paprika

2 heaping tablespoons cilantro

2 tablespoons Harissa butter, or to taste

1 teaspoon lime zest

1/2 cup Parmesan cheese, grated

Directions

Place a metal rack in the bottom of your Instant Pot; then pour in 1 cup of water. Lay the ears of corn on the rack. Secure the lid.

Choose the "Manual" setting and cook for 8 minutes under HIGH pressure. Now, use the Quick pressure release.

In a small mixing dish, thoroughly combine the salt, black pepper, smoked paprika, cilantro, Harissa butter, and lemon zest. Drizzle the mixture over the ears of corn.

Afterward, roll them in grated Parmesan cheese and serve immediately.

Herbed Baby Potato Snack

(Ready in about 15 minutes | Servings 4)

Ingredients

12 baby potatoes, halved

1/2 stick butter

1 tablespoon fresh lime juice

1 teaspoon fresh rosemary

1 teaspoon fresh thyme

1/2 teaspoon coarse salt

1 tablespoon dill, minced

Fresh chopped chives, to serve

Directions

Lower a rack onto the bottom of your cooker; pour in 1/2 cup of the water.

Throw in the potatoes and close the lid; set the timer for 10 minutes. Once cooking is complete, use a quick release. Taste your potatoes for the doneness.

Add the butter, lime juice, and seasonings; toss to coat well. Then, serve topped with fresh chopped chives.

Zesty Baby Bok Choy

(Ready in about 10 minutes | Servings 4)

Ingredients

1 cup water

4 baby Bok choy, split horizontally

1 teaspoon soy sauce

1 teaspoon lime zest

1 tablespoon fresh lime juice

1 teaspoon sesame oil

1 teaspoon agave nectar

3/4 teaspoon seasoned salt

1/2 teaspoon freshly ground black pepper, or to taste

2 tablespoons sunflower seeds

Directions

Add the water to the inner pot; place the steamer basket on top. Add the Bok choy to the steamer basket. Secure the lid.

Select "Manual" setting and cook under HIGH pressure for 4 minutes. Once cooking is complete, perform a quick release.

Next, transfer steamed Bok choy to a large-sized bowl; toss with the rest of the above ingredients; toss to combine. Bon appétit!

Amazing Acorn Squash Snack

(Ready in about 20 minutes | Servings 8)

Ingredients

1/2 cup water

4 small-sized acorn squash, halved

1 tablespoon sesame oil

2 tablespoons soy sauce

1/4 teaspoon sea salt

1/4 teaspoon red pepper

1/4 teaspoon pumpkin pie spice

Directions

Place a rack in the bottom of the cooker. Pour in the water; lower the squash onto the rack.

Cover and cook under HIGH pressure for 20 minutes.

Meanwhile, thoroughly whisk all remaining ingredients.

Transfer the squash to a serving platter; drizzle prepared sauce over all. Enjoy!

Roasted Pepper and Tomato Dip

(Ready in about 15 minutes | Servings 12)

Ingredients

2 tablespoons canola oil

2 roasted bell peppers, chopped

1 parsnip, chopped

1 carrot, chopped

1 onion, diced

3 ripe tomatoes, peeled, cored and sliced

1/2 cup water

3 tablespoons sugar

1/2 teaspoon red pepper flakes

Seasoned salt and ground black pepper, to taste

1/2 teaspoon dried rosemary

1 teaspoon dried thyme

1 teaspoon dried oregano

Directions

Select "Sauté" setting and heat the oil; then, add the peppers, parsnip, carrot, onion, and tomatoes. Sauté it for 3 minutes, until the vegetables are just tender.

Stir in the other ingredients. Cover and cook for 5 minutes.

Afterward, remove the lid according to the manufacturer's instructions. Serve with dippers of choice.

Honey-Glazed Wax Beans Snack

(Ready in about 10 minutes | Servings 6)

Ingredients

1 ½ pounds yellow wax beans

1 tablespoon butter

1 tablespoon mild honey

1 cup vegetable stock

1 teaspoon lemon zest, finely grated

Directions

Add wax beans to the Instant Pot. Select "Manual" setting and set the timer for 4 minutes.

Remove the lid by realizing pressure. Toss the beans with the remaining ingredients; toss to coat. Bon appétit!

Dad's Jalapeño Bean Dip

(Ready in about 20 minutes | Servings 16)

Ingredients

1 (15-ounce) can beans, rinsed and drained

1 tablespoon corn oil

2 garlic cloves, minced

1 cup red onions, finely chopped

1/2 cup fresh corn kernels

1 tablespoon soy sauce

1/2 cup tomato puree

1/4 cup pickled jalapeño slices, finely minced

Sea salt and ground black pepper, to your liking

1 teaspoon dried dill weed

1 teaspoon cayenne pepper

Directions

Add the beans to the cooker and choose the "Bean/Chili" button.

While the beans are cooking, in the saucepan, heat the oil and sauté the other ingredients; cook until tender.

Carefully open the cooker; add the sautéed mixture to the cooker. Stir to combine well.

Now, puree the mixture in a food processor, working in batches. Serve with dippers of choice.

Sage Brussels Sprouts with Vidalia

(Ready in about 10 minutes | Servings 4)

Ingredients

1 tablespoon butter

1 cup Vidalia onions, cut into rings

1 teaspoon dried dill weed

3-5 leaves sage, chopped

1/2 cup water

22 Brussels sprouts, cut in half

Sea salt and freshly ground black pepper, to taste

Directions

Preheat your cooker on "Sauté" mode; next, melt the butter and sauté Vidalia onions, along with dill and chopped sage; sauté them approximately 2 minutes or until aromatic and tender.

Now, dump the water and Brussels sprouts into the inner pot. Season with salt and black pepper to taste.

Lock the lid and cook an additional 2 minutes on HIGH pressure. Lastly, use the Quick pressure release. Serve with blue cheese dip if desired. Enjoy!

Sunday Cauliflower Snack

(Ready in about 5 minutes | Servings 4)

Ingredients

3 cups cauliflower florets

1/2 cup Prosecco

1/4 teaspoon dried dill weed

1/2 teaspoon dried thyme

1/2 teaspoon ground cumin

1/2 teaspoon chili powder

1 teaspoon seasoned salt

1/4 teaspoon black pepper, freshly cracked

Directions

Throw all ingredients into the inner pot of your cooker.

Cook under HIGH pressure for 2 minutes. Open your Instant Pot by realizing the pressure.

Serve at room temperature and enjoy!

Salsa and Refried Bean Dip

(Ready in about 5 minutes | Servings 12)

Ingredients

15 ounces fat-free canned refried beans

2 tablespoons mild salsa

1 tablespoon cilantro, chopped

Tortilla chips, to serve

Directions

Empty the can of beans into the cooker. Choose the "Bean/Chili" mode.

Add the salsa and cilantro. Stir until everything is well combined.

Lastly, puree the mixture in a food processor, working in batches. Serve with tortilla chips and enjoy!

Bean and Watercress Dipping Sauce

(Ready in about 5 minutes | Servings 12)

Ingredients

1 16-ounce can Great Northern beans, drained and rinsed

2 tablespoons extra-virgin olive oil

1/4 cup watercress, chopped

Seasoned salt and freshly ground pepper, to taste

1 teaspoon cayenne pepper

Directions

Add the beans to the cooker. Choose the "Bean/Chili" mode.

Stir all remaining ingredients into the cooker. Stir to combine.

Afterward, puree the mixture in a food processor. Serve with crackers and enjoy.

Delicious Steamed Asparagus

(Ready in about 10 minutes | Servings 6)

Ingredients

1 cup shallots, chopped

1 pound asparagus spears

1 teaspoon sesame oil

1 teaspoon granulated garlic

1/2 teaspoon shallot powder

1/2 red chili

2 tablespoons Prosecco

1/2 teaspoon cayenne pepper

Sea salt and ground white pepper, to your liking

Directions

Choose "Sauté" setting and cook the shallots until tender or 2 minutes.

Throw in the other ingredients. Now, cook it for 2 minutes under HIGH pressure.

Afterward, use the Quick pressure release. Serve with mayonnaise. Bon appétit!

Garbanzo Bean and Spinach Dip

(Ready in about 35 minutes | Servings 12)

Ingredients

4 cups water

1 cup garbanzo beans

1 shallot, peeled and minced

1 teaspoon red pepper flakes

2 garlic cloves, minced

1 cup spinach leaves

Sea salt and ground black pepper, to your liking

2 tablespoons tahini

1/4 cup extra-virgin olive oil

Directions

Add the water and garbanzo beans to the inner pot.

Lock the lid onto the pressure cooker; select "Manual" mode and cook for 25 minutes. Turn off the heat; drain garbanzo beans.

Add all ingredients, except oil, to a bowl of your food processor. Now, gradually and slowly pour the oil in a thin stream. Blend until everything is well incorporated.

Sprinkle pepper flakes over all and serve.

Mexican-Style Corn Dip

(Ready in about 10 minutes + chilling time | Servings 12)

Ingredients

4 cups corn kernels, frozen

1/2 cup red onions, finely chopped

2 (8-ounce) packages cream cheese, softened

3/4 cup mayonnaise

1/2 (7-ounce) can green chilies, diced

1/2 teaspoon red pepper flakes, to taste

Sea salt, to taste

2 (1 ounce) packages taco seasoning mix

1/2 cup chopped fresh cilantro, or to taste

Directions

Place the corn kernels in the Instant Pot. Choose "Steam" setting and cook for 3 minutes. Now, let it cool completely.

Add the remaining ingredients; stir until everything is well combined. Serve chilled and enjoy!

Cream Cheese and Pumpkin Dip

(Ready in about 15 minutes | Servings 12)

Ingredients

1 cup butternut pumpkin, diced

1 ¼ cups cream cheese, room temperature

2 teaspoons ground cumin

1 heaping tablespoon coriander, finely chopped

1/2 teaspoon pumpkin pie spice mix

Seasoned salt and ground black pepper, to taste

1/2 teaspoon paprika

2 tablespoons Greek yogurt

Directions

Throw diced pumpkin into the inner pot and cook using the "Steam" mode for 10 minutes. Drain the pumpkin and return it back to the pot.

Fold in cream cheese; beat the mixture with an electric mixer until your desired consistency is reached.

Add the other ingredients. Continue to beat until the mixture is uniform and creamy. Serve with wafers and enjoy!

Collard Green and Water Chestnut Dip

(Ready in about 15 minutes | Servings 12)

Ingredients

2 (10-ounce) boxes collard greens, thawed and drained

1 (16-ounce) container sour cream

1 cup mayonnaise

1/2 teaspoon basil

1 teaspoon dried parsley

Kosher salt and ground black pepper, to your liking

1 (4-ounce) can water chestnuts, drained and chopped

Directions

Set the trivet in an electric pressure cooker. Combine all ingredients in the baking dish; mix well. Wrap the baking dish with an aluminum foil and make a foil sling.

Close the lid properly and cook for 9 minutes on the "Manual" setting. Serve at room temperature and enjoy.

Thyme Polenta Bites

(Ready in about 30 minutes | Servings 6)

Ingredients

4 cups water

1 tablespoon butter

1 teaspoon dried thyme

1 teaspoon cayenne pepper

1 teaspoon salt

1/2 teaspoon ground black pepper

1/4 teaspoon capsicum spice

1 cup dry polenta

Directions

Add the water, butter, thyme, cayenne pepper, salt, and black pepper to the inner pot. Select "Sauté" setting. After pressure is released, open the lid according to the manufacturer's directions.

Immediately stir in the capsicum and polenta; make sure to stir frequently. Close the lid and choose the "Manual" mode; set the timer for 7 minutes.

After that, use the Quick release method. Pour the polenta mixture into a cookie sheet. Refrigerate it about 30 minutes and cut into small squares.

Warm Cheesy Corn Dip

(Ready in about 10 minutes | Servings 12)

Ingredients

4 cups corn kernels, frozen

2 cloves garlic, minced

1 small-sized onion, finely chopped

1 jalapeno pepper, diced, or more to taste

1 (8-ounce) carton sour cream

2 (8-ounce) packages cream cheese

Kosher salt, to your liking

2 (1-ounce) packages taco seasoning mix

2 cups Mexican cheese blend, shredded

Directions

Add the corn to the inner pot of your cooker. Press the "Steam" button and cook for 3 minutes. Let it cool completely.

Add the remaining ingredients, except for cheese blend; stir until everything is well incorporated. Serve warm topped with shredded Mexican cheese blend.

Piquant Cornmeal Squares

(Ready in about 20 minutes | Servings 6)

Ingredients

2 cups chicken broth

2 cups water

1 tablespoon olive oil

1 teaspoon grated orange rind

1/2 teaspoon ground black pepper

1 teaspoon salt

1 teaspoon chili powder

1 teaspoon cumin powder

1 teaspoon dried minced garlic

1 tablespoon dried cilantro flakes

1 cup yellow cornmeal

Directions

Throw all ingredients, except cilantro and cornmeal, into the inner pot of your Instant Pot. Select "Sauté" mode. After pressure is released, open the lid.

Now, throw in the cilantro and cornmeal; make sure to stir continuously. Close the lid and choose the "Manual" setting; set the timer for 7 minutes.

Lastly, use the Quick release method. Pour the mixture into a rimmed baking sheet. Refrigerate approximately 1 hour and cut into squares. Enjoy!

Ranch Corn Dip

(Ready in about 10 minutes | Servings 12)

Ingredients

4 cups corn kernels, frozen

1 (8-ounce) package sour cream

1 (1 ounce) package ranch dressing mix

Sea salt, to taste

1/2 teaspoon ground black pepper, or to taste

1 cup Cheddar cheese, shredded

Directions

Throw the corn kernels into the inner pot; press the "Steam" button and cook for 3 minutes. Next, allow pressure to drop down naturally and remove the lid.

Add the other ingredients, except for cheese. Give it a gentle stir, garnish with dippers, and serve topped with shredded Cheddar cheese.

Bean and Olive Dip

(Ready in about 10 minutes | Servings 12)

Ingredients

1 pound kidney beans, soaked overnight

3 tablespoons olive oil

2 garlic cloves, minced

1/2 cup Italian-style salad dressing

2 tablespoons tomato ketchup

A pinch of cardamom

1 teaspoon capers

2 sprigs thyme, finely minced

1/4 teaspoon ground black pepper

1/2 teaspoon salt

Sliced black olives, for garnish

Directions

Throw the beans into the inner pot. Lock the lid onto the cooker.

Choose "Bean/Chili" button. Unlock and open the pot.

Add all remaining ingredients, except black olives; stir to combine. Serve topped with black olives and drizzled with some extra olive oil. Enjoy!

Orange-Glazed Brussels Sprout

(Ready in about 12 minutes | Servings 4)

Ingredients

2 pounds Brussels sprouts, trimmed

1/4 cup orange juice, freshly squeezed

1 tablespoon butter

2 tablespoons brown sugar

1/2 teaspoon salt, or to taste

1/2 teaspoon red pepper flakes, or to taste

Directions

Place all items in an electric pressure cooker.

Push the "Manual" button; set the timer for 4 minutes; cook until Brussels sprouts are fork tender.

Use the Quick-release method to return the pot's pressure to normal. Unlock and open the pot. Serve at room temperature.

Peppery Tomatillo Dip

(Ready in about 10 minutes | Servings 12)

Ingredients

1 pound tomatillos, chopped

2 Serrano peppers, seeded and minced

1 onion, finely chopped

2 cloves garlic, minced

4 sprigs fresh cilantro, thick stems and roughly chopped

Salt and ground black pepper, to taste

1 teaspoon cayenne pepper

Directions

Throw the tomatillos, Serrano peppers, onion, and garlic into your Instant Pot. Next, choose "Bean/Chili" setting; set the timer for 10 minutes.

Carefully unlock and open the cooker.

Stir in the remaining ingredients; stir until everything is well mixed. Serve with tortilla chips.

Sunday Easy BBQ Wings

(Ready in about 15 minutes | Servings 8)

Ingredients

2 pounds wings

1 cup honey BBQ sauce

Kosher salt, to taste

3/4 teaspoon ground black pepper

1 teaspoon smoked paprika

1 teaspoon dried rosemary

1/2 teaspoon dried marjoram

1 teaspoon dried basil

1/2 cup water

1/4 cup brown sugar

2 bay leaves

5-6 black peppercorns

Directions

Preheat your cooker on "Sauté" function and brown the wings on all sides.

Combine all ingredients in the cooker. Cook under HIGH pressure for 10 minutes.

Then, perform the Natural pressure release and open the cooker. Eat warm and enjoy!

Piquant Turkey Thighs

(Ready in about 1 hour | Servings 8)

Ingredients

1 pound turkey thighs, tips removed and sectioned

1 cup turkey broth

2 garlic cloves, peeled and minced

1 teaspoon onion powder

1 teaspoon dried thyme

1 teaspoon dried sage

1/2 teaspoon dried basil

Kosher salt and ground black pepper, to taste

Directions

Set your cooker to "Sauté"; brown the turkey thighs on all sides.

Throw in the rest of the ingredients; lock the lid onto the cooker. Choose "Poultry" setting and cook the turkey for 1 hour. Taste the turkey for doneness.

Serve with toothpicks and the dipping sauce of choice. Enjoy!

Tomatillo and Avocado Dipping Sauce

(Ready in about 10 minutes | Servings 12)

Ingredients

1 pound tomatillos, chopped

2 cloves garlic, minced

1 cup shallots, finely chopped

2 tablespoons extra-virgin olive oil

Salt and ground black pepper, to taste

1 tablespoon fresh lime juice

2 avocados, pitted and chopped

1 teaspoon cayenne pepper

Directions

Place the tomatillos in the cooker. Next, choose "Bean/Chili" mode; set the timer for 10 minutes.

Use the Quick-release method to return the pressure to normal; open the cooker.

Throw in the other ingredients. Transfer the mixture to your food processor. Pulse until coarsely chopped. Serve and enjoy!

One-Pot Sticky Chicken Wings

(Ready in about 1 hour | Servings 5)

Ingredients

10 chicken wings, tips removed and sectioned

1 cup soy sauce

3 tablespoons mirin

1 teaspoon granulated garlic

1 teaspoon shallot powder

1 teaspoon dried sage

1/2 teaspoon red pepper flakes, crushed

1/2 teaspoon dried basil

3/4 teaspoon salt

1/2 teaspoon ground black pepper, to taste

Directions

Preheat your cooker on "Sauté" function; sauté the chicken wings until just browned.

Throw in the other ingredients; lock the lid onto the cooker. Choose "Poultry" function; set the machine to cook at LOW pressure for 1 hour. Unlock and open the pot.

Use the Quick-release method to drop the pressure back to normal. Serve immediately and enjoy!

Italian-Style Cocktail Meatballs

(Ready in about 35 minutes | Servings 10)

Ingredients

1 pound lean ground beef

1/2 pound lean ground pork

1/2 teaspoon seasoned salt

1/2 teaspoon ground black pepper

2 Italian plum tomatoes, chopped

1 yellow onion

1 cup tomato ketchup

1 teaspoon granulated garlic

1 teaspoon red pepper flakes, crushed

1 teaspoon dried oregano

1 teaspoon dried basil

Directions

Turn your cooker to "Sauté" mode. In a mixing dish, thoroughly combine the meat, salt, and ground black pepper. Form the mixture into small meatballs (the size of golf balls).

Sear the meatballs on all sides, turning occasionally. Then, turn the cooker to the "Meat/Stew" setting.

Next, add all remaining ingredients to the Instant Pot. Cook for 35 minutes.

Afterward, use the Quick-release method to bring the pot's pressure back to normal. Open the cooker and serve this appetizer warm. Bon appétit!

Chicken Wings Adobo

(Ready in about 25 minutes | Servings 16)

Ingredients

1 tablespoon olive oil

1 teaspoon adobo seasoning

3/4 cup BBQ sauce

4 pounds chicken wings, frozen

Directions

Dump all ingredients into the inner pot of your Instant Pot. Lock the lid onto the cooker.

Choose "Soup" mode. Afterward, use the Quick-release method to bring the pot's pressure back to normal.

Serve with dipping sauce of choice. Bon appétit!

The Ultimate Chicken Wings

(Ready in about 15 minutes | Servings 8)

Ingredients

2 pounds wings

2 tablespoons vegetable oil

3/4 cup soy sauce

Salt and ground black pepper, to taste

1 teaspoon dried rosemary

1/2 teaspoon dried marjoram

1 teaspoon cayenne pepper

1/2 cup rice milk

2 tablespoons honey

3-4 black peppercorns

Directions

Preheat your cooker on "Sauté" mode; now, brown the wings on all sides.

Add the other ingredients to the cooker. Cook for 10 minutes under HIGH pressure.

Afterward, use the Natural pressure release and carefully open your Instant Pot. Serve and enjoy!

Quick and Easy Carrot Coins

(Ready in about 20 minutes | Servings 6)

Ingredients

1 tablespoon butter

1 tablespoon sugar

1/2 cup water

1/2 teaspoon paprika

1 teaspoon grated orange peel

1/4 teaspoon coarse salt

1 pound carrots, trimmed and cut into coins

Directions

Simply throw all ingredients, except carrots, into your Instant Pot. Select "Sauté" function and cook for just 30 seconds; make sure to stir continuously.

Stir in the carrot coins. Lock the lid onto the cooker. Set the machine to "Steam" function. Cook for 15 minutes under HIGH pressure.

After that, uncover and select "Sauté" setting. Cook until cooking liquid has evaporated. Enjoy!

Turkey Sausage Dip

(Ready in about 15 minutes | Servings 10)

Ingredients

1 tablespoon butter

1/2 pound ground turkey sausage

2 Roma tomatoes, chopped

1 onion, chopped

2 cloves garlic, sliced

8 ounces cream cheese

Salt and freshly cracked black pepper, to your liking

Directions

Preheat your cooker on "Sauté" mode; then, melt the butter and cook turkey sausage until it is browned. Add the rest of the above ingredients.

Lock the lid onto the pot. Set the machine's timer to cook 15 minutes under HIGH pressure.

Afterward, release the cooker's pressure naturally. Enjoy!

Greek-Style Tomato and Olive Dip

(Ready in about 25 minutes | Servings 16)

Ingredients

2 tablespoons olive oil

2 garlic cloves, finely minced

1 cup scallions, chopped

1 teaspoon dried basil, crushed

1 teaspoon dried rosemary, crushed

1 teaspoon dried oregano, crushed

1 (28-ounce) can crushed tomatoes

1 cup vegetable stock

Sea salt and cracked black pepper, to your liking

1/2 cup Kalamata olives, pitted and chopped

Crumbled Feta cheese, to serve

Directions

Choose the "Sauté" button on your cooker and heat olive oil. Now, sauté the garlic and scallions for 2 to 2 ½ minutes or until they're softened.

Add all remaining ingredients, except Feta cheese; give it a good stir.

Lock the lid onto the pot and cook for 20 minutes under HIGH pressure. After that, use the Quick-release method to bring the pressure back to normal.

Serve topped with Feta cheese and garnished with pita bread. Bon appétit!

Parmesan Zucchini Appetizer

(Ready in about 5 minutes | Servings 4)

Ingredients

3 cups zucchini, cut into halves lengthwise

2 tablespoons vegetable stock

2 tablespoons apple cider

1 teaspoon garlic powder

1/4 teaspoon salt

1/4 teaspoon black pepper, preferably freshly ground

1/2 teaspoon dried oregano

1/2 teaspoon dried rosemary

1 teaspoon dried basil

Grated Parmesan cheese, to serve

Directions

Throw all ingredients, except Parmesan cheese, into the inner pot of your cooker.

Bring to HIGH pressure and set the timer for 1 minute.

Use the quick-release method to bring the pressure back to normal. Scatter Parmesan cheese over all. Serve right away.

Summer Shrimp Dip

(Ready in about 15 minutes + chilling time | Servings 12)

Ingredients

1 tablespoon extra-virgin olive oil

1 onion, chopped fine

2 garlic cloves, smashed

2 cans shrimp

A few dashes of paprika

1 (8-ounce) package cream cheese, plus

3⁄4 cup mayonnaise

2 tablespoons ketchup

1/2 teaspoon dried basil leaves, crushed

Sea salt and ground black pepper, to taste

Directions

Preheat your cooker on "Sauté" setting; heat the oil. Then, sauté the onion and garlic for 3 to 4 minutes or until tender and fragrant.

Then, stir in the shrimp and cook a few minutes more. Allow the mixture to cool slightly.

After that, stir in the remaining ingredients. Mash all ingredients and chill the mixture before serving. Serve and enjoy!

DESSERTS

White Wine-Poached Apples

(Ready in about 20 minutes | Servings 6)

Ingredients

1 bottle white wine

1 ½ cups sugar

6 firm apples, peeled

3-4 whole cloves

1 vanilla bean

1 cinnamon stick, broken in half

1 small-sized lemon, cut into rounds

Directions

Add white wine and sugar to the cooker; stir until the sugar is dissolved. Add the rest of the above ingredients and gently stir to coat. Secure the lid.

Select "Manual" and cook at HIGH pressure for 8 minutes.

Once pressure cooking is done, use a natural release. Reserve 2 cups of cooking liquid. Choose "Sauté" setting and cook the sauce until it reduces by half, approximately 10 minutes.

Serve the pears along with the sauce. Bon appétit!

Easy Country Applesauce

(Ready in about 15 minutes | Servings 20)

Ingredients

2 ½ pounds apples, peeled, cored, and cut into wedges

1/4 cup brown sugar

1/2 teaspoon ground cardamom

1 teaspoon cinnamon

3/4 cup apple juice

1 tablespoon lemon juice

1/2 teaspoon anise star, ground

Directions

Add all ingredients to the cooker, stir, and close the lid; cook under HIGH pressure for 4 minutes.

Once cooking is complete, use the Natural pressure release. Now, carefully open the lid.

Stir the mixture with a potato masher, breaking up large chunks. Enjoy!

Carrot Rice Pudding with Dried Cherries

(Ready in about 35 minutes | Servings 6)

Ingredients

1 cup Arborio rice

2 ¾ cups milk

1/2 cup carrot, shredded

A pinch of salt

1/4 cup packed brown sugar

1 large egg, well beaten

1 teaspoon vanilla extract

1/2 teaspoon coconut extract

1/2 teaspoon ground cinnamon

1/4 teaspoon ground ginger

1/2 cup coconut, shredded

1/2 cup dried cherries

Directions

Add the rice, milk, carrot, and salt to the cooker; stir to combine. Secure the cooker's lid.

Select "Manual" mode and cook for 12 minutes under HIGH pressure. Once cooking is done, perform the Natural release.

Select "Sauté" mode and add the sugar, egg, vanilla and coconut extract; stir well. Once the mixture begins to boil, press the "Cancel" button. Add the cinnamon, ginger, coconut, and dried cherries.

Serve at room temperature. Enjoy!

Star Anise Bread Pudding

(Ready in about 25 minutes | Servings 6)

Ingredients

2 tablespoons butter

4 cups Aniseed stale bread, cubed

3 eggs, beaten

2 cups milk

1 ¼ cups heavy cream

1/2 cup dried prunes, pitted and chopped

1/2 cup brown sugar

1 teaspoon cinnamon powder

1/2 teaspoon ground anise star

A pinch of salt

1 teaspoon vanilla paste

Directions

Pour 2 cups of water into the Instant Pot. Place the rack at the bottom.

Then, butter the casserole dish that will fit in the inner pot. Throw bread cubes into the casserole dish.

In a bowl, combine the rest of the above ingredients; combine until everything is well incorporated. Pour the mixture over the bread cubes. Top with two layers of foil.

Select "Steam" setting and set the timer for 15 minutes. Let the puddings stand until the steam dies down and carefully lift them out. Serve.

Walnut Pumpkin Cake

(Ready in about 35 minutes | Servings 10)

Ingredients

1 ½ cups all-purpose flour

1 teaspoon baking soda

1 teaspoon pumpkin pie spice

1 teaspoon vanilla extract

A pinch of salt

1/2 cup applesauce

1 cup brown sugar

1/2 teaspoon ginger, grated

1 cup pumpkin purée

1 cup walnuts, chopped

Confectioners' sugar, to serve

Directions

In a mixing dish, combine the flour, baking soda, pumpkin pie spice, vanilla extract, and salt.

In a separate bowl, combine applesauce, sugar, ginger, pumpkin purée, and walnuts; mix until everything is well incorporated.

Now, fold the applesauce mixture into the flour mixture. Spoon the batter into a lightly greased cake pan. Cover with foil.

Add 1 ½ cups of water to your cooker. Lower a metal rack onto the bottom of your cooker. Lower prepared cake pan onto the rack. Cook for 25 minutes under HIGH pressure.

Dust your cake with confectioners' sugar. Enjoy.

Peach and Apricot Cobbler

(Ready in about 35 minutes | Servings 6)

Ingredients

1 cup all-purpose flour

1/3 cup sugar

1 teaspoon baking powder

1/2 teaspoon baking soda

A pinch of salt

2 tablespoons cold butter

1/3 cup buttermilk

1 cup frozen peaches, pitted, peeled and sliced

2 cups frozen apricots, pitted and halved

1/3 cup water

1 tablespoon cornstarch

1 teaspoon pure vanilla extract

1 teaspoon lime juice

1/4 teaspoon ground cloves

1/2 teaspoon grated nutmeg

Directions

In a bowl, combine together the flour, 1 tablespoon of sugar, the baking powder, baking soda, and salt. Cut in the butter and mix until it resembles a coarse meal. Set the dough aside.

Add the buttermilk; mix just until moistened.

Select "Sauté" setting; add the peaches, apricots, water, remaining sugar, cornstarch, vanilla extract, and lime juice. Now, add the cloves and nutmeg to the Instant Pot; stir.

Cook for 3 minutes; press the "Cancel" button.

Then, form the dough into the balls and nestle them on top of the fruit (you should have 8 balls). Secure the lid and select "Manual" setting; cook at HIGH pressure for 10 minutes.

Afterward, use a natural release. Serve warm.

Nectarine and Mango Tapioca Pudding

(Ready in about 10 minutes | Servings 2)

Ingredients

1/3 cup small pearl tapioca, soaked and rinsed

1 cup milk

1 cup coconut water

1/2 cup sugar

1 teaspoon lemon zest, grated

1 teaspoon vanilla paste

1 cup nectarine, diced

1 cup mango, diced

Directions

Add 1 cup of water to the inner pot; then, insert the rack.

Next, throw the tapioca into a heat-proof bowl. Add the milk, coconut water, sugar, lemon zest, and vanilla paste. Add the heat-proof bowl to the cooker.

Secure the lid and choose "Manual" mode; cook under HIGH pressure for 8 minutes.

While the mixture is still warm, add the nectarine and mango. Gently stir and serve at room temperature.

Chocolate and Coconut Tapioca Pudding

(Ready in about 10 minutes | Servings 4)

Ingredients

1 cup small pearl tapioca, soaked and rinsed

4 cups coconut milk

1 cup water

3/4 cup sugar

1/2 teaspoon coconut extract

3/4 teaspoon vanilla extract

1 teaspoon ground cinnamon

1 cup chopped chocolate

Coconut flakes, to serve

Directions

Pour 1 cup of water into the inner pot; place the rack at the bottom.

Then, add the tapioca, coconut milk, water, sugar, coconut extract, vanilla extract, and cinnamon to a heat-proof bowl. Lower the heat-proof bowl onto the rack.

Secure the lid and choose "Manual" setting; cook for 8 minutes under HIGH pressure.

While it is still warm, fold in the chocolate; stir to combine well. Serve topped with coconut flakes. Enjoy!

Autumn Pear Dumplings

(Ready in about 30 minutes | Servings 8)

Ingredients

1 (8-ounce) can crescent rolls

1 pear, cored, peeled, and cut into 8 wedges

4 tablespoons butter

1/2 cup brown sugar

1/4 teaspoon orange extract

1/4 teaspoon vanilla extract

1/4 teaspoon grated nutmeg

1/2 teaspoon ground cloves

1/2 teaspoon ground cinnamon

3/4 cup pear cider

Directions

Preheat the Instant Pot by selecting "Sauté" button.

Now, roll the dough out flat; roll each wedge of pear in 1 crescent roll. Add the butter, sugar, orange extract, vanilla extract, nutmeg, cloves, and cinnamon.

Arrange the dumplings at the bottom of your Instant Pot. Drizzle the pear cider over all. Now, secure the cooker's lid.

Select "Manual" mode and cook under HIGH pressure for 10 minutes.

Once cooking is done, use the Natural pressure release. Serve at room temperature.

Sago Pudding with Dates

(Ready in about 10 minutes | Servings 4)

Ingredients

1 cup small pearl tapioca, soaked and rinsed

4 cups almond milk

1 cup water

1/3 cup sugar

2 tablespoons molasses

1/2 teaspoon pure vanilla extract

1/2 teaspoon pure almond extract

1/2 teaspoon ground cardamom

1 teaspoon ground cinnamon

1 cup dates, pitted and chopped

Directions

Pour 1 cup of water into the inner pot; lay the metal rack on the bottom.

Then, add all ingredients to a heat-proof bowl. Lower the heat-proof bowl onto the rack.

Secure the lid and choose "Manual" setting; cook for 8 minutes using a HIGH pressure. Serve warm.

Rice Pudding with Almonds

(Ready in about 15 minutes | Servings 4)

Ingredients

1 cup jasmine rice

3 cups chocolate almond milk

1 cup water

1/3 cup brown sugar

1 tablespoon maple syrup

1 teaspoon vanilla extract

A pinch of salt

1/2 teaspoon ground cardamom

Slivered almonds, for garnish

Directions

Add the rice, chocolate almond milk, water, and brown sugar to the inner pot. Then, stir in maple syrup, vanilla extract, salt, and cardamom.

Choose "Manual" setting; use [+ -] button to select 12 minutes. After that, use rapid pressure release. Once the pressure has been released carefully open the lid.

Divide rice pudding among four serving bowls; serve topped with slivered almonds. Enjoy!

Rice Pudding with Prunes

(Ready in about 15 minutes | Servings 4)

Ingredients

1 cup white rice

2 ¼ cups water

1/2 cup white sugar

1/4 cup honey

1/4 teaspoon grated nutmeg

1 cup evaporated milk

3 egg yolks

1/2 cup prunes, pitted and chopped

Whipped topping

Directions

Throw the rice and water into the pressure cooker; cook for 8 minutes under HIGH pressure.

Carefully open the cooker with the Natural release method. Throw in all remaining ingredients, except whipped topping.

Cook under heat until the mixture thickens. Spoon the rice pudding into individual bowls and serve topped with whipped topping.

Bread Pudding with Raisins and Pecans

(Ready in about 15 minutes | Servings 6)

Ingredients

2 tablespoons butter

4 cups Italian bread, cubed

3 eggs, beaten

2 cups almond milk

1 ¼ cups heavy cream

1/2 cup raisins, pitted and chopped

1/2 cup sugar

1/2 teaspoon cardamom powder

1 teaspoon cinnamon powder

A pinch of salt

1 teaspoon vanilla paste

1 cup pecans, chopped

Directions

Pour 2 cups of water into your cooker. Place the metal rack at the bottom.

Now, butter the casserole dish. Stir bread cubes into the casserole dish.

In a mixing bowl, combine the other ingredients. Pour the mixture over the bread cubes. Place two layers of foil over it.

Select "Steam" mode and set the timer for 15 minutes. Serve warm.

Chocolate Pudding with Walnut Crunch

(Ready in about 30 minutes | Servings 6)

Ingredients

2 tablespoons cocoa powder

4 cups rice milk

1 cup Arborio rice

1/2 teaspoon freshly grated nutmeg

1/2 cup brown sugar

1/2 teaspoon hazelnut extract

1 teaspoon vanilla extract

2 ounces bittersweet chocolate, chopped

1/2 cup walnuts, toasted and coarsely chopped

2 tablespoons caster sugar

1 tablespoon egg white, lightly beaten

Directions

In the inner pot, place cocoa powder, milk, Arborio rice, nutmeg, sugar, hazelnut, and vanilla.

Next, select "Manual" mode and 12-minute cook time. Carefully remove the lid and immediately fold in the bittersweet chocolate.

To make the Hazelnut crunch, preheat the oven to 300 degrees F. Toss together walnuts, sugar, and egg white. Spread the mixture on a cookie sheet.

Bake your crunch for about 15 minutes; make sure to stir occasionally. Allow your crunch to cool fully. Serve your pudding topped with walnuts crunch. Bon appétit!

Chocolate Wine Poached Pears

(Ready in about 15 minutes | Servings 4)

Ingredients

1 cup of dry red wine

2 whole cloves

1 cinnamon stick

1 vanilla bean, split lengthwise

4 pears, cored

4 tablespoons semi-sweet chocolate chips, melted

Directions

Place red wine, cloves, cinnamon stick, and vanilla bean in your cooker; stir to combine.

Add the pears to your cooker making sure they are not touching each other. Cook under HIGH pressure for 6 minutes.

Carefully open the lid and discard the pears. Spoon the wine sauce over each pear. Drizzle melted chocolate over each pear. Enjoy!

Berry and Honey Pudding

(Ready in about 20 minutes | Servings 6)

Ingredients

3 cups whole milk

1 cup water

1 ¾ cups Arborio rice

1 teaspoon orange rind, grated

1/2 cup brown sugar

2 tablespoons honey

1 cup mixed berries

Directions

Simply throw all ingredients, except the honey and mixed berries, into your cooker.

Choose "Manual" mode; adjust the machine's timer to 12 minutes. Use the Natural pressure release and open the cooker.

Divide the pudding among six serving bowls. Drizzle with honey and top with berries. Bon appétit!

Pressure Cooked Apple and Apricot Compote

(Ready in about 10 minutes | Servings 8)

Ingredients

1 pound Golden Delicious apples, cored and diced

6 dried prunes, halved

2 tablespoons Sherry

1/2 cup caster sugar

3-4 whole cloves

1 cinnamon stick

1 vanilla bean, split in half

Directions

Simply throw all ingredients into a steel bowl. Gently stir to coat.

Set a metal rack in the bottom of the electric pressure cooker. Lower the steel bowl onto the rack.

Choose "Steam" setting and cook for 5 minutes under HIGH pressure; use the steam release.

Serve at room temperature sprinkled with chopped nuts of choice. Bon appétit!

Winter Berry Compote

(Ready in about 10 minutes | Servings 8)

Ingredients

1 cup black currants

1 cup strawberries

1 cup blackberries

4 cups water

1/2 cup sugar

1/2 teaspoon cardamom pods

1 teaspoon cinnamon stick

1 tablespoon anise star

1 vanilla pod

Directions

Simply throw all ingredients into an ovenproof dish.

Lay the trivet on the bottom of your cooker. Lower the ovenproof dish onto the trivet. Choose "Steam" function; then, adjust 5-minute cook time using the [+-] button.

Serve at room temperature with a scoop of whipped cream. Bon appétit!

Ginger Rice Pudding with Walnuts

(Ready in about 20 minutes | Servings 6)

Ingredients

1 cup water

3 cups whole milk

1 ¾ cups Arborio rice

1/4 teaspoon ground cinnamon

1/2 teaspoon pure vanilla essence

1 (1/2-inch) piece fresh ginger, peeled and grated

2 large-sized egg yolks, beaten

1/2 cup brown sugar

2 tablespoons agave nectar

1 cup walnuts, chopped medium coarse

Directions

Add all ingredients, except the agave nectar and walnuts, to the inner pot.

Now, select "Manual" mode; adjust the machine's timer for 12 minutes. Use the Natural pressure release and carefully open the cooker according to the manufacturer's instructions.

Divide the pudding among six individual bowls. Top with agave nectar and walnuts. Bon appétit!

Winter Fruit Compote with Ginger Syrup

(Ready in about 10 minutes | Servings 8)

Ingredients

4 cups water

6 dried prunes, pitted and halved

6 dried apricots, halved

2 cups dried raisins

1 vanilla pod

3-4 whole cloves

1/2 cup caster sugar

1 tablespoon candied ginger, sliced

Directions

Add all items to an ovenproof dish. Lay the metal trivet on the bottom of an electric pressure cooker. Lay the ovenproof dish on the trivet.

Now, choose "Steam" function; set the machine's timer for 5 minutes. Use the Natural pressure release and carefully open the lid. Serve warm.

Easy Macadamia Cheesecake

(Ready in about 35 minutes + chilling time | Servings 10)

Ingredients

1 ¼ cups digestive biscuits, crumbled

5 tablespoons coconut butter, at room temperature

1 pound cream cheese

1/3 cup caster sugar

3/4 cup macadamias, finely chopped

2 eggs, room temperature

1/4 cup sour cream

2 tablespoons flour

1/2 teaspoon grated ginger

1/2 teaspoon coconut extract

1/2 teaspoon vanilla extract

Directions

In a bowl, beat the biscuits with coconut butter. Butter the inside of a springform pan. Then, press the biscuit mixture into the bottom of the spring-form pan.

Pour 2 cups of water into your cooker. Lay a metal trivet on the bottom of the cooker.

In a food processor, mix the cream cheese together with caster sugar and macadamias. Fold in the eggs, one at a time.

Add the remaining items. Puree until everything is well combined.

Spoon the batter into the springform pan. Cook under HIGH pressure for 25 minutes. Serve well chilled.

Yummy Chocolate-Orange Cup Custard

(Ready in about 15 minutes | Servings 6)

Ingredients

2 cups whole milk

4 ounces bittersweet chocolate, chopped

A few strips of orange rind

2 whole eggs, beaten

1/3 cup granulated sugar

1/2 teaspoon ground anise star

1/2 teaspoon ground cloves

3/4 teaspoon vanilla essence

2 cups water

Directions

Scald the milk in a small-sized saucepan. Allow it to cool slightly and add the chocolate and orange rind; whisk thoroughly.

In a measuring cup, whisk the eggs with sugar; now, add the milk mixture in a thin stream, whisking constantly.

Throw in the anise, cloves, and vanilla essence. Pour the mixture into six individual custard cups; cover each cup with aluminum foil.

Place a rack in your pressure cooker. Add the water. Lower 3 custard cups onto the rack. Place another rack on top of the cups; top with another 3 cups.

Close and lock the lid. Cook for 8 minutes under HIGH pressure. Use the Natural pressure release and open the lid. Serve with a dollop of whipped cream and enjoy!

Fig and Almond Pudding

(Ready in about 15 minutes | Servings 4)

Ingredients

1 cup jasmine rice

2 ¼ cups water

1/2 cup granulated sugar

1/4 cup honey

1/4 teaspoon nutmeg, preferably freshly grated

1/2 teaspoon pure vanilla extract

1/2 teaspoon pure almond extract

1 cup milk

3 egg yolks

1/2 cup dried figs, pitted and chopped

1/2 cup almonds, toasted and chopped

Whipped topping, to serve

Directions

Throw jasmine rice and water into the inner pot of your cooker; cook for 8 minutes under HIGH pressure.

Now, open the cooker using the Natural release method. Add all remaining ingredients, except the almonds and whipped topping.

Cook until the mixture thickens. Divide the pudding among individual bowls and serve topped with chopped almonds and whipped topping. Enjoy!

Lemon Cup Custard

(Ready in about 15 minutes | Servings 6)

Ingredients

2 cups whole milk

Freshly grated zest of 1 lemon

2 whole eggs, beaten

1/3 cup sugar

1/2 teaspoon ground anise star

1 teaspoon lemon oil

1/4 teaspoon vanilla extract

2 cups water

Directions

Scald the milk in a pan. Allow it to cool slightly and add the grated zest of the lemon; whisk thoroughly.

In a mixing dish, whisk the eggs with sugar; slowly and gradually pour in the milk mixture; whisk until thoroughly combined.

Add the anise star, lemon oil, vanilla extract. Pour the custard mixture into six (4–6-ounce capacity) custard cups; cover each cup with aluminum foil.

Place a rack in your cooker. Add the water. Lower 3 custard cups onto the rack. Place another rack on top of the cups; top with another 3 cups.

Close and lock the lid. Cook for 8 minutes under HIGH pressure. Use the Natural pressure release and open the lid according to the manufacturer's directions. Serve the custard with a sprinkle of crystallized ginger.

Cherry Carrot and Rice Pudding

(Ready in about 20 minutes | Servings 6)

Ingredients

1 cup medium-grain white rice

1 ½ cups carrots, grated

3 cups water

1/2 cup honey

1/2 teaspoon grated ginger

1/2 teaspoon ground cinnamon

1 tablespoon almond butter

1 cup dried cherries

Directions

Add all ingredients to the inner pot. Select "Rice" setting.

Afterward, perform the Natural pressure release and carefully open the cooker. Serve chilled and enjoy!

Mango Rice Pudding

(Ready in about 15 minutes | Servings 4)

Ingredients

1 cup medium-grain white rice

2 ¼ cups water

1/2 cup sugar

A pinc of salt

Finely grated zest of 1 lemon

1/2 teaspoon pure vanilla extract

1 cup milk

1/4 cup dried mango, diced

Whipped topping, to serve

Directions

Throw the rice and water into the inner pot; cook under HIGH pressure for 8 minutes.

Now, open the cooker using the Natural release method. Add all remaining ingredients, except for whipped topping.

Divide the pudding among 4 bowls and serve topped with whipped topping. Bon appétit!

Aromatic Fig and Papaya Compote

(Ready in about 12 minutes | Servings 6)

Ingredients

1/2 cup water

1/2 pound dried papaya

1/2 pound dried figs

1 cup cranberry juice

1/4 cup sugar

3-4 whole cloves

1 vanilla bean

Directions

Throw all ingredients into the inner pot of the Instant Pot.

Close and lock the lid; choose "Manual" setting. Cook for 9 minutes under HIGH pressure.

Afterward, perform the Normal release method to drop the pressure. Serve warm or at room temperature.

Poached Dried Pineapple with Yogurt

(Ready in about 10 minutes | Servings 6)

Ingredients

1 ½ pounds dried pineapple

1 cup pineapple juice

1/4 cup honey

3-4 whole cloves

1 teaspoon anise star

1 vanilla bean, split lengthwise

Plain yogurt, to serve

Directions

Simply add all ingredients, except yogurt, to the inner pot.

Lock the lid onto the pot, and choose the "Manual" button. Adjust the timer to 9 minutes.

Turn off the machine. Let the pressure return to normal naturally, about 10 minutes.

Unlock and open your cooker. Serve topped with plain yogurt.

Rich Chocolate Tapioca Pudding

(Ready in about 10 minutes | Servings 2)

Ingredients

1/3 cup small pearl tapioca, soaked and rinsed

1 cup whole milk

1 cup water

4 tablespoons cocoa powder

2 large egg yolks, slightly beaten

1/2 cup sugar

1 teaspoon orange zest, grated

1 teaspoon vanilla paste

Whipped cream, to serve

Directions

Add 1 cup of water to the inner pot; place the metal rack in the cooker.

Stir the tapioca into a heat-proof bowl. Add the milk, water, cocoa powder, egg yolks, sugar, orange zest, and vanilla paste. Put the heat-proof bowl into the cooker.

Secure the lid and select "Manual" function; cook for 8 minutes under HIGH pressure.

Afterward, allow the pudding to cool completely. Stir the cooled pudding; gently fold in the whipped cream; mix to combine. Bon appétit!

Harvest Fruit Compote

(Ready in about 10 minutes | Servings 6)

Ingredients

1/2 pound dried pear

1/2 pound dried apple

1/2 pound prunes

1 cup apple juice

1 teaspoon grated orange rind

1/4 cup honey

2 cinnamon sticks

3-4 whole cloves

1 vanilla bean, split lengthwise

Plain yogurt, to serve

Directions

Simply throw all ingredients into the inner pot of your Instant Pot.

Lock the lid onto the pot and select the "Manual" mode. Adjust the timer to 10 minutes.

Turn off the cooker and let the pressure return to normal naturally.

Unlock and open your cooker. Serve in individual bowls and enjoy!

Brown Rice Pudding with Dark Raisin

(Ready in about 15 minutes | Servings 6)

Ingredients

1 ¾ cups whole grain brown rice

3 cups whole milk

1 cup water

2 large egg yolks, beaten

1/2 cup brown sugar

2 tablespoons maple syrup

1/2 teaspoon allspice

1 cup dark raisin

Directions

Add all ingredients to the inner pot.

Now, select "Manual" mode; adjust the machine's timer for 15 minutes. Use the Natural pressure release; open the cooker.

Divide the pudding among 6 dessert bowls. Serve warm.

Picnic Perfect Fruit Crisp

(Ready in about 20 minutes | Servings 6)

Ingredients

2 pears, cored and diced

5-6 apricots, pitted and sliced

1 apple, cored and diced

1 tablespoon freshly squeezed lemon juice

1/4 cup sugar

1/2 cup old-fashioned oats

1/4 cup self-rising flour

1 teaspoon cinnamon powder

1/2 teaspoon pure vanilla essence

1/2 teaspoon freshly grated nutmeg

4 tablespoons butter

1 cup warm water

Directions

Drizzle fresh lemon juice over the fruit. In a mixing dish, combine the sugar, oats, flour, cinnamon, vanilla, nutmeg, and butter.

Arrange the fruit on the bottom of a baking dish. Spread prepared sugar/oat mixture over the fruits.

Pour the water into your Instant Pot. Place a metal rack on the bottom. Cover the baking dish with a piece of aluminum foil and lower it onto the rack.

Secure the lid; now, use "Beans" function and adjust the cooker's timer to 15 minutes. Afterward, remove the cooker's lid and serve.

Blueberry Oatmeal Dessert

(Ready in about 10 minutes | Servings 4)

Ingredients

2 cups blueberries

3 cups water

2 tablespoons agave syrup

1/2 teaspoon cardamom pods

1 cinnamon stick, split in half

1 teaspoon vanilla paste

1 ½ cups oatmeal, cooked

Directions

Throw blueberries into an ovenproof dish. Now, coat them with the water; let stand for 5 minutes.

Stir in the agave syrup, cardamom pods, cinnamon stick, and vanilla paste.

Lay the rack on the bottom of your cooker. Lower the dish onto the rack. Secure the lid. Select "Steam" mode and cook for 6 minutes.

Once cooking is done, use the Quick release. Serve over cooked oatmeal.

Winter Citrus Fruit Delight

(Ready in about 10 minutes | Servings 6)

Ingredients

3 mandarin oranges, peeled and sliced

2 tangerines, peeled and sliced

1 pink grapefruit, peeled and sliced

1 ½ cups sweet orange Muscat wine

2 ½ cups water

A few strips of orange curls

3 tablespoons agave nectar

1 (1-inch) piece of ginger, peeled and thinly sliced

3-4 whole cloves

1 anise star pod

1 vanilla pod

Directions

Throw your ingredients into an ovenproof dish.

Place the trivet in your Instant Pot. Lay the ovenproof dish on the trivet. Choose "Steam" function and cook for 5 minutes. Afterward, use the steam release.

Discard the cloves, star anise, and vanilla pod from compote. Serve warm over ice cream.

Healthy Cardamom Rice Pudding

(Ready in about 20 minutes | Servings 6)

Ingredients

1 ¾ cups whole grain brown rice

4 cups unsweetened vanilla almond milk

2 large egg yolks, beaten

1/4 coconut palm sugar

2 tablespoons honey

1/2 teaspoon ground cardamom

1 vanilla bean, split lengthwise

Directions

Throw all ingredients into the inner pot of your pressure cooker.

Next, select "Manual" mode; lock the lid onto the pot and adjust the timer to 15 minutes. After that, let its pressure return to normal naturally, approximately 10 minutes; open the cooker.

Serve in individual bowls and enjoy!

Dried Cherry Dessert

(Ready in about 10 minutes | Servings 4)

Ingredients

2 cups dried tart cherries

3 cups water

1/2 teaspoon crystallized ginger

2 tablespoons honey

1/2 teaspoon ground cloves

1 cinnamon stick, split in half

1 teaspoon vanilla paste

2 tablespoons buttermilk

1 ½ cups oatmeal, cooked

Directions

Add the cherries to an ovenproof baking dish. Pour in the water; let stand approximately 10 minutes.

Stir in the other ingredients, except for oatmeal.

Place the rack inside. Lower the baking dish onto the rack. Secure the cooker's lid; press the "Steam" key; cook for 6 minutes.

Once cooking is done, use the Natural pressure release. Serve over cooked oatmeal and enjoy!

Bing Cherry and Apple Compote

(Ready in about 10 minutes | Servings 8)

Ingredients

1/2 pound bing cherries, pitted

1/2 pound apples, cored and diced

1 tablespoon brandy

3 tablespoons orange juice

1/2 cup sugar

A pinch of salt

1 cinnamon stick

1 vanilla bean, split lengthwise

1 tablespoon Chia seeds

Directions

Place all ingredients, except Chia seeds, in a steel bowl. Set a metal rack in your cooker. Lower the bowl onto the rack.

Choose "Steam" mode and cook under HIGH pressure for 6 minutes. Then, use the steam release. Serve topped with Chia seeds and cream. Enjoy!

Cardamom Tapioca Pudding with Mango

(Ready in about 10 minutes | Servings 4)

Ingredients

1 cup water

1 cup small pearl tapioca, soaked and rinsed

4 cups milk

1/4 cup honey

3/4 teaspoon vanilla extract

A pinch of fine salt

1 teaspoon ground cardamom

Mango slices, to serve

Directions

Pour the water into your cooker; lower the metal rack onto the bottom.

Then, add all ingredients, except mango, to a heat-proof bowl. Lower the heat-proof bowl onto the metal rack.

Lock the lid onto the pot; choose the "Manual" button; cook under HIGH pressure for 8 minutes.

Allow tapioca pudding to cool slightly. Serve topped with mango and enjoy!

Mom's White Chocolate Pudding

(Ready in about 15 minutes | Servings 6)

Ingredients

2 cups heavy cream

6 ounces white chocolate, chopped

4 large egg yolks, beaten, at room temperature

2 tablespoons sugar

1 vanilla bean, seeds scraped out

1/2 teaspoon rum extract

Grated semisweet chocolate, to decorate

Directions

Melt and warm the cream in a small-sized saucepan over low heat.

Pour the warm cream over the white chocolate in a mixing bowl; whisk until everything is completely melted. Fold in the egg yolks and whisk to combine.

Now, add the sugar, vanilla, and rum extract. Pour the mixture into 6 heat-safe ramekins; cover each portion tightly with foil.

Set the pressure cooker rack in an electric pressure cooker; pour in 2 cups of water. Lower the ramekins onto the rack. Lock the lid onto the pot.

Set your Instant Pot to cook at HIGH pressure for 15 minutes. Afterward, reduce the pressure. Unlock and open your Instant Pot. Serve chilled, topped with grated chocolate. Bon appétit!

White Rice Pudding with Cherries Jubilee

(Ready in about 15 minutes | Servings 6)

Ingredients

1 ¾ cups white medium grain rice

4 cups unsweetened vanilla almond milk

2 egg yolks, beaten

1/2 caster sugar

2 tablespoons honey

1/2 teaspoon ground cloves

1 vanilla bean, split lengthwise

Cherries jubilee, to serve

Directions

Throw all ingredients, except for cherries jubilee, into the inner pot.

Choose "Manual" mode; lock the lid onto the pot and adjust the timer to 15 minutes. Next, release the pressure with the Natural release method; open the cooker.

Serve in large goblets topped with cherries jubilee.

Sunday Espresso Pudding

(Ready in about 15 minutes | Servings 6)

Ingredients

1 cup half-and-half

1 cup heavy cream

1 tablespoon instant espresso powder

1/2 cup caster sugar

1 large egg

4 large egg yolks, at room temperature and whisked

1/4 teaspoon vanilla paste

1/2 teaspoon ground anise star

Directions

Whisk the half-and-half, heavy cream, and espresso powder in a large-sized bowl.

Whisk in the sugar, egg, and egg yolks until smooth and uniform; add vanilla and anise star and stir to combine. Scrape the mixture into six heat-safe ramekins; cover each portion with foil.

Set the pressure cooker rack in your Instant Pot; pour in 2 cups water. Stack the ramekins on the rack. Lock the lid onto the pot.

Set the machine to cook under HIGH pressure for 15 minutes. Reduce the pressure. Turn off the machine and let its pressure return to normal naturally.

Unlock and open the pot. Serve chilled.

Butterscotch Bread Pudding

(Ready in about 20 minutes | Servings 6)

Ingredients

2 cups water

2 tablespoons butter, melted

1 loaf day-old bread, torn into small pieces

1 cup butterscotch chips

2 cups milk

1 ¼ cups heavy cream

3 eggs, beaten

1/2 cup firmly packed light brown sugar

1/2 teaspoon ground cardamom

1 teaspoon cinnamon powder

A pinch of salt

1 teaspoon vanilla essence

3/4 cup pecans, chopped

Directions

Pour the water into the cooker. Lay the pressure cooker rack at the bottom.

Then, brush the casserole dish with the melted butter. Throw bread pieces into the casserole dish.

In a bowl, combine the remaining ingredients, except pecans; mix until well combined. Pour the mixture over the pieces of bread. Scatter chopped pecans over the top. After that, top everything with two pieces of aluminum foil.

Choose "Steam" setting and set the machine's timer for 15 minutes. Serve at room temperature.

Peppermint Candy Pudding

(Ready in about 15 minutes | Servings 6)

Ingredients

1 cup half-and-half

1 cup heavy cream

1 teaspoon nutmeg, preferably grated

1/2 cup sugar

1 large egg

4 large egg yolks, at room temperature and whisked

1/4 teaspoon vanilla paste

1/2 teaspoon peppermint extract

2 candy canes, crushed

Directions

Beat the half-and-half, heavy cream, and nutmeg in a mixing bowl.

Throw in the sugar, egg, and egg yolks, vanilla, and peppermint extract. Spoon the mixture into six heat-safe ramekins.

Set the metal rack in your cooker; pour in 2 cups water. Stack the ramekins on the metal rack. Lock the lid onto the pot.

Set the machine to cook under HIGH pressure for 15 minutes. Then, turn off the machine and let its pressure return to normal naturally.

Unlock and open the pot. Sprinkle the crushed candy over the pudding and serve chilled.

Orange and Mango Tapioca Pudding

(Ready in about 15 minutes | Servings 6)

Ingredients

1 cup small pearl tapioca

1 cup water

3 cups non-dairy milk

1/3 cup caster sugar

A pinch of salt

1/2 teaspoon vanilla extract

1/4 teaspoon orange extract

1 orange, peeled and chopped

2 ripe mangos, chopped

Directions

Add the tapioca, water, milk, sugar, and salt to the Instant Pot.

Push "Manual" button and use [+ -] function to select 12-minute cook time. Once the cooking is complete, use the Natural pressure release.

Add vanilla and orange extract; stir to combine well.

Divide the pudding among six dessert bowls; serve topped with orange and mango.

Croissant Pudding with Apricots

(Ready in about 25 minutes | Servings 6)

Ingredients

2 cups water

2 tablespoons butter

8 croissants, torn into pieces

3 eggs, beaten

1 ½ cups milk

1 ¼ cups heavy cream

1/2 cup apple juice

1/2 cup dried apricots, pitted and chopped

1/2 cup sugar

1 teaspoon cinnamon powder

1/2 teaspoon ground cardamom

A pinch of kosher salt

1/4 teaspoon vanilla extract

Whipped cream, for serving

Directions

Prepare your Instant Pot by adding the water; insert the steam rack.

Then, take a casserole dish that will fit in the inner pot. Then, butter the casserole dish; stir in the croissants.

In a measuring cup, whisk the remaining ingredients, except for whipped cream; whisk thoroughly. Pour the mixture over the croissants. Cover with aluminum foil.

Select "Steam" function and cook for 15 minutes. Let it cool slightly before serving. Serve with whipped cream and enjoy.

Fig and Date Rice Pudding

(Ready in about 20 minutes | Servings 6)

Ingredients

3 cups water

1 ½ cups carrots, grated

1 cup medium grain rice

1/2 cup caster sugar

1/4 teaspoon ground cloves

1/2 teaspoon ground cinnamon

1 tablespoon butter, softened

1/2 cup figs, chopped

1/2 cup dates, pitted and sliced

Directions

Throw everything into the inner pot of your Instant Pot. Choose "Rice" mode.

Perform the Natural pressure release. Serve at room temperature. Bon appétit!

Nana's Berry Custard Pie

(Ready in about 40 minutes + chilling time | Servings 6)

Ingredients

4 cups milk

1/3 cup sugar

3 eggs

3 egg yolks

1/2 teaspoon pure vanilla extract

1/2 cup blueberries

1/2 cup raspberries

2 cups water

Directions

In a saucepan, cook milk and sugar over medium-high heat; bring it to a boil and set aside.

In a mixing dish, beat the eggs with egg yolks. Stir 2 tablespoons of the warm milk mixture into the eggs; add the vanilla and mix to combine.

Reduce the heat; simmer an additional 4 minutes, stirring frequently.

Then, brush a baking dish with a nonstick cooking spray; spoon the mixture into the baking dish. Nestle blueberries and raspberries in the batter; press with a wide spatula. Cover with foil.

Add the water to your cooker; set the trivet and lay the soufflé dish on the trivet. Cook another 30 minutes. Refrigerate and serve well-chilled.

Rice Custard with Zante Currants

(Ready in about 40 minutes | Servings 6)

Ingredients

2 2/3 cups whole milk

1 cup half-and-half

2 large eggs, at room temperature

2 large egg yolks, at room temperature

2 cups long-grain white rice, cooked

1/3 cup caster sugar

1/3 cup Zante currants

2 tablespoons dark rum

1 tablespoon vanilla extract

1 teaspoon ground cardamom

A pinch of kosher salt

Directions

Butter the inside of a high-sided soufflé dish. Set a rack inside an electric pressure cooker; pour in 2 cups water.

In a mixing bowl, whisk the milk, half-and-half, eggs, and egg yolks until smooth and uniform. Whisk in the rice, sugar, currants, rum, vanilla, cardamom, and salt; pour the mixture into the buttered soufflé dish. Cover with aluminum foil.

Make an aluminum foil sling. Lock on the lid. Set the machine to cook under HIGH pressure for 30 minutes. Reduce the pressure.

Turn off the machine and release the pressure for 10 minutes. Unlock and open the cooker. Enjoy!

Rice Pudding with Dried Cherries and Pistachios

(Ready in about 20 minutes | Servings 6)

Ingredients

1 cup Arborio rice

1 ½ cups carrots, grated

1 tablespoon rose water

3 cups water

1/2 cup sugar

1 teaspoon lemon zest

1/2 teaspoon ground cinnamon

2 tablespoons butter, softened

1/2 cup dried cherries

1/2 cup pistachios, chopped

Directions

Throw everything, except for pistachios, into the inner pot. Choose "Rice" setting.

Afterward, perform the Natural pressure release. Serve at room temperature, topped with chopped pistachios.

Melt-in-your-Mouth Raisin Croissant Pudding

(Ready in about 25 minutes | Servings 6)

Ingredients

2 cups water

Nonstick cooking spray

8 croissants, torn into pieces

3 eggs, beaten

4 cups half-and-half

1/2 cup sugar

1/2 cup pineapple juice

3/4 cup raisins

1 teaspoon cinnamon powder

A pinch of kosher salt

1/2 teaspoon vanilla extract

Directions

Prepare your cooker by adding the water and the steam rack.

Treat a casserole dish with a nonstick cooking spray. Add the croissants.

In a mixing bowl, whisk the other ingredients; whisk until thoroughly combined. Pour the mixture over the croissants and cover with foil.

Choose "Steam" setting and cook for 15 minutes. Once the cooking is completed, use a natural release. Turn your cooker off and carefully remove the lid. Bon appétit!

Traditional Cherry Clafouti

(Ready in about 20 minutes | Servings 6)

Ingredients

2 cups sour cherries, pitted

3/4 cup sour cream

4 large egg yolks

1/3 cup honey

1/4 cup whole milk

1/2 teaspoon ground cinnamon

1/4 teaspoon ground cardamom

1 tablespoon vanilla extract

A pinch of kosher salt

1/2 cup all-purpose flour

Directions

Butter the inside of a soufflé dish. Set the rack inside your pressure cooker; pour in 2 cups water.

Arrange the cherries in the bottom of the soufflé dish. In a large-sized bowl, whisk the sour cream, egg yolks, honey, and milk.

Now, add the cinnamon, cardamom, vanilla, and salt and continue whisking until smooth and creamy. Stir in the flour and mix until it is completely dissolved. Spread the batter over the cherries.

Then, create an aluminum foil sling and lock the lid onto the pot. Set the machine to cook under HIGH pressure for 18 minutes. Reduce the cooker's pressure.

Turn off the machine. Allow the pressure to come down naturally. Unlock and open the pot. Let it cool slightly before serving. Enjoy!

Old-Fashioned Stuffed Apples

(Ready in about 10 minutes | Servings 4)

Ingredients

2 cups water

1/3 cup rolled oats

1/3 cup sugar

2 tablespoons walnuts, chopped

1/4 teaspoon freshly grated nutmeg

1/2 teaspoon ground cloves

8 apples, cored, scoop out the seeds

2 tablespoons butter, melted

Directions

Prepare your cooker by adding the water and a pressure cooker rack.

Then, combine the oats, sugar, walnuts, nutmeg, and cloves. Stuff the apples; arrange them on the rack; dot with melted butter.

Select the "Manual" setting and 4-minute cook time. Afterward, use the Quick pressure release. Serve right away.

Carrot and Rice Pudding with Dates

(Ready in about 15 minutes | Servings 4)

Ingredients

3 cups water

1/2 pound carrots, grated

1 cup basmati rice

A pinch of kosher salt

1/4 teaspoon cinnamon, ground

1/2 teaspoon ground cloves

1 tablespoon ghee, softened

1/2 cup dates, pitted and chopped

Directions

Add all ingredients to your cooker. Turn the cooker on "Rice" mode.

Lastly, perform the Natural pressure release. Serve warm and enjoy!

Black Cherry Almond Pudding

(Ready in about 15 minutes | Servings 8)

Ingredients

2 cups jasmine rice

2 cups milk

1/2 cup caster sugar

1/2 teaspoon pure vanilla essence

1/4 teaspoon pure almond extract

1/2 teaspoon anise seeds

1 teaspoon cinnamon powder

1 cup black cherries

2 tablespoons almonds, slivered

Directions

Put the rice, milk, sugar, vanilla, almond extract, anise seeds, and cinnamon powder into your Instant Pot. Choose "Manual" setting and 12-minute cook time.

Serve topped with black cherries and slivered almonds. Bon appétit!

Sweet Orange Risotto

(Ready in about 10 minutes | Servings 4)

Ingredients

2 ½ cups milk

3/4 cup Sunrice Arborio rice

1/3 cup sugar

1/2 cup heavy cream

1 teaspoon orange extract

1 teaspoon vanilla extract

1 cup fresh orange segments

Candied orange peel, for garnish

Directions

Add the milk, rice, and sugar to the inner pot. Lock the lid onto the cooker. Then, cook for 7 minutes under HIGH pressure.

Stir in the sugar, heavy cream, orange extract, vanilla extract, and orange. Stir until everything is well incorporated.

Serve garnished with candied orange peel. Enjoy!

French-Style Pear Clafouti

(Ready in about 20 minutes | Servings 6)

Ingredients

Nonstick cooking spray

2 cups ripe Bartlett pears, cored and diced

1/4 cup whole milk

3/4 cup sour cream

1/3 cup sugar

4 large-sized egg yolks

1/2 teaspoon lemon zest, grated

1/4 teaspoon ground allspice

1/4 teaspoon ground cardamom

1 tablespoon vanilla extract

A pinch of kosher salt

1/2 cup all-purpose flour

Directions

Treat the inside of a soufflé dish with a nonstick cooking spray. Set the rack inside your pressure cooker; pour in 2 cups water.

Arrange the pears in the bottom of the soufflé dish. In a mixing dish, whisk the milk, sour cream, sugar, and egg yolks.

Now, add the lemon zest, allspice, cardamom, vanilla extract, and salt; continue whisking until smooth and uniform. Throw in the flour; stir until everything's completely dissolved. Spread the batter over the pears.

Then, create an aluminum foil sling; lock the lid onto the pot. Cook under HIGH pressure for 18 minutes. Reduce the cooker's pressure.

Turn off the machine and allow the pressure to come down naturally. Unlock and open the pot. Bon appétit!

Cinnamon Bread Pudding with Currants and Almonds

(Ready in about 20 minutes | Servings 6)

Ingredients

2 cups water

Nonstick cooking spray

4 cups stale cinnamon bread, torn into pieces

3 eggs, whisked

2 cups whole milk

1 tablespoon rum

1/2 teaspoon nutmeg, preferably freshly grated

1/2 teaspoon ground cloves

1/2 teaspoon pure almond extract

1/2 teaspoon pure vanilla extract

1/2 cup dried Zante currants, chopped

2 tablespoons almonds, chopped

Directions

Prepare your cooking pot by adding the water. Place the rack at the bottom of the pot.

Grease a casserole dish with a nonstick cooking spray. Throw in cinnamon bread pieces.

In a mixing bowl, combine the eggs, milk, rum, nutmeg, cloves, almond extract, and vanilla extract. Pour the egg/milk mixture over bread cubes in the casserole dish.

Scatter Zante currants and almonds over the top. Cover the dish with wax paper.

Select "Steam" mode and adjust the timer to 15 minutes. Serve warm. Bon appétit!

Quick and Easy Crème Brule

(Ready in about 15 minutes | Servings 4)

Ingredients

3/4 cup sugar

2 cups warm 35% heavy cream

1 teaspoon vanilla paste

4 egg yolks, large

A pinch of salt

1 cup water

3 teaspoons granulated sugar

Directions

Beat the sugar, heavy cream, vanilla paste, egg yolks, and salt in a mixing bowl. Then, pour the mixture into 4 ramekins and wrap them with foil.

Add the water and pressure cooker rack to the inner pot. Lower the ramekins onto the rack.

Choose "Manual" setting and 4-minute cook time. Transfer your Crème Brule to the refrigerator and let it stand at least 3 hours.

Top with granulated sugar; now, place the ramekins under the broiler in order to caramelize the sugar. Bon appétit!

Winter Red Wine Poached Plums

(Ready in about 15 minutes | Servings 4)

Ingredients

1 pound plums, pitted and halved

1 cup red wine

1 cinnamon stick

1 vanilla bean

4-5 whole cloves

1/4 cup agave nectar

Directions

Place the plums on the bottom of the cooking pot. In a mixing bowl, combine the rest of the above ingredients; whisk thoroughly. Pour the wine mixture over the plums.

Cover and choose "Manual" setting. Cook for 10 minutes under HIGH pressure. Lastly, use the Normal release method. Serve warm and enjoy!

Spiced Poached Pears

(Ready in about 15 minutes | Servings 4)

Ingredients

4 pears, pitted and halved

1 navel orange, quartered

1 cup red wine

1 lemon, thinly sliced

1 cinnamon stick

1 vanilla bean, split, seeded

4-5 whole cloves

1/4 cup honey

Directions

Place the pears on the bottom of the cooking pot.

Add the rest of the ingredients and toss to coat well.

Lock the lid onto the cooking pot and choose "Manual" mode. Cook for 10 minutes under HIGH pressure. Afterward, use the Normal release method. Bon appétit!

Date and Walnut Sweet Risotto

(Ready in about 25 minutes | Servings 6)

Ingredients

1 ¾ cups Sunrice Arborio rice

4 dried dates, pitted and chopped

3 cups rice milk

1 cup water

1/4 cup agave nectar

Fresh juice of 1 orange

1/2 cup walnuts, chopped

Directions

Throw all ingredients into the cooking pot. Give it a good stir.

Lock the lid onto the cooking pot. Select the "Manual" setting; cook under HIGH pressure for 12 minutes.

Once cooking is done, use a quick release. Serve warm or at room temperature.

Father's Day Oatmeal Dessert

(Ready in about 10 minutes | Servings 4)

Ingredients

2 peaches, pitted and diced

4 plums, pitted and halved

1 cup steel-cut oats

1 cup coconut milk

1/4 teaspoon ground cinnamon

1/2 teaspoon ground cloves

1/2 teaspoon pure vanilla extract

2 cups water

1 cup brown sugar

Directions

Add all ingredients to the inner pot. Then, choose "Manual/Adjust" setting.

Cook for 5 minutes under HIGH pressure. Let the pressure come back to normal naturally and carefully open the cooker's lid. Serve well-chilled. Bon appétit!

Winter Cashew Pudding

(Ready in about 20 minutes | Servings 6)

Ingredients

2 cups water

4 cups stale French bread, cubed

1 tablespoon coconut butter, melted

2 cups whole milk

3 eggs plus, beaten

2 egg yolks, beaten

1/2 cup prunes, coarsely chopped

1/2 cup Sultanas, coarsely chopped

1/2 teaspoon cinnamon powder

A pinch of salt

1/2 teaspoon pure almond extract

1 teaspoon pure vanilla extract

Chopped cashews, for garnish

Directions

Prepare your cooker by adding the water and steam rack. Arrange the bread cubes in the bottom of a well-greased casserole dish.

In a mixing dish, combine all of the above ingredients, except for cashews; mix to combine. Spoon the mixture over the bread cubes; cover with an aluminum foil.

Lock the lid onto the cooker. Choose "Steam" function on your Instant Pot; adjust the time to 15 minutes.

Once cooking is done, unlock and open the pot. Carefully remove the lid and serve garnished with chopped cashews.

Easiest Plum Dumplings Ever

(Ready in about 20 minutes | Servings 8)

Ingredients

1 (8-ounce) can crescent rolls

8 plums

4 tablespoons butter

1/2 cup sugar

1/4 teaspoon grated nutmeg

1/2 teaspoon ground anise star

1/2 teaspoon ground cinnamon

1/4 teaspoon vanilla extract

3/4 cup apple cider

Directions

Preheat an electric pressure cooker by selecting "Sauté" function.

Next, roll the dough out flat; roll each plum in 1 crescent roll. Add the butter, sugar, nutmeg, anise, cinnamon, and vanilla.

Place the dumplings on the bottom of your pressure cooker. Drizzle the apple cider over all. Now, secure the lid.

Select "Manual" function; cook under HIGH pressure for 10 minutes. Once cooking is done, use the Natural pressure release. Serve at room temperature and enjoy!

Poached Fruits with Vanilla Frozen Yogurt

(Ready in about 15 minutes | Servings 4)

Ingredients

6 dried figs

8 prunes

5 allspice berries

3 pieces candied ginger

1 cup port

1 cinnamon stick

1 vanilla bean, split, seeded

4-5 whole cloves

1 (3 x 1-inch) orange rind strips

1/4 cup honey

Directions

Place the figs, prunes, allspice berries, candied ginger on the bottom of your cooker.

Add the remaining ingredients; gently stir to coat.

Lock the lid onto the cooker and choose "Manual" setting. Cook for 10 minutes under HIGH pressure. Lastly, use the Normal release method. Bon appétit!

Holiday Eggnog Bread Pudding

(Ready in about 20 minutes | Servings 6)

Ingredients

2 cups water

Nonstick cooking spray

4 cups stale cardamom bread, torn into pieces

3 eggs, whisked

1 cup whole milk

2 cups eggnog

1/2 teaspoon nutmeg, preferably freshly grated

1/2 teaspoon ground cloves

1/2 teaspoon pure vanilla extract

Warm maple syrup, for serving

Directions

Prepare your cooker by adding the water and rack to the bottom of the pot.

Generously grease a casserole dish with a nonstick cooking spray. Throw in bread pieces.

In a mixing bowl, combine all remaining ingredients, except maple syrup. Pour the egg/milk mixture over bread cubes.

Cover the dish with wax paper or foil.

Select "Steam" setting and cook for 15 minutes under HIGH pressure. Serve topped with warm maple syrup. Bon appétit!

Date and Hazelnut Cake

(Ready in about 1 hour | Servings 10)

Ingredients

2 sticks butter

1 cup caster sugar

1 cup self-rising flour

1/2 teaspoon baking soda

1 teaspoon baking powder

3 eggs, beaten

2 egg yolks, beaten

1 teaspoon orange rind, grated

1/2 cup dried dates, pitted and chopped

1/2 cup hazelnuts, chopped

1/2 teaspoon vanilla extract

1/2 teaspoon ground cinnamon

1/2 teaspoon ground cloves

1 tablespoon rum

Whisked double cream, for garnish

Directions

In a casserole dish, cream the butter with sugar. Add the flour, baking soda, and baking powder. Fold in the eggs and egg yolks.

Throw in the grated orange rind, dates, hazelnuts, and vanilla extract. Add the cinnamon, cloves, and rum; stir until everything is well combined.

Add 2 cups of water to your cooker. Place a pressure cooker rack inside; lower the casserole dish onto the rack.

Select "Manual" mode, HIGH pressure, and 50-minute cook time. Decorate with the double cream. Bon appétit!

Banana Bread Pudding

(Ready in about 20 minutes | Servings 6)

Ingredients

2 cups water

Nonstick cooking spray

4 cups stale sweet bread, torn into pieces

3 eggs, whisked

1 cup whole milk

2 tablespoons bourbon

1/2 cup sugar

2 bananas, sliced

1/2 teaspoon ground cloves

1/2 teaspoon pure vanilla extract

Directions

Add the water and rack to the bottom of the pot.

Generously grease a baking dish with a nonstick cooking spray. Stir the bread pieces into the baking dish.

In a mixing dish, combine all remaining ingredients. Pour the liquid mixture over bread cubes. Cover the dish with wax paper.

Select "Steam" function and cook under HIGH pressure for 15 minutes. Bon appétit!

Coconut and Banana Rice Pudding

(Ready in about 20 minutes | Servings 6)

Ingredients

1 ¾ cups Arborio rice

1 cup water

2 ripe bananas, mashed

3 cups coconut milk

Zest and juice of 1 orange

1/2 teaspoon ground cardamom

1/2 teaspoon vanilla extract

1/4 cup candied ginger, diced

1/2 cup shredded coconut

Directions

Add all ingredients, except the coconut, to your cooker.

Select "Manual" setting and adjust the time to 12 minutes. Lock the lid onto the pot.

Reduce the pressure and carefully remove the lid; serve well-chilled, topped with shredded coconut. Enjoy!

Cranberry Eggnog Bread Pudding

(Ready in about 20 minutes | Servings 6)

Ingredients

2 cups water

Nonstick cooking spray

1 pound panettone, crust removed, cut into cubes

3 eggs, whisked

3 tablespoons amaretto liqueur

1 cup whole milk

2 cups eggnog

1/2 teaspoon nutmeg, preferably freshly grated

1/2 teaspoon ground cloves

1/2 teaspoon pure vanilla extract

1 cup dried cranberries

Whipped cream, for serving

Directions

Prepare your cooker by adding the water and rack to the bottom of the pot.

Then, take a nonstick cooking spray and grease a casserole dish. Throw in bread cubes.

In a mixing dish, combine all remaining ingredients, except whipped cream. Pour the egg/amaretto mixture over bread cubes in the casserole dish. Cover the dish with foil.

Select "Steam" function and cook under HIGH pressure for 15 minutes. Serve topped with whipped cream. Bon appétit!

Delicate Lemon Pudding Cake

(Ready in about 22 minutes | Servings 6)

Ingredients

1 pound Cottage cheese

4 large eggs, at room temperature

1/2 cup caster sugar

2 tablespoons fresh lemon juice

2 teaspoons finely grated lemon zest

1 teaspoon pure vanilla extract

1/4 cup all-purpose flour

Directions

Set the rack inside an electric pressure cooker; pour in 2 cups of water. Butter the inside of a baking pan.

Place the cheese, eggs, sugar, lemon juice, lemon zest, and vanilla extract in a food processor. Cover and process until uniform and smooth. Add the flour and process until smooth.

Spoon the batter into the prepared baking pan; cover with foil. Make an aluminum foil sling. Use the sling to lower the baking pan onto the rack.

Lock the lid onto the cooker. Cook under HIGH pressure for 22 minutes. Let the pressure return to normal naturally, about 15 minutes. Unlock and open the pot. Enjoy!

Chocolate Dream Dessert

(Ready in about 20 minutes | Servings 6)

Ingredients

2 cups water

2 cups milk

1 ¾ cups Sunrice rice

1/2 cup walnuts, chopped

1/4 cup cocoa powder

1/4 cup sugar

1/4 teaspoon grated nutmeg

1/2 teaspoon ground cinnamon

2 cups ripe bananas, mashed

Directions

Put all ingredients into the inner pot; stir until everything is well combined.

Choose "Manual" setting and adjust the time to 12 minutes.

Dust with some extra granulated sugar if desired and serve. Bon appétit!

Plum Crisp with Ice Cream

(Ready in about 25 minutes | Servings 6)

Ingredients

1 teaspoon orange rind, grated

1/4 cup flour

1/2 cup old-fashioned oats

1/4 cup sugar

1 teaspoon ground cinnamon

1/2 teaspoon ground cloves

1/4 teaspoon grated nutmeg

A pinch of sea salt

4 tablespoons butter, softened

1 pound plums, cored, peeled and thinly sliced

1 cup warm water

Directions

In a mixing dish, combine the orange rind, flour, oats, sugar, cinnamon, cloves, nutmeg, salt, and butter. Next, layer the plums and crisp mixture in a baking dish, ending with the layer of crisp mixture. Cover dish with foil.

Pour 1 cup of water into the inner pot; add the rack to the cooker. Place the baking dish on the rack.

Secure the lid. Choose the "Beans" button; cook for 15 minutes.

Once pressure cooking is completed, use a natural release; carefully remove the lid. Serve with a dollop of vanilla ice cream if desired.

Coconut and Orange Dessert Risotto

(Ready in about 20 minutes | Servings 6)

Ingredients

2 cups coconut milk

2 cups water

1 ¾ cups Arborio rice

1/2 cup shredded coconut

1/4 cup candied ginger, diced

1/4 cup honey

1/4 teaspoon ground cloves

1/2 teaspoon ground anise seed

Navel orange segments, to serve

Directions

Place the ingredients in the inner pot; give it a good stir.

Choose "Manual" setting; cook for 11 minutes under HIGH pressure.

Serve in individual bowls topped with navel oranges. Bon appétit!

Sweet Pecan Zucchini Bread

(Ready in about 40 minutes | Servings 10)

Ingredients

1/2 cup applesauce

3 eggs

1/2 stick butter, at room temperature

1 ½ cups caster sugar

1 tablespoon orange juice

1 teaspoon vanilla extract

1 teaspoon almond extract

2 cups zucchini, peeled and grated

2 ½ cups all-purpose flour

1/2 teaspoon ground cloves

1/2 teaspoon cinnamon powder

1/2 teaspoon baking powder

1 teaspoon baking soda

1/2 cup pecans, chopped

1/2 cup chocolate chips

Directions

In a mixing dish, combine the applesauce, eggs, butter, sugar, and orange juice. Then, stir in the vanilla extract and almond extract. Throw in the grated zucchini; stir to combine.

In another mixing dish, combine the other ingredients. Stir in the egg mixture; stir to combine well.

Put a rack into the cooker; pour in 1 ½ cups water. Then, scrape the batter into a buttered baking dish that will fit your cooker. Place the baking dish on the metal rack.

Choose the "Manual" button and 25-minute cook time. Afterward, use the Natural pressure release. Dust with powdered sugar and serve.

Dark Chocolate and Hazelnut Desserts

(Ready in about 15 minutes | Servings 6)

Ingredients

1 ½ cups dark chocolate

1 stick butter, softened

3/4 cup caster sugar

1/2 teaspoon ground cloves

1/2 teaspoon vanilla extract

1 teaspoon hazelnut extract

1/2 teaspoon cardamom powder

1/4 cup white flour

3 whole eggs

Directions

Melt dark chocolate and butter in a microwave. Stir in the other ingredients and beat using an electric mixer.

Divide the batter among 6 ramekins. Secure the lid. Select "Manual" setting and cook for 6 minutes. Use the Quick release pressure.

Let your cakes cool on a wire rack before serving. Enjoy!

Chocolate Challah Bread Pudding

(Ready in about 35 minutes | Servings 6)

Ingredients

8 slices Challah, torn into bite-sized pieces

3 tablespoons butter, melted

2 cups milk

1 cup water

4 whole eggs

2 egg yolks

2 tablespoons bourbon

1/2 teaspoon vanilla extract

A pinch of kosher salt

1 tablespoon honey

1/4 cup caster sugar

1/4 teaspoon grated nutmeg

2 tablespoons walnuts, chopped

1 cup chocolate chips

Directions

First, add the pieces of Challah to a lightly buttered baking dish. Now, make the custard by mixing the other ingredients.

Pour the custard mixture over the bread in the baking dish. Cover with foil.

Add a pressure cooker rack and water to the Instant Pot. Secure the lid.

Select "Manual" setting; set the cooker's timer for 25 minutes. Afterward, do the Natural pressure release. Bon appétit!

Pumpkin and Sour Cream Pudding

(Ready in about 25 minutes | Servings 4)

Ingredients

Nonstick cooking spray

1 ½ cups pumpkin, canned

1/2 cup dark brown sugar

2 eggs, beaten

2 tablespoons molasses

1 teaspoon vanilla paste

2 tablespoons flour

1/2 teaspoon ground cardamom

1/4 teaspoon ground cloves

1 teaspoon ground cinnamon

1/2 cup sour cream

Directions

Lightly grease the inside of a soufflé dish using a nonstick cooking spray; reserve.

In a bowl, combine the pumpkin, sugar, eggs, molasses, and vanilla paste. Whisk in the flour, cardamom, cloves, and cinnamon.

Scrape the mixture into the prepared soufflé dish. Cover with foil. Create an aluminum foil sling.

Place the rack in a cooker. Pour in 2 cups of water. Add the soufflé dish to the cooker. Lock the lid onto the cooker.

Cook for 22 minutes under HIGH pressure. Afterward, open the cooker. Now, fold in the sour cream and serve well-chilled.

Poached Chocolate Pears

(Ready in about 10 minutes | Servings 4)

Ingredients

1 cup sweet dessert wine

2 whole cloves

1 cinnamon stick

1/2 teaspoon vanilla paste

4 Anjou pears, cored

4 tablespoons semi-sweet chocolate chips, melted

Directions

Add all ingredients, except chocolate chips, to your pressure cooker. Cook for 5 minutes under HIGH pressure; use rapid pressure release.

Carefully open the lid. Transfer the pears to the individual custard bowls. Drizzle 1 tablespoon of the melted chocolate over each pear. Enjoy!

White Chocolate and Banana Pudding

(Ready in about 20 minutes | Servings 6)

Ingredients

2 cups water

2 cups milk

1 ¾ cups short grain rice

1/2 cup sugar

2 tablespoons honey

1/4 teaspoon nutmeg, preferably freshly grated

1/2 teaspoon ground cinnamon

1/4 teaspoon ground anise seed

1 teaspoon vanilla extract

2 cups ripe bananas, mashed

Directions

Add all ingredients to the inner pot; give it a good stir.

Lock the lid onto the cooker. Choose "Manual" mode and adjust the time for 12 minutes.

Once cooking is complete, use a natural release. Bon appétit!

Plum and Fig Oatmeal Dessert

(Ready in about 15 minutes | Servings 6)

Ingredients

1/4 cup flour

1/2 cup old-fashioned oats

1/4 cup sugar

1/2 teaspoon pure almond extract

1 teaspoon pure vanilla extract

1/4 teaspoon ground anise star

1 teaspoon cinnamon powder

1/2 teaspoon grated nutmeg

4 tablespoons butter

6 plums, pitted and sliced

3 dried figs, chopped

1 cup warm water

Directions

Combine the flour, oats, sugar, almond extract, vanilla extract, anise star, cinnamon powder, nutmeg, and butter. Arrange the plums in a baking dish.

Place oat crisp mixture over the plums. Scatter chopped figs over all.

Cover the dish with foil. Add the water and trivet to the cooker.

Lower the baking dish onto the trivet. Next, choose "Beans" setting; set the timer for 15 minutes. Carefully open the lid. Serve and enjoy!

Double-Chocolate Pudding

(Ready in about 15 minutes | Servings 6)

Ingredients

1/2 ounce bittersweet chocolate, chopped

6 ounces semisweet chocolate, chopped

6 tablespoons sugar

1 ½ cups light cream

A pinch of salt

4 large egg yolks, whisked

1 tablespoon vanilla extract

1/2 teaspoon almond extract

Lightly whipped cream, for serving

Directions

Combine the chocolate and the sugar in a mixing bowl. Warm the light cream in a pan.

Next, pour the warmed cream over the chocolate; whisk until everything is melted. Add the egg yolks, vanilla extract, and almond extract.

Spoon the mixture into six heat-safe ramekins. Cover them with foil.

Place the rack in an electric pressure cooker; pour in 2 cups water. Place the ramekins on the rack. Lock the lid onto the cooker.

Cook under HIGH pressure for 15 minutes. Reduce the pressure; serve with whipped cream.

Carrot-Rice Pudding with Currants

(Ready in about 20 minutes | Servings 6)

Ingredients

1 ½ cups carrots, grated

3 cups water

1 cup Arborio rice

1/2 cup honey

1/2 teaspoon fresh ginger, grated

1/2 teaspoon ground cinnamon

2 tablespoons nut butter of choice

1 cup Zante currants

1/2 cup pecans, finely chopped

Directions

Add all ingredients to the inner pot. Select "Rice" function.

Once the pressure cooking is done, perform the Natural pressure release.

Now, carefully open the cooker. Serve chilled and enjoy!

Chip Challah Bread Dessert

(Ready in about 25 minutes | Servings 6)

Ingredients

8 slices Challah, torn into small-sized pieces

3 tablespoons melted butter

2 cups milk

4 whole eggs plus 2 egg yolks

2 tablespoons orange juice

1 cup water

1/2 teaspoon almond extract

1/4 teaspoon vanilla extract

A pinch of salt

1/4 cup sugar

1/2 teaspoon ground cloves

2 tablespoons walnuts, chopped

Directions

Throw the Challah into a lightly greased baking dish. Now, prepare the custard by mixing the other ingredients, except for walnuts.

Pour the custard mixture over the Challah pieces. Scatter chopped walnuts over all. Cover with a piece of foil.

Insert a steaming rack in your cooker and pour in 2 cups water.

Select "Manual" function and cook for 25 minutes under HIGH pressure. Afterward, do the Natural pressure release. Bon appétit!

Aromatic Baked Apples with Prunes

(Ready in about 15 minutes | Servings 6)

Ingredients

6 apples, cored

1/2 cup dried prunes, pitted and chopped

1/2 cup water

1/2 cup apple brandy

2 whole cloves

1 vanilla bean, cut in half lengthwise

1 cinnamon stick

1/3 cup honey

1/4 cup brown sugar

Directions

Arrange the apples in the base of an electric pressure cooker. Stir in the other ingredients.

Select "Manual" mode and set the machine's timer for 10 minutes. Perform the Natural release method.

Serve immediately with a dollop of whipped cream. Enjoy!

Download a PDF file with photos of all the recipes by following the link below:

Made in the USA
Middletown, DE
29 November 2016